MEDIEVAL COMIC TALES

MEDIEVAL COMIC TALES

EDITED BY DEREK BREWER

Second Edition

D. S. BREWER

First published 1973
D. S. Brewer, Cambridge

Second edition 1996

ISBN 0 85991 430 5 hardback
ISBN 0 85991 485 2 paperback

D. S. Brewer is an imprint of Boydell & Brewer Ltd
PO Box 9, Woodbridge, Suffolk IP12 3DF, UK
and of Boydell & Brewer Inc.
PO Box 41026, Rochester, NY 14604–4126, USA

British Library Cataloguing in Publication Data
Medieval comic tales. – 2nd ed.
  1. Short stories   2. Short stories, Medieval
  3. Humorous stories   4. Humorous stories, Medieval
  I. Brewer, Derek, 1923–
  808.8'31 [FS]
  ISBN 0859914305
  ISBN 0859914852 pbk

Library of Congress Cataloging-in-Publication Data
Medieval comic tales / edited by Derek Brewer. – 2nd ed.
     p.   cm.
  Includes bibliographical references.
  ISBN 0–85991–430–5. – ISBN 0–85991–485–2 (pbk.)
  1. Tales, Medieval. I. Brewer, Derek, 1923– .
  PN667.M4   1996
  808.83'917–dc20   95–52450

The paper used in this publication meets the minimum requirements
of American National Standard for Information Sciences –
Permanence of Paper for Printed Library Materials, ANSI Z39.48–1984

Printed in Great Britain by
St Edmundsbury Press Ltd, Bury St Edmunds, Suffolk

CONTENTS

ENGLISH TALES

translated by Derek Brewer, Fellow of Emmanuel College and Emeritus Professor of English in the University of Cambridge

ITALIAN TALES

translated by Derek Brewer

GERMAN TALES

translated by David Blamires, Reader in German at the University of Manchester

DUTCH TALES

translated by David Johnson, Professor of English at Florida State University, Tallahassee

MEDIEVAL LATIN TALES

translated by Michael Lapidge, Fellow of Clare Hall and Professor of Anglo-Saxon, Norse and Celtic at the University of Cambridge

vii

PREFACE

Medieval comic tales in modern English translation need no introduction to be, for the most part, enjoyable. Much of their comedy rests on human conditions we still enjoy or endure. Telling funny stories is a normal human activity which doubtless cave-men enjoyed, and flourishes as much, or more than ever, today. As always the better stories give an insight into human conditions and circumstances, give relief and cheerfulness to lives that may be drab or miserable. At this point the wise reader, in search of no more than relaxation and life-enhancing enjoyment, will abandon this Preface and Introduction and go straight to the texts. Afterwards there can be a return for fruitful critical activity.

There is a great deal more of interest, pleasure and understanding to be gained, without losing the humour, and even increasing it, by closer consideration of the literary experience offered by these and the many hundreds of other medieval comic tales. Such consideration leads to deeper understanding of literature in general, and of literary theory. Although the aim of this book is primarily to introduce an informal, and inevitably rather arbitrary, selection of European medieval comic tales, with the minimum of scholarly apparatus, the Introduction briefly offers a lead into the general topic. The topic has not been neglected since the first edition of this collection, in 1973, and comic tales continue to offer a rich as well as entertaining field of enquiry. They appeal equally to the general reader, the student of literary courses, and the scholar, the critic, the anthropologist. The deeper literary questions raised by consideration of tragedy are equally raised by consideration of comedy. Besides raising the puzzling question of the nature of humour, consideration of comic tales offers insight into the nature of narrative, especially in the form of traditional literature, into the relations between orality and literacy, the significance of plot and its relation to characterisation, and into the social contexts of class, country and period. They are a valuable key to cultural history. Although the tales are European and even occasionally world-wide in distribution, they also enjoy a strong particularity. Most notably, they release us from the bonds of theory based on post-seventeenth-century, European literature, which is only a tiny, if enormously significant segment of the world's literature, based on special and relatively unusual assumptions.

The present collection is a revised and expanded edition of *Medieval Comic Tales* (Cambridge: D.S. Brewer), first published in 1972. That edition was one of the first two books published by that press, and bore a few marks of haste and inexperience in publishing, though it was well received. It would not have been possible without the generous co-operation of the distinguished scholars who made their own selections and translations of the tales from various foreign languages. With one welcome recruit, Dr D.F. Johnson, these scholars, twenty-five years later, now risen to even greater heights of academic glory, have kindly looked over the original texts but have needed to make few alterations. They are not responsible for any of the views expressed in the Introduction, which is new. There are some additional texts in French, English, German, and Dutch. There are some new notes. The editorial assistance of Caroline Palmer who also modernised *Howleglass* and the patient efficiency of Pru Harrison and the staff of what is now the larger firm of Boydell and Brewer are gratefully acknowledged. I am grateful also to the helpful staff of Cambridge University Library, and for the use of its resources.

Derek Brewer
June 1995

INTRODUCTION

I

There are thousands of medieval comic tales, some independent narratives, others occurring incidentally in long poems, in romances, chronicles, sermons, collections of moral fables, or as dramatic farces. The collection made here is but a small example, excluding farces and also the beast-fable, but otherwise representative of all but the very crudest or the dullest.

Within the vast and miscellaneous variety of comic stories there are many overlaps and repetitions. Although for obvious reasons we rely on the written records there is ample evidence that these stories drifted between oral and written forms. There is no clear demarcation. They must also have appealed to all classes of people, but the nature of the evidence reveals that the literate, the courtly and merchant classes savoured and preserved them. Though they were appreciated by, and especially in the earlier periods improved and preserved by clerics, especially as sermon anecdotes, 'exempla', they are predominantly secular in tone. This in itself gives them added interest in a period dominated by the ecclesiastical culture. At the same time we cannot make too clear a distinction between ecclesiastical and lay, any more than we can between courtly and 'bourgeois' (that much abused word), oral and literate, learned and ignorant. The boundaries are vague, and despite many divisions in society there was inevitably much in common.

The origins of the stories are equally uncertain. Many seem to have come ultimately from India, perhaps further afield. Some came from classical antiquity. Many must have been generated, as comic stories are now, from absurd incidents in daily life, suitably polished and exaggerated. They have a pleasing mixture of fantasy and realism. They are based on the human constants and self-contradictions of ordinary life, of the needs of food, drink, defecation, love, sex, money; and also on the potentially comic horror of death. Everything is seen in a comic spirit though it could equally be the subject of pathos, pity, tragedy. For many reasons these highly readable tales are worth further study.

The supreme examples are by the great writers Chaucer and Boccaccio and for that very reason, because they are so well known and many times translated, no examples from their work are given here. But the experienced reader will note that several tales here are also told by Chaucer and Boccaccio (e.g. the German 'The Smith in the Baking-Trough' (p. 120) as Chaucer's *Miller's Tale*'). Except in the transcendence of their genius they are of the same kind as the writers of the present collection, even if their art makes them somewhat different.

II

A sense of humour is common to all cultures and periods. But the ways it is embodied in jokes, stories, dramas etc. are historically conditioned, and therefore variable, as is the estimation in which humour is held and the degree to which its manifestations are studied. Whom and what we may laugh at, and when, undergo considerable change. For example, for many centuries in all cultures the physically handicapped were thought uproariously comic. Plato in the *Philebus* (355 B.C.) sees 'the weak as a justifiably prime target for humour. For Aristotle (in *Poetics*) the ludicrous was based in deformities, defects, and ugliness which are neither destructive nor painful'.[1] These have been the targets for humour ever since, until 'political correctness' in the 1990s attempted to ban jokes on such subjects, surely with good reason. Yet to judge from the British popular press, from advertising and casual remarks, humour, fun, laughter, have never been so highly valued as now. In all British advertisements for potential friends, 'partners', etc. GSOH (good sense of humour), is a prime requisite. Humour is also nowadays usually regarded as subversive, and subversion is, at least in Western literary circles, more highly valued than ever before. Thus it is that though a 'good sense of humour' is one of the currently most highly valued human qualities, at least in Britain, the fundamental aggressiveness of humour is at least obliquely recognised.[2] In order to enjoy the expression of humour there must be a certain limitation of sympathy. There must also be a certain sympathetic group feeling, which the expression of humour warms and consolidates. In consequence, as has always been realised, we feel better for sharing a joke or a comic tale: we feel a sense of community. 'Communities' imply 'outsiders'. The identification of 'outsiders' of various kinds enhances group

1   For a useful primarily psychological survey see the article 'Humour', by A.J. Chapman and N.P. Sheehy, in *The Oxford Companion to the Mind*, ed. R.L. Gregory (Oxford: Oxford University Press, 1987), 320–23. For a comprehensive bibliography see Don. L.F. Nilsen, *Humor Scholarship: A Research Bibliography* (Bibliographies in Popular Culture 1, Westport, Conn.: Greenwood Publishing Group, Inc., 1993). For a series of literary studies see *A Cultural History of Humour from Antiquity to the Present Day*, ed. J. Bremner, R. Dekker, H. Roodenburg (Oxford: The Polity Press, 1995). See also the journal *Humour Studies*.

2   On the aggressiveness of jokes see Hannjost Lixfeld, 'Jokes and Aggression', in *German Volkskunde*, ed. and trans. James R. Dow and Hannjost Lixfeld (Bloomington: Indiana University Press, 1986), 229–43, with much bibliographical information. See also J.C.H. Davies, *Ethnic Humour Around the World* (Bloomington and Indianapolis: Indiana University Press, 1990). Davies is inclined to deny the aggressiveness of many ethnic jokes, but develops a valuable sociological theory.

feeling. The comic tales of the European Middle Ages invite us to share some of their most spontaneous pleasures, and also, because of the ambivalent nature of humour, their natural, if sometimes repressed, apprehensions, fears, obsessions. We have also to lend imaginative sympathy sometimes to their reprehensible prejudices, such as anti-feminism of various kinds, their cruelty to vulnerable outsiders. We may sometimes laugh a little shamefacedly. Fortunately the passage of time, and the non-responsible nature of art, allow us to follow the advice of Chaucer, who understood these matters, at the end of the highly comic *Nun's Priest's Tale*, to take 'the fruit, and let the chaff be still'.

No general study of humour was made in the Middle Ages. It is an interesting question whether such a quality, or entity, was even recognised. There was some discussion of comedy and tragedy, usually of a learned and rather muddled kind, based on an inadequate study of classical sources. Discussions of comedy rarely do more than imply humour. While comic tales abound, some curious responses also emerge. The fourteenth-century John Arderne, writing about 1380, writes of the Bible and other 'tragedies' as sources for humorous stories of a good and decent kind that doctors can use to make their patients laugh and so improve their health.[3]

The cultivation of humour for health reasons becomes more prominent in the Renaissance and has been re-iterated by modern medical science. But the kind of funniness enjoyed in the Renaissance was very similar to the traditional and medieval forms. The humour of *Don Quixote* and Falstaff is essentially medieval and they were enjoyed as straightforwardly absurd until the Romantic period. Romanticism brought about a marked change in our attitude to the comic. Falstaff came to be taken seriously, and Romanticism turned *Don Quixote* into a sad book, from which it has hardly recovered, as shown by P.E. Russell in a valuable essay.[4] The process continues. We are

---

[3] M. Wolterbeck, *Comic Tales of the Middle Ages: An Anthology and Commentary* (New York, Westport, Conn., and London: Greenwood Press, 1991) collects, classifies and translates Latin texts from the Carolingian period to the twelfth-century Renaissance. E.R. Curtius gives a series of examples of medieval observations on the comic in *European Literature and the Latin Middle Ages*, trans. W.R. Trask (London: Routledge and Kegan Paul, 1953), 417–35. Madeline Doran, *Endeavours of Art* (Wisconsin: University of Wisconsin Press, 1954: paperback edn 1964), 105ff discusses the diffusion of the fourth-century grammarians' ideas on tragedy and comedy. Comedy for them becomes assimilated to our notion of 'romance', and of pieces, usually narrative, with a happy ending. Hence, ultimately, Dante's *Divina Commedia*, rarely comic in our sense, but a narrative with a happy ending, though deeply serious in content. H.A. Kelly, *Tragedy and Comedy from Dante to pseudo-Dante* (Berkeley, London: University of California Press, 1989).

[4] P.E. Russell, '*Don Quixote* as a Funny Book', *Modern Language Review* 64 (1969), 312–26.

more sympathetic to suffering since the Romantic extension of sensibility (which is surely a gain), and we no longer pass pleasant Sunday afternoons laughing at the antics of the mentally sick, as was still common in Bedlam Hospital in eighteenth-century London. Nevertheless there can be no doubt that Cervantes and two centuries of readers in Europe did find madness comic, as well as the cruel and pointless deceits inflicted on Don Quixote and Sancho Panza, especially in the second volume. Any reader of the present volume will recognise Cervantes' continuation in part of the roughness, satire, and unsympathetic sanity of medieval comic tales in the string of farcical events in which Don Quixote is involved, as well as the way in which the genius of Cervantes extends and transcends his model by associating it with romance, and by making it more humane and profound, as A. Close shows.[5]

Towards the end of the nineteenth century scholarship, mostly of an antiquarian nature, began to study comic literature, with often justified contempt or apology, and apparently for any other reason than that it had at least once been thought funny. Its 'realism' is often an expected nineteenth-century attraction, though from Aristotle onwards comedy was associated with the 'low' or realistic style. Also in the nineteenth century began to develop the idea, of which the earliest expression I have noted is Pater's, that humour is always subversive.[6] Some jokes may be, but many are not. Much popular humour derides the odd or the original and reinforces 'normal', i.e. 'conservative' attitudes.

Perhaps the most stimulating book on medieval humour is that by M. Bakhtin.[7] He argues that medieval humour represents the whole community and is itself holistic in accepting the physical, excremental, degrading aspects of life as cheerful and festive. He uses the concept of the 'carnivalesque' to describe the topsy-turvidom, the irresponsible but life-enhancing quality of some medieval humour. It is an entrancing book, but granting the highly metaphorical nature of the word 'carnivalesque' it can only apply

5   A. Close 'Cervantes' Aesthetics of Comic Fiction and his concept of "La Verdad de la Historia" ', *The Modern Language Review*, 89 (1994) 88–106. I am grateful to Dr Close for discussion and information about jests and comedy.

6   W. Pater, *The Renaissance* 1, 26, quoted in *Middle English Humorous Tales in Verse*, ed. G.H. McKnight (Boston and London: D.C. Heath and Co., 1913). McKnight's introduction is excellent, and covers much omitted in the present Introduction, especially on beast epic.

     Freud's theory of humour is too complex to discuss here but he supports the notion that jokes are subversive. So also Mary Douglas, 'Jokes', *Implicit Meanings* (London: Routledge and Kegan Paul, 1975).

7   M. Bakhtin, *Rabelais and His World*, trans. H. Lowolsky (Cambridge, Mass.: M.I.T. Press, 1968).

to certain aspects of medieval humour, as a glance at the following stories
will show. It is perhaps most applicable to Till Eulenspiegel, (in English,
'Howleglass') the obscene trickster figure, amongst whose descendants we
may number Falstaff, but who is endemic in human society. Even in the late
twentieth century there are distinguished men boasting in their memoirs of
the dishonest, deceitful and disgracefully anti-social behaviour of their
earlier or not so earlier days, and receiving much praise, admiration and
financial advantage from doing so. The 'festive', carnival spirit perceived by
Bakhtin is not restricted to the medieval period, though it was less admired
then than in our day by the dominant official culture. An advantage for the
modern study of comedy is that the 'carnivalesque' now dominates modern
literary culture. Thus a contemporary drama critic writes of a modern
American (United States) play in London, Killer Joe by Tracy Letts:

> The play is cynical, sick, exploitative and gross, but schlock horror
> doesn't come much funnier than this. I'm ashamed to admit that I
> loved every minute of it.[8]

How seriously to take such publicly proclaimed shame may be questioned
but the judgement is clear, and might be applied to much contemporary art,
film and literature.

It applies rather less to much medieval comedy but Bakhtin helped to
restore comedy to a place in the wholeness of medieval vernacular literature
as illustrated in, for example, The Canterbury Tales. Bakhtin's purpose was to
remind us of the comic lest we pay too much attention to the serious.

III

At no period has there emerged a general theory of the nature of humour
other than that it arises from the juxtaposition of incongruous elements
upon a common basis. (If there is nothing in common there can be no
effective juxtaposition). The most obvious general example of the juxtaposition of incongruities in all races and periods is that between, on one side,
human spiritual, intellectual, moral and social aspirations and necessities,
and on the other, the wilfulness or recalcitrance of our equally human
physical nature, the grossness, greed and selfishness of our craving bodies.
This juxtaposition of the generally mental against the material sides of
humanity may when one side strongly predominates produce tragedy. For
comedy something of a balance between the two sides is required, and a
certain limitation of sympathy either way; comedy can never be extreme nor

---

8   Charles Spencer, The Daily Telegraph, London, Tuesday, 24 January 1995, p. 17.

single-minded, which is why its ambiguities may have profound implications for the nature of human life. This was clearly sensed in the Middle Ages, whose greatest authors are often great humorists. The exaltation of tragedy as a solitary extreme which is alone truly expressive of the human condition is a characteristic of twentieth-century literary theory.

The juxtaposition of and incongruity between mental and material is immensely complex and variable in balance and detail. In the Middle Ages the mental may be regarded as those aspects of spiritual, mental and social life which aim at order; which are self-conscious and purposive; which, through self-discipline, envisage long-term benefits to the individual within a social harmony, whereby the individual most fully realises himself by transcending his or her (usually physical, or physically-based) limitations. In consequence the mental aspects of life may be regarded as expressed by the 'official' culture. It was either ecclesiastical or courtly – they overlapped; though some aspects of courtly culture, e.g. those concerned with sexual love, were 'unofficial' in regard to the ecclesiastical culture. In either case the cultural pattern was hierarchical, authoritarian and aggressive.

Inevitably the dynamic official cultures work *against* some aspects of human nature. By our given physical nature we all wish to gratify our multiple physical needs and desires as soon, as fully, as variously, and as frequently as possible. We are all (though only in part and some more than others) lazy, lecherous, greedy, domineering, selfish, irrational, erratic, dishonest and cowardly – all the things the official cultures tell us not to be. The various expressions of our idleness, wilfulness and insubordinate recalcitrance may be regarded as forming an 'unofficial' or 'counter' culture – or cultures. The 'unofficial' element may be summed up as preferring spontaneous expression rather than calculated response; immediate and certain short-term personal gratification, rather than long-term general benefits, however transcendental. It takes pleasure in reversals, 'the world upside-down'. The clash between the mental and the materialistic makes up the human story, tragic or comic. The comic tends to favour the materialistic side.

These are very rough-and-ready generalisations. The various cultures which made up the whole of such a vast, ancient, complex and diversified segment of human society as Europe in the Middle Ages require much more analysis. For example, the dominant ecclesiastical official culture was a form, or series of forms, of Christianity. Yet Christianity has built into its very heart a profound and paradoxical self-criticism, and self-reversal, as well as important 'unofficial' elements, such as hostility to 'the world', taking no thought for the morrow, etc. Historically Christianity itself had begun as an 'unofficial' culture, though not a culture lower than the dominant one. So the official ecclesiastical culture, like most cultural forms, had its own share of self-contradictions.

On the other hand the 'unofficial' cultures were also rooted in necessity and physical reality; in joy, therefore, as well as death. Not all unofficial spontaneous action, or physical desires, are purely personal or self-regarding. The 'unofficial' cultures included attractive patterns of loving and hating and social organisation that far antedated Christianity, and were not always happily accommodated by medieval Christianity – uninhibited sexuality, for example. In other words 'unofficial' culture is also in various ways positive and creative too, not merely rebellious. In particular, at both courtly and lower social levels the 'unofficial' culture gave a much more generally important place to women. For to the 'official' ecclesiastical culture women were, extraordinary as it must seem (and with one major exception, the worship of the Blessed Virgin Mary), largely unofficial.

The sociological division into 'official' and 'unofficial' is also a psychological one; it exists within almost everyone. It is out of the ambivalence created by this division that much medieval, and some later humour, arises.

The subject-matter which attracts humour is naturally that where we feel both strongly and ambivalently. Sex and death are the obvious candidates to head the top of the list. Perhaps there was greater ambivalence about death in the Middle Ages because everyone believed, at least 'officially', in personal immortality, as probably few now do. Blasphemy had a certain nervous daring, rather than coarse hostility. Marriage, with its built-in juxtaposition of at least two incongruous elements, man and woman, strongly, and in the Middle Ages indissolubly, yoked, is another topic essentially comic. (Progressively easier and more frequent divorce will presumably take the comedy out of marriage). When dead husbands can be procured, comic tales about marriage can score heavily, with sex and death and even blasphemy included as well. Jokes about excrement and farting, and coarse expressions about the anus, are fairly common. Some of the ambivalence which creates comedy arises from the tensions between physical need and equally natural physical disgust, in the absence of modern sanitation and privacy. Less personal, but important for comedy, are subjects like official tyranny and corruption – like the wide-spread story represented here by the Stricker's 'The Judge and the Devil' (pp. 95–7), essentially the same as Chaucer's 'Friar's Tale'. Certain groups of people traditionally attract mockery – shrewish wives, stupid husbands, the physically deformed, for example. The misbehaviour of parish priests is another subject of mockery. The clash between official and unofficial elements to do with authority, learning, money, sex, is obvious here, though not always simple. Parish priests may be mocked by laymen, but also by university clerks, superior to priests in wit and learning, and also by socially superior courtiers or courtly clerics, as seems to be the case in some French *fabliaux*. In the early sixteenth century, as occurs in *A Hundred Merry Tales*, there may be also a Humanist and reforming bias against priests. Friars are another group of clerics who figure usually to their own disadvantage, as in Chaucer's 'Summoner's Tale', and 'Don Hugh of Leicester', in comic tales. Other groups who offer an obvious target for humour are foreigners, where the 'official' side is native and the 'unofficial' foreign. These 'ethnic jokes' are now not only 'politically incorrect' but often illegal in Britain and some of the United States. There is an Irish joke in *The Hundred Merry Tales*. (No. XIII, not given here.) Ethnic jokes seem to be universal but we notice an outcrop of jokes about Welshmen in England in the early sixteenth century, presumably following an influx of the Welsh with the Tudors. Shakespeare keeps this latter interest going at the end of the century with his Fluellen in *King Henry V*, and, along with Scotsmen and Irishmen, they are still subjects for jokes in England, like Poles in Germany, Belgians in France, and so forth, though the world-wide pleasure in the ethnic joke is now in some countries becoming illegal. The same jokes may be used in different countries against different nationalities.[9] The elderly and the silly (often the same), and the weak, as well as the pompous, are constantly regarded as fair game. Oddly enough, the young as a group seem much less often to be regarded as comic.

Physical disaster is sometimes the subject of humour as well as an instrument by which it is created. Chaucer is much less rough than most, but even in Chaucer the fooled and deceived old husband of 'The Miller's Tale' has his arm broken for him in addition to his other misfortunes. Sacchetti's Ser Benghi is knocked about almost as brutally as Don Quixote, and we are clearly expected, in one of Sacchetti's favourite phrases, to 'nearly burst with laughter' at the spectacle. A modern reader is much more likely to be shocked by the brutality and callousness towards suffering of medieval humour than by sexual indecency. All humour depends on some limitation, as well as extension, of sympathy, and there is little pity for physical pain, though there is also no sadism, in this hard medieval world. The close connection said to exist in modern pornography between sex and violence does not appear. Pornography is probably a specifically historical phenomenon arising in the Renaissance, with strong Neoclassical associations, for it is first found in England in the seventeenth century when the attempt was made closely to associate words with things in the material sense, and when metaphor and the generally symbolic, imprecise nature of language were first seriously attacked in the name of science.[10]

When considering medieval writing one must remember, first, the hardness

9 See Davies, *Ethnic Humour*, above, n. 2.
10 Derek Brewer, 'Some Observations on the Development of Literalism and Verbal Criticism', *Poetica* (Tokyo, 1974), 71–95.

of physical life for everyone in a technologically and medically primitive culture which made pain commonplace; and second, that language was not so closely bound to naturalistic representation as it has tended to be later. The apparently 'commonsense' close bond between 'word' and 'thing', so important for the development of modern industrial Western European culture, only begins to be significant from the seventeenth century onwards. Furthermore, medieval humour, like all pre-seventeenth century humour, is based on the stresses and strains of agrarian communities. Agrarian communities are hierarchical, patriarchal, aggressive, collective, harsh, deeply conservative, and closely bound to the soil. It is interesting that though lords may be mocked and some knights foolish, the class feudal structure is not mocked.

One of the pleasures of comic writing has always been its 'realism', that is, its vivid evocation of the details of the material everyday world. Such physical details, particularly of our own bodies, are often a comic stumbling-block to the mind's aspirations or schemes. The very notion of 'body and soul' is a potential joke, and the body, doomed to decay and death, wilful and recalcitrant, often undignified, looked rather 'unofficial' to the Middle Ages. Physical detail also supplies the necessary basis to fantastically farcical plots, so that we can fully imagine and enjoy them, wildly improbable as they are, like Chaucer's 'Miller's Tale' and 'Reeve's Tale', their numerous analogues, and the stories of this anthology.

'Realism' is historically associated with derision, no doubt partly at any rate because pre-industrial society usually believed that true reality does not consist in the tangible visible surface of things, which may mislead, and which therefore deserves some degree of disdain. It is natural to find that most medieval comedy (perhaps most comedy?) is derisive or satirical. 'Derision' is a better concept than 'satire' though it may include satire. Derision is a general attitude of humorous, superior contempt, very characteristic of medieval humour. Satire is a more literary concept, with associations of ostensible desire to improve, or at least a desire to measure behaviour against moral standards and find it wanting. Satire seeks respectability. Derision is the self-confident, cheerful and not very malicious contempt felt by the safe for the vulnerable. A sense of superiority has rightly been felt to be an important component of a sense of humour, even if not the only component.

Thus it is that in the end, *pace* Bakhtin, and accepting much of his holism, medieval humour, with some exceptions, is conservative, hearty, and expressive of an ultimately 'official' point of view. It is rarely genuinely subversive. This is true even of Chaucer and Shakespeare. The supreme example is Falstaff. He is the very incarnation of the 'unofficial' culture; always taking immediate gratifications; self-indulgent in sex and drink;

totally unreliable; a liar; and a coward. Most of his jokes arise exactly out of the tension between 'official' and 'unofficial', and his witty inversions which set up the 'unofficial' instead of the 'official' – for example, Hal as King, with a cushion on his head for a crown, holding court in a pub. This inversion, granted Shakespeare's genius of evocation, is why we love Falstaff, for though he suffers the diseases of self-indulgence – gout and pox – he is, until the very end, the unofficial culture apparently triumphant: he never seems to suffer pain or even a hangover; fat as he is, he can run, even if he lards the lean earth as he does so; he is always merry; and he even gets away with his cowardice on the field of battle by being rewarded for bravery. It loses the whole point of Falstaff to argue, as since the Romantic period some have done, that because we love him he must be admirable; as, for example, brave. We love him because he is *not* admirable. He is a glorious fantasy-figure embodying our self-indulgent short-term physical desires, which is why this huge hill of flesh, this stuffed cloak-bag of guts, seems so very material. But in the end he is repudiated, as for social sanity he must be. Shakespeare and Chaucer and almost all writers until the Romantics, whatever their knowledge of the 'unofficial' culture and their sympathy for it, are in the end on the side of the 'official' culture. They are Prince Hals, enjoying the 'unofficial' with a strong fundamental reservation from and condemnation of it; the ambivalence makes the cómedy. Romanticism changed that, by extending sympathy towards, or exalting, the 'unofficial' culture in all sorts of radical ways. Writers identified themselves much more with the 'unofficial', as Blake, the early Wordsworth, Byron and others did. Many writers would henceforth identify themselves with the 'unofficial' culture not as deplorable (which had happened before) but as admirable. They considered themselves, or were forced to be, 'outsiders' from the 'official' culture, which itself of course developed. Much of the complex comedy even of Dickens, no outsider in any deep sense, is 'anti-official'. Perhaps the final stage of this Romantic development is the comedies of Charlie Chaplin, whose poor, down-trodden, hungry and sex-hungry, deceitful and dishonest little tramp is surprisingly and delightfully often successful in his war against the rich, efficient, well-informed, bigger, stronger, conventional, superior world. Charlie represents in some ways the Romantic hero's war against society in its comic aspect. But Romanticism does not really favour comedy, as is seen by the changed reception of *Don Quixote*. The enthusiasm, total conviction, absolute commitment, unequivocal passion, evangelical fervour, which mark Romanticism, do not favour the ambivalence of comedy. Charlie Chaplin is comic because in the end he wishes to be rich and conventional, while he is neither. He is not fully Romantic but has a comic ambivalence. He is not very characteristic of literary culture in the late twentieth century.

IV

The literary forms used for medieval narrative comedy are varied and can be only briefly mentioned here. Humour itself is often found in primarily serious contexts. There are touches of humour in the *Iliad*, while in the *Odyssey* occurs the famous story of Hephaistos (Vulcan), husband of Aphrodite (Venus), who entrapped Ares (Mars) with Aphrodite in a golden net when they were in bed together and showed them to the gods, who only laughed. (*Odyssey* VIII, 266 ff.). So ancient are comic stories about marriage and sex, the silliness of old husbands, the faithlessness of wives. Some ancient burlesque poems were attributed to Homer but they are lost, except for the *Batrachomyomachia*, 'The Battle of Frogs and Mice', which may date from the fifth century B.C. Thus some comic tales in verse and some literary parody are very early, and a distinction could be made between serious and light verse. Among classical poets Ovid is perhaps the greatest humorist, as well as the great manipulator of rhetoric and pathos. His work was well-known throughout the Middle Ages.

Comedy seems to have won more esteem in the Classical period on the stage, where the great name is Aristophanes. It is also worth remembering that the Greek dramatic trilogy was concluded with a farce, though none survives. Classical stage comedy died out about the first century A.D. but mimes and pantomimes, comic turns by actors, jugglers, tumblers, continued in unbroken succession throughout the Middle Ages. The fourth century grammarians' remarks about comedy became understood to apply to narrative rather than to drama, and as such are more significant for the understanding of medieval romance – stories with happy endings. The connection of comedy with romance is close, and many serious romances have deliberately comic episodes, which themselves may deserve to rate as comic tales.

In prose narrative there may be comic anecdotes as illustrations or digressions in a generally serious work, but the earliest example of a collection of comic tales, which may be said to suggest the *genre*, appears to be the Milesian Tales written in Greek and attributed to Aristides of Miletis in the second century B.C. They have a reputation for being mainly erotic and sometimes obscene, but none survives. They were no doubt regarded as unworthy of serious consideration and preservation. 'Milesian Tales' came to be descriptive of erotic comic stories in general. Such stories might be digressions in longer works of the same or different general character. Petronius Arbiter (d. A.D. 66) wrote a prose fictional narrative of which part survives, the *Cena Trimalchionis*, and which seems to have been influenced by Milesian Tales. The most famous example is the anecdote he tells of the Widow of Ephesus, a story which is traditionally cynical about the endurance of a widow's love for her dead husband, involving marriage, sex and death, with a touch of the macabre. It also has an aesthetic neatness which gives much pleasure.

Quintilian the rhetorician (born about 35 B.C.) in his *Institutio Oratoria* devoted a chapter (VI, iii) to jests, apophthegms, witty remarks, as they might be used in oratory, and in which he appears to refer to the existence of jest-books. (VI, iii, 63).

The great development of collections of tales in Europe took place from the late eleventh century onwards, together with so much else of cultural significance for which the twelfth century is so important. An early example is the collection of anecdotes, jests, and fables including some that are comic, made by the Spaniard known as Petrus Alphonsus, born in 1062. They are traditionally regarded as a part of Spanish literature and some examples are represented in the present collection in the section of Spanish tales, but they were written in Latin and might have appeared in the Latin section. The collection was widely influential for centuries in Europe. Also notable for its early appearance is the Latin romance, as it is best regarded, *Ruodlieb*, which, as often in romance, has at times a comic tone, and comic episodes, of which an example has been given below (pp. 145–7). In the twelfth and following centuries a number of compilations of stories appears, of which a proportion at least were intended to be amusing, mainly for the purpose of supplying sermon-writers with illustrative anecdotes.[11] The narratives are brief and schematic: it was for others to work them up, as *Dame Sirith* is in the present volume (pp. 47–51), by some cleric who liked to exercise a talent for versifying in the vernacular. Preachers also developed them in sermons to rouse up the drowsy. The most striking example of such working up of known stories, whether sermon, *exempla* or folk-tales of diverse origins, is the body of poems in French now known as *fabliaux*, of which a number are represented in the present volume. Their origins and authors (where known) are mixed. For example the story of Aristotle and Alexander, given from a Latin version (p. 170), also appears in a French *fabliau* of about the same date by Henri d'Andeli, apparently a courtier and a cleric in Paris.[12] It is now generally agreed that the *fabliaux* are mostly courtly in origin, a sort of counterpoise to romance. There are some hundred and sixty-odd extant, mostly composed in the late twelfth and thirteenth centuries, dying out in the fourteenth.

The *fabliaux* as a genre have attracted most attention from modern scholars.

---

11 J.T. Welter, *L'exemplum dans la littérature religieuse et didactique du Moyen Age* (Paris, 1927).

12 See the discussion, following a translation, in R. Hellman and R.F. O'Gorman, *Fabliaux* (London: Arthur Barker Ltd, 1963), 177–79.

More valuable studies have been devoted to them than can be noted here. The materiality of the subject-matter, the emphasis on the physical human body, with the paradoxical, metaphorical and even metaphysical implications of this, have been emphasised by Charles Muscatine and R. Howard Bloch, extending the work of Bakhtin.[13] Bloch speaks of

> the exclusiveness of their sexual and scatological obscenity, their anti-clericalism, antifeminism, anti-courtliness, the consistency with which they indulge the senses, whet the appetites (erotic, gastronomic, economic) . . . (p. 11)

So summary a statement, though not without truth, is excessive, omitting necessary qualifications. Not all are without warmth, sensuality, even kindness, but certainly most are deeply misogynistic.

Muscatine writes of the *fabliaux*'s cosmos which

> has its own rather formidable integrity. The recurrence in text after text of the same attitudes and values makes clear that we are not dealing here with a random miscellany of jokes, having a rather random miscellany of tendencies, but with a body of literature expressing a consistent value system. (p. 153)

It is this value system which he calls 'materialistic hedonism' or 'hedonistic materialism'. He argues that the system is coherent, has an historical life of its own and a specific place in medieval French culture. 'It is particularly receptive to the high valuation of cleverness or wit' (p. 154), and exemplifies 'a kind of individualism if not egalitarianism in which wit levels distinction of station and gender and opens the prospect of pleasure to whoever can manage it.' Muscatine believes that this ethos has 'enough resemblance to one widely to be found in modern American society (to take an example) that it does not need much proving'. It is 'a value system that coexists along with an indeterminate number of other value systems in a wide range of individuals in the culture' (p. 157). He argues that the 'ethos of the *fabliaux* is too important in human experience to ignore . . . It simply cannot be swept over to the margins as an example of childish truancy. Indeed it celebrates values that are perhaps too central to the human condition, too essentially comic to allow us to hold it steadily in mind as a particular historical phenomenon at all.' (p. 165).

Such reflections are not true of all comic tales but are of value in opening

---

[13] C. Muscatine, *The Old French Fabliaux* (New Haven and London: Yale University Press, 1986); R.H. Bloch, *The Scandal of the Fabliaux* (Chicago and London: The University of Chicago Press, 1986).

up consideration of a whole area of human life, and one that nowadays we are little likely to be able to ignore, at least in modern literature. It has its place apart from or indeed at odds with currently under- valued qualities of beauty, honour, justice, trust, kindness, self-sacrifice, and most of all, genuine love. The actual experience of reading many French *fabliaux* in an admittedly artificial situation without mitigation of other forms of writing is in the end a dismal one. It is like spending a whole evening in a degraded barrack room. The analogy is not unjust. The obsession with drink, defecation and sex in a male society devoted to war, and with drink and the pursuit of women as its only recreations, cut off from home and family and intellectual life, with the constraints only of the most external physical discipline, is not dissimilar to that ethos partially represented by the *fabliaux*. It is a world of harsh comedy: that ancient archaic world of primitive popular derisive humour which depends upon a total lack of sympathy with the victims and with those who do not conform to the norms of that world. The contradictions it creates, depending upon frustration and the occasional inversion of superior to inferior, are indeed comic, as well as harsh. It is salutary to contemplate them. But it is an extraordinarily narrow world, concentrating so mindlessly on material pleasure. It is conspicuous for its sympathy with greed, dishonesty, treachery, brutality, unfairness and unkindness. Every man's hand is against the others. It is a world without beauty, without general thought (there is plenty of death but no thought about it). It is curiously and irresponsibly blinkered, not only in its sympathies, but in relation to that very materialistic sequence of cause and effect which it is supposed to celebrate, for in a world where copulation is so vigorously sought, birth is very infrequent. It is a world of mutually destructive individuals, a world of trickery and brutal victimisation, seen resolutely from the point of view of the successful villain, or, to put him (rarely her) at his most favourable, the victor. Although one laughs, one is also saddened and ashamed. Why should we laugh at hunchbacks, or all the other victims, even if two millennia or more of our ancestors have done so?

In so far as a *fabliau* ethos does exist it is parasitic on true values. It can only be funny if it is seen in contradistinction to a different world, because the comedy derives from the violation of trust and love. Yet if it is also true that the world we know and live in does partly correspond to the *fabliaux* world, it is also necessary to realise that comedy is almost as various as life itself. As the following collection shows, by no means all *fabliaux*, let alone all comic tales, are as hedonistic, ruthless and indecent as represented. Many find humour in the immoral biter bit, and are on the side of trust and goodness, accepting conservative, conventional, 'official' values.

These are complex matters of the relationship between life and literature, subtly treated by Muscatine, Bloch and others. Before leaving this brief opening-up of the questions, it should again be remarked that almost all the story collections made before the sixteenth century contain, like *The Canterbury Tales*, a Gothic mixture of comic and serious tales. When we isolate the medieval comic, as the present collection does, we partly exaggerate and partly denature it. Probably the first collection devoted only to comedy is the collection of jokes made by Poggio Bracciolini, written in Latin, in the middle of the Humanist fifteenth century, rapidly popular in many manuscripts, printed many times in Europe from 1477 onwards.[14] This is more properly and usually called a jest book, a collection of brief anecdotes and witty, or would-be witty, remarks. The first such collection in English is a brief selection of Poggio's less indecent jests printed by Caxton, *The Fables of Alfonce and Poge* (London, 1484), which also includes a few tales from Petrus Alphonsus. The concentration on a single genre, even the concept of a genre, belongs to the Humanists of the Renaissance. Of such generic collections *The Hundred Merry Tales* (1526), generously represented in the present book because its material is medieval, is the outstanding example in English of the late medieval period.

In genuine medieval collections, therefore, the impact of *fabliaux* is much reduced because the individual items are a small proportion of a great variety of other tales. It must also be remembered that when referring to the *fabliaux*, as to all this traditional European narrative, we are dealing with a European phenomenon which is both oral and literate. No European country has a monopoly of such stories, though preferences and inclinations can be seen. Within the repetitions are variations. The French *fabliaux* of the thirteenth century number some 160, not really a very large number. They bring the art of the dirty comic story in verse to a high pitch. As Muscatine suggests they have a special appeal for modern literary culture and therefore have attracted much scholarly attention. But the stories themselves, and much that is implicit in any ethos they may express, can be matched in the many similar agrarian communities of Europe, in many languages. Rarely can these tales be used as a key to any one particular class, or country, or ethos, or *mentalité*, except with the greatest caution, and only with careful attention to the 'surface' detail of the verbal realisation. The deeper structure, being traditional, is likely to have a more general relationship to human needs than to a particular social moment.

---

[14] For a recent scholarly edition see his *Liber Facetiarum* in *Opera Omnia* con una premessa di R. Fubini, 4 vols (Monumenta politica et philosophica rariora, Series II, 4–7, Torino, 1964–69), Vol. I.

V

There is, beside the *fabliaux*, another strand of comic tales that can be isolated, and which establishes itself in the fifteenth century with perhaps rather more claim to the status of a minor genre, though its roots go deep in the past. This is the sequence of comic tales or episodes all associated with one individual trickster-figure, notably Till Eulenspiegel.

The concept itself of the trickster-figure we owe to Radin's study of American Indian mythology,[15] an origin which serves to remind us that we are dealing with a common human phenomenon, as well as with its specific historical expression.

The trickster's name is self-explanatory. He (rarely 'she', though Chaucer's Wife of Bath approaches that function) is the awkward, upsetting, malicious, deceitful person who usually gets away with the unpleasant tricks he plays on vulnerable, which means middle- and lower-class, people. Never, I think, does he play his savage tricks on nobles or bishops, though they patronise him and enjoy the troubles he brings on others. He is clearly to be associated with the professional fool and court jester, discussed in Welsford's classic work, though the fool might take a licence with his noble master, for which also he might pay dearly.[16]

The history of Till Eulenspiegel (= the Owl-mirror, an enigmatic name doubtless meant to insult the reader) appears to have a curious beginning in Old English versions of a dialogue between Solomon and a character called Marcolf, which reflects a general European tradition of questions and short answers on philosophical or theological topics. Gradually Solomon's challenger Marcolf turns into a crude peasant-like character who controverts Solomon's proverbial wisdom with sardonic practical truths.[17] The dialogues developed in France and Germany; a dialogue between Solomon and Marcolf, translated from the German, was printed in English in Antwerp in 1492. The Marcolf-figure, ugly, disruptive, rude, anarchic, but patronised by kings and bishops, had his analogues in roguish priests in Germany, such as Parson Amis in the thirteenth century and the Parson of Kalenborow of the fourteenth, who were the heroes of comic tales in verse.

Till Eulenspiegel represents the culmination of such figures, developed, it

---

15 Paul Radin, *The Trickster: A Study in American Indian Mythology* (with commentaries by Karl Kerényi and C.G. Jung, London, 1956).

16 Enid Welsford, *The Fool: His Social and Literary History* (London: Faber and Faber, 1935. Anchor Edition, New York: Doubleday and Company Inc., 1961). See also *The Fool and the Trickster: Studies in Honour of Enid Welsford*, ed. P.V.A. Williams (Cambridge: D.S. Brewer, 1979).

17 John Wardroper, *Jest upon Jest* (London: Routledge and Kegan Paul, 1970), 76.

seems, in Germany or the Low Countries in the fifteenth century. The stories told of him were in many cases those that had been told of the earlier tricksters. Eulenspiegel became immensely popular all over Northern Europe, appealing to high and low. His adventures, originally in German, were put into Latin verse in Utrecht in 1538, in Frankfurt in 1557, for the benefit of learned men. The earliest known version is a book printed in Strassburg in 1515, rather handsomely, with 261 pages, 86 different wood-cuts, and 95 tales, each one about Till Eulenspiegel. Only one copy survives, to be found in the British Library.[18]

The first English translation, entitled *Howleglass*, was printed c.1410–20 apparently in Antwerp, and the first printed in England was by William Copland in about 1528, and again in 1530. It is from Copland's translation that the modernisations in the present collection were made. Scholars like Gabriel Harvey, and the playwright Ben Jonson, loved Howleglass. As re-marked, some stories are traditional, some are new. *Howleglass* is notable for peculiarly disgusting scatological pranks and the complete absence of any sexual interest.

Somewhat similar reflections could be made about the 'ethos' represented by Howleglass as about the *fabliaux*, with the added interest of the way in which filth is used as an instrument of destruction and perhaps of power.[19] Realism, low life, the upsetting of order, mockery by the adoption of a ridiculously literalistic interpretation of orders, characterise the stories.

All the stories are attached to the one figure, Howleglass. There is of course no interest in characterisation or plot, but he is the prototype of a whole series of what have been called jest book heroes, rascally figures, usually in England well-educated gentlemen, who swindle and torment the tradespeople, innkeepers, etc. on whom they prey. They in their turn culmi-nate in the character of Falstaff – a process I have discussed elsewhere,[20] and as remarked above, the type is always with us. Nowadays however the

---

18 For a translation of this first version, with bibliographical etc. information, see *A Pleasant Vintage of Till Eulenspiegel*, translated from the edition of 1515, with introd-uction and critical appendix, by Paul Oppenheimer (Middleton, Conn.: Wesleyan University Press, 1972). See also the World's Classics edition, *Till Eulenspiegel: His Adventures*, translated by Paul Oppenheimer (Oxford: Oxford University Press, 1995). Cf. Werner Röcke, *Die Freude am Bösen* (München: Wilhelm Fink Verlag, 1987), especially 228–51.

19 For discussion of the general topic see Mary Douglas, *Purity and Danger* (London: Routledge and Kegan Paul, 1975). Regrettably *Howleglas* does not come within her field.

20 Derek Brewer, 'Elizabethan Merry Tales and *The Merry Wives of Windsor*: Shakespeare and Popular Literature', in *Chaucer to Shakespeare: Essays in Honour of Shinsuke Ando*, ed. T. Takamiya and R. Beadle (Cambridge: D.S. Brewer, 1992), 145–61.

particularly American and modern European obsession with hygienic clean-
liness (commented on by Davies) seems to have driven out the scatological
element, leaving us obsessed with sex.

Since Eulenspiegel is in the main a German creation, the stories repre-
senting him have been placed with earlier German stories, though the
adaptation of the English translation, sometimes extending even to English
place-names, would justify his appearance among the English Tales.

VI

A word of regret must be offered for the fact that Italian comic stories are
rather under-represented in this volume in terms of bulk. The main paradoxical reason is that Boccaccio's *Decameron* is so outstanding an achieve-
ment, and so readily available in translation, that there is the less need for
Italian tales here. Boccaccio is fully medieval in his selection of stories,
which are from the general international fund, and in the mixture of comic
with serious tales. The difference lies in the bulk, the artistry, and the vast
amount of scholarship and criticism devoted to them which cannot be
touched on here. Much of what can be said in general of medieval comic
tales applies to Boccaccio's comic tales, though it may be noted that southern Europe seems much less interested in scatology and correspondingly
more interested in varieties of sexual experience.

The Italians were early in the field with collections of stories in the
vernacular, the earliest in Italian being the *Cento novelle antiche*, otherwise
known as *Il Novellino* of the thirteenth century. They are brief and rather
pallid anecdotes. But up to 1587 there were some seventeen collections,
including the *Decameron* (c.1350). These collections of what are now called
the *novella* draw as usual on the international stock but the Italians in turn
influenced European literatures. Shakespeare was apparently indebted to
them for the plots of a number of plays. The stories are serious and tragic as
well as comic – Boccaccio's most famous story from the *Decameron* was not
of the comic type, but the tale of patient Griselda, not funny at all, though
with a happy ending.

The *novella* in Europe from the fourteenth to the seventeenth centuries
has been well anatomised in its subject-matter and more artistic forms by
Clements and Gibaldi.[21] Here we have space only to note, in relation to the
Italian tales, that the vein of everyday secular realism, characteristic of
medieval comic tales in general, seems well-developed, along with a certain

---

[21] R.J. Clements and J. Gibaldi, *Anatomy of the Novella* (New York: New York
University Press, 1977).

artistic and social polish. It is no accident that popular in nature as the stories are, the narrative setting is usually that of the gentry. (The difference, for example, between Chaucer's setting of *The Canterbury Tales* amongst many social levels, and Boccaccio's setting of well-educated young ladies and gentlemen, escaping from life and death in the plague, is worth meditating on.) But Sacchetti has no such setting. His anecdotes are separated, held together by the personality of the storyteller, so that his realism is the more striking, even if his art is less memorable. Like most good storytellers he gives his incidents and characters a local habitation and a name, even if he is retelling a wide-spread folktale, such as his story of Bernabò Visconti. He also uses some familiar motifs, and his humour, derisive though not malicious, is of the usual popular kind. He is amused by seeing pomposity deflated. Yet there is a certain man-of-the-world geniality, and originality, an anecdotal variety, a personal quality, in his telling, which distinguishes him from the more impersonal tone, of, for example, Straparola's famous but much later collection, the *Piacevoli notti*, of 1550–53. Granted the *Decameron* in the background, Sacchetti is a good representative of the Italian comic tale.

VII

The network of tales, with no specific source, sometimes perhaps ultimately of Eastern origin, gives a strong impression of the interrelatedness of Western European culture, along with a sense of marked originality in telling; a perfect base for comparative study, though one there is no space for here. The stories told in Latin are the most international of all, since told in the learned *lingua franca* of Europe. The immense popularity of *Pamphilus* (from which we derive our modern word *pamphlet*) represents the great spread of influence from Latin. Though popular, it is different in tone from many comic tales. It is longer, semi-dramatic, flowery in style, deriving from the twelfth century. Perhaps Chaucer in 'The Miller's Tale' takes a hint or two from it, two centuries later. The subject matter is cynical and the love story no more than that of a rape. Yet it has been found entertaining and no doubt has a truth to life, though we should beware of literalism.

Equally literary (not literalistic) but a great contrast in style are the brief summaries of comic plots in Latin. They are well-worth considering as giving the germ or nucleus of tales which preachers and secular tale tellers embroidered to suit circumstances. They offer a fruitful field for comparison, and are of importance for the way we understand the story and for the theory of literature.

VIII

The relation between the 'germ' or 'nucleus' of a story and its elaboration, and often the re-elaboration, or the abbreviation of a previously heard elaboration, affects the nature of traditional literature, of which the medieval comic tale is only one example.[22] Much of what can be said of it equally concerns epic, romance, lyric, ballad. The theory of literature has sometimes neglected the lessons that can be learnt, even in the field of narrative, from traditional literature. Comparisons of different versions of the same story are a good beginning.

Medieval comic tales are conditioned by their transmission and variable social contexts. They are rooted in social story-telling, remembered by the teller, and adjusted by him or her to the interests of the group. They are popular in the sense that these circumstances once applied to all social levels, at a period when the varying classes of society, whatever their inequalities and injustices, inevitably lived cheek-by-jowl in agrarian communities of relatively low technology.

These stories are therefore also a part of oral folklore, and take their place along with wonder-tales, romance themes, tragedies. The great record of the types of the folk tale by Aarne and Thompson therefore includes the types of the majority of the plots of the stories in the present selection, though these were not chosen for that reason.[23] The study of folk tale in Britain has with a few honourable exceptions been neglected, though United States and Continental European scholarship have done much.

The long history that a particular nucleus of a story may have is illustrated from Aarne-Thompson Tale Type 1791, there called *The Sexton carries the Parson*, of which the English version here is taken from *The Hundred Merry Tales* (1526), *About the Miller Who Stole the Nuts*. Possibly it takes its origin

---

22 For example K. Franzel, in his excellent *Theory of Narrative* (Cambridge: Cambridge University Press, 1984), devotes virtually no space to the relation between nucleus and elaboration when the nucleus is already given. If the story is already known that must affect how the characters are developed. It often accounts for a certain gap between what kind of a person the character is represented to be, and the actions attributed to him or her, in any particular version of a known story. It also affects the nature of description, causality (or its absence) and point of view. In traditional stories action precedes characterisation. Pattern, often of a psychological kind, predominates over realistic cause-and-effect, even if cause-and-effect (e.g. maturation, etc.) also appears to operate. Cf. Derek Brewer, *Symbolic Stories* (Cambridge: D.S. Brewer, 1980).

23 A. Aarne and S. Thompson, *The Types of the Folktale*, FF Communications no. 184, second revision (Helsinki: Academia Scientiarum Ferrica, 1973).

from the thirteenth century French *fabliau* 'Estula' (= 'Are you there?' and = also the name of a talking dog). Many other versions of the tale are recorded, for example in the fifteenth-century preacher's monumental compilation, the *Summa Predicantium* of John of Bromyard; in the famous Continental collections by J. Gobii, *Scala Celi*, Lübeck, 1476; J. Pauli, *Schimpf und Ernste*, Strassburg, 1535; in the *Alphabetum Narratiorum*, once attributed to Etienne de Besançon, a preacher's collection of useful tales in French of the fifteenth century; and the fifteenth century translation of this as *An Alphabet of Tales*, (number 333 ed. EETS, O.S. 127). The version in *A Hundred Merry Tales* is the most elaborate and amusing. After that in English it turns up in a mid-eighteenth century chapbook, *A New Riddle Book or a Whetstone for Dull Wits*, Derby, and then in the nineteenth century it was collected orally in Gaelic, with the sheep changed into an ox (which would have been much heavier to carry, but more suited to the local farming). Aarne-Thompson record dozens of local 'sightings'. As recently as the 1950s it has been collected in South Georgia, U.S.A.[24]

The variations in the story, and the story itself, provide subject-matter for reflections rather different from those provoked by modern thought about the *fabliaux*. Truly the subject-matter is secular, and deals with the horror of corpses, which, as in so many medieval comic tales, are a cause of both fear and laughter. (I hope to write a study of 'the comedy of corpses' before I become one myself.) Corpses are material, with a puzzling relation to the non-material ghost – the soul is not thought of. Theft again is a topic, introduced without moralising, though inducing guilt in the thieves. Graveyards are familiar places, but can seem sinister at night. In the variants the superficial elements may change, the sheep become an ox, or disappear altogether, as may the graveyard.

Consider the nature of the humour here, and the basic attitudes involved. The story is neither socially rebellious nor moralistic, nor sexual, nor scatological, nor religious, nor satirical, nor particularly derisive, nor the embodiment of daydreams of maturation like the wonder-tale. Mistaken identities, guilt-feelings, perhaps even a touch of the awe of judgement in secular terms, all appear. The story depends on the needs and stresses of an agrarian

---

[24] For the Gaelic see *Waifs and Strays of Celtic Tradition*, Argyllshire Series No. V, collected by the Revd John Gregorson Campbell (London: David Nutt, 1895), 3–6. For South Georgia, see *Storytellers: Folktales and Legends from the South*, ed. J.A. Burison (Athens and London: The University of Georgia Press, 1978). The *fabliau* is to be found in A. de Montaiglon and G. Raynaud, *Recueil général et complet des fabliaux* (Paris: Librairie des Bibliophiles, 1872–90, 6 vols) discussed by R.H. Bloch (see Notes to French Tales). For a devastating criticism of Bloch, see B.N. Sargent-Baur, 'Philology Through the Looking-Glass', *Towards a Synthesis?*, ed. K. Busby (Amsterdam/Atlanta GA: Rodopi, 1993) 97–118.

society, where all the instances of it occur, and one would not expect to find it in a purely industrial or post-industrial fully secularised society. The story, after a history of some five or six centuries, will probably disappear as its social, economic and mental basis disappears.

In such transmission there is no hard and fast line between oral and literate. Oral storytellers exist, I am told, in the clubs of Northern England, whose tales are so indecent, and politically so incorrect, that the BBC refuses to transmit them. Here is a nice example of the ambivalently subversive nature of humour. In so far as the stories violate the norms of decency they are subversive. But they also, it would seem, express a deep conservatism in some social attitudes – the racism, sexism, etc. that have been practised for millennia past in all societies. They rely on stereotyped characters, on traditional attitudes, expected patterns of narrative. They conserve even as they violate traditional norms. Other storytellers, less offensive, regularly appear at British pop-festivals and nowadays even at learned medieval conferences.

IX

Finally, a brief word may be added about the English examples given in the present selection, added to the first edition of this book. There are a considerable number of comic tales in English, especially from the fifteenth century, which have been printed in nineteenth-century collections, and it has been decided to include some of these using as a basis the texts of the learned new edition by Professor Furrow.[25]

The stories illustrate more widely still the nature of medieval and perhaps general humour. They are examples of international Tale Types, with widespread analogues. Some exist nevertheless in only one text. Again they are items in a whole series of quite different texts, moral, religious, practical, etc., bound up in one manuscript. Some exist, despite their medieval origins, only in chapbook form of the seventeenth century. None can thus be said to speak for the peasantry, or any other class. They are genuinely popular literature. That being said, the actual texts vary in literary polish. The fifteenth century poems, *The Lady Prioress*, *The Tale of the Pot*, *Dom Hugh*, *The Friar and the Boy*, are told with vigour but without sophistication. They

---

25 See, for example, *Remains of the Early Popular Poetry in England*, ed. with introduction and notes by W. Carew Hazlitt (London: John Russell Smith, 4 vols, 1864–66); *Shakespeare Jest-Books*, ed. with introduction and notes by W. Carew Hazlitt (London: Willis and Sotheran, 3 vols, 1864); *Ten Fifteenth Century Comic Poems*, ed. Melissa M. Furrow (New York and London: Garland Publishing Inc., 1985).

are not courtly in style and the versification is rough and ready. These particular versions obviously derive from the moderately prosperous 'middle classes', to use a convenient but rather anachronistic term. They are from small towns and villages, dependent, like Jack's father in *The Friar and the Boy*, on sending cattle out to graze in the neighbouring pasture. There are merchants, knights, farmers, monks, friars, of the usual sort.

These tales are hardly subversive. *The Lady Prioress*, with analogues in the *Decameron* (Day 9, Tale 1), French fourteenth-century farce, and elsewhere, is a joke against lecherous suitors, where the Lady Prioress preserves her virginity and the safety of her soul. *The Tale of the Pot*, demotic but not indecent or excremental, shows the amendment of a feckless husband by his brother, a priest. *The Friar and the Boy*, very popular for a couple of centuries more, mocks the stereotypes of the harsh stepmother and the friar, but the revenge taken is not savage. *Dom Hugh*, for all its possible origin in a lost French *fabliau*, is a small-town story which depends on the well-known widespread joke of the corpse which keeps on turning up again, (about whose symbolism some interesting reflections might be made) and the lecherous monk gets short shrift from the virtuous married couple. In this story of the middle classes the husbands rely on their wives for good advice, and live in harmony. Yet it is certainly a *fabliau*.

The stories from *A Hundred Merry Tales* are different, not so much in subject-matter as in sophistication. It is traditionally called a jest book but is also a collection of comic tales. The subjects are traditional – ignorant priests, shrewish wives, silly husbands, etc., and as always we are conscious of the agrarian community, with its small villages and towns. But London and wider intellectual horizons are in the background, for all the traditional nature and terse prose of the stories. They include early ethnic jokes in English – one about the Irish (no. 13) and no less than eight about the Welsh.[26] The other stories are told at the expense of the ignorant or stupid, as are most traditional jokes. The collection emanates from the Humanist circle of Sir Thomas More, though the probable collector and writer was John Rastell, More's brother-in-law, an interestingly versatile man who eventually became a fervent Protestant.[27] The first edition of *A Hundred*

[26] The earliest ethnic joke in English may be the reference to chattering Irish priests in the thirteenth-century *Owl and Nightingale*, ed. J.W.H. Atkins (Cambridge: Cambridge University Press, 1922) 322 and note. I owe this reference to E.G. Stanley. There were Latin precedents; also Langland, *Piers Plowman*, B XX, 220. Chaucer jokes about Flemings.

[27] See Brewer, as in n. 20; *An Hundred Merry Tales and Other English Jestbooks of the Fifteenth and Sixteenth Centuries*, ed. P.M. Zall (Lincoln: University of Nebraska Press, 1963). For Rastell see Introduction to *The Pastyme of People and A New Boke of Purgatory*, by J. Rastell, *with a facsimile of 'The Pastyme'*, ed. A.J. Geritz, *The*

Merry Tales was in folio size, but handier, smaller and doubtless cheaper formats soon followed. They were popular enough to be read to pieces, and hardly any copies survive, apart from a few fragments.

X

Sixteenth-century humour shows little change from what had prevailed for millennia, except in the wider spread and the accession of new material. There was a decided increase in comic writing in the sixteenth and seventeenth centuries, due no doubt to the spread of printing, but relying still on oral transmission as well, which continues to the present day.

It is sometimes argued that there was a fundamental change in the sense of humour in the latter part of the seventeenth century, at any rate in England, and that there was less laughter. On all grounds, including not least Restoration Comedy, the eighteenth century novel, and the plethora of jest books, both propositions seem improbable, despite undoubted considerable changes of taste. It is to be hoped that at least the change was not so great as to prevent a modern reader's amusement at some, at least, of the tales that follow. They are only brief and personal selections of many hundreds of possibilities. Some kinds of stories, for example the beast-fable or beast-epic, are almost ignored here, for they tend to constitute a class of their own, with special qualities beside humour. There is also little satire as such here. Similarly, this Introduction can only touch on a few of the aspects of the tales, without any attempt at full coverage even of the material here. But what is here may prove both entertaining and instructive in itself, while inciting others to explore further in the rich fields of medieval literature.

Renaissance Imagination, vol. 14 (New York and London: Garland Publishing Inc., 1985).

FRENCH TALES

1. The Goodman who Saved Another from Drowning

It happened one day that a fisherman putting out to sea in a boat was just about to cast a net, when right in front of him he saw a man on the point of drowning. Being a stout-hearted and at the same time an agile man, he jumped up and, seizing a boathook, thrust it towards the man's face. It caught him right in the eye and pierced it. The fisherman hauled the man into the boat and made for the shore without casting any of his nets. He had the man carried to his house and given the best possible attention and treatment, until he had got over his ordeal.

For a long time, that man thought about the loss of his eye, considering it a great misfortune. 'That wretched fellow put my eye out, but I didn't do *him* any harm. I'll go and lodge a complaint against him – why, I'll make things really hot for him!' Accordingly he went and complained to the magistrate, who fixed a day for the hearing. They both waited till the day came round, and then went to the court. The one who had lost an eye spoke first, as was appropriate. 'Gentlemen,' he said, 'I'm bringing a complaint against this worthy, who, only the other day, savagely struck me with a boathook and knocked my eye out. Now I'm handicapped. Give me justice, that's all I ask. I've nothing more to say.'

The other promptly spoke up and said 'Gentlemen, I cannot deny that I knocked his eye out, but if what I did was wrong, I'd like to explain how it all happened. This man was in mortal danger in the sea, in fact he was on the point of drowning. I went to his aid. I won't deny I struck him with my boathook, but I did it for his own good: I saved his life on that occasion. I don't know what more I can say. For God's sake, give me justice!'

The court was quite at a loss when it came to deciding the rights of the case, but a fool who was present at the time said to them 'Why this hesitation? Let the first speaker be thrown back into the sea on the spot where the other man hit him in the face, and if he can get out again, the defendant shall compensate him for the loss of his eye. That, I think, is a fair judgement.' They they all cried out as one man 'You're absolutely right! That's exactly what we'll do.' Judgement was then pronounced to that effect. When the man heard that he was to be thrown into the sea, just where he had endured all that cold water before, he wouldn't have gone back there for all the world. He released the goodman from any liability, and his earlier attitude came in for much criticism.

In the light of this incident, you can take it from me that it's a waste of time to help a scoundrel. Rescue a guilty thief from the gallows, and he will never like you for it. A wicked man will never be grateful to anyone who does him a good turn: he'll forget all about it; it will mean nothing to him.

On the contrary, he would be only too glad to make trouble for his benefactor if he ever saw him at a disadvantage.

2. The Peasant and his Two Donkeys

Once upon a time there lived near Montpellier a peasant who used to load two donkeys with the manure he had collected for spreading on the land. One day, having loaded his donkeys, he speedily set out with them for the town, driving them along with some difficulty and with frequent shouts of 'Gee up there!' After a while he turned into the street where the apothecaries were. Their apprentices were busy pounding away at their mortars, mixing spices. Now, as soon as the peasant smelled those spices, he couldn't have walked another step, not even if you had given him a hundred silver marks; he simply fainted on the spot, and fell down like a dead man. Then great was the consternation of the passers-by, who exclaimed 'Mercy on us! Just look, that man has dropped dead!' – and they couldn't think why. As for the donkeys, they just stood there quietly, in the middle of the street. They didn't mind, for donkeys don't usually keep moving unless they are told to.

A local worthy, who had been in the street when it happened, came forward and said to the bystanders 'Gentlemen, if any of you would like to see this good man recover, I'll cure him, for a consideration.' A townsman at once said to him 'Cure him right now, and you shall have twenty shillings from my pocket.' 'Certainly,' the other replied. He took the pitchfork with which the peasant used to urge on his donkeys, lifted up a forkful of manure and held it close to his nose. As soon as the peasant got a whiff of the manure and lost the scent of the spices, he opened his eyes and jumped to his feet, saying that he felt perfectly all right. In his delight at being thus cured, he swore he would never pass that way again, if he could avoid it.

In the light of this anecdote I would like to remind you that he who puts aside all pride acts sensibly and reasonably. No man should be false to his origins.

3. The Three Hunchbacks

Gentlemen, if you will forbear and listen just for a little while, I will tell you a tale in rhyme about a strange thing which happened, and every word of it is true.

Once upon a time, in a certain town (I've forgotten the name of the place, but let's say it was Douai) there dwelt a townsman, living quietly from his own modest resources. He was a handsome man and well liked, the very best sort of citizen. Though by no means wealthy, he was sufficiently well off to be highly thought of in the locality. He had a beautiful daughter, so beautiful that she was a delight to behold: indeed, to tell you the truth, I don't believe Nature ever shaped a creature more fair. This is not the place for me to describe her beauty in detail, for if I attempted to do so, I might easily go astray; it is therefore better that I should say nothing about it here, rather than risk inaccuracy.

In the same town there was a hunchback – I never saw one so misshapen. His head was an ample size, and I fancy Nature must have taken great pains in fashioning him. He was quite unlike any normal person, in fact he was really hideous. He had this huge head, and an ugly shock of hair, a short neck, and broad shoulders which were all hunched up. Anyone who tried to describe him fully would be a fool to waste his time: he was too hideous for words. All his life he had been intent on amassing a large fortune. Take it from me, he was frightfully rich; indeed, if my source is to be trusted, no one in the town was as rich as he was. So much for the hunchback and his achievements.

Because of his large fortune, his friends gave him that beautiful girl in marriage, but she was so lovely that after marrying her he was never free from anxiety. The hunchback was so jealous that there could be no peace of mind for him. The doors of his house were kept closed all day. He would never admit anyone to the house unless the man brought something with him, or came to borrow money. All day long the hunchback would sit on the threshold.

One Christmas, three hunchbacked minstrels turned up at his address. They all said they wanted to spend that feast-day with him, because there was no one in the town with whom they could have fared better, since he was of the same kind as themselves, as much a hunchback as they were. So the master of the house led them up the stairs (for the house had an outside staircase). The meal was ready and they all sat down to dinner – a very fine and sumptuous dinner too, I must say. The hunchback was neither miserly nor mean, and he entertained his fellows lavishly. They had bacon and peas, and capons too, and finally, when the meal was over, I believe the host gave

5

each of the three hunchbacks twenty Paris shillings. Then he forbade them ever to appear again in the house or the grounds: if they were ever caught there again, they would get a severe ducking in the cold water of the river (for the house, a large, spacious building, stood on the river-bank). When the hunchbacks heard that, they left the house readily enough and with beaming faces, for they considered that they had had a very good day. Soon after that, the owner left the house too, and crossed the bridge.

The lady, who had heard the hunchbacks singing and revelling, had all three of them brought back, for she wanted to hear them sing. Then she had the doors firmly closed. And while the hunchbacks were singing and making merry with the lady of the house, why, her husband came back: he hadn't been away very long. The lady heard her husband arrive, and clearly recognized his voice. She didn't know what on earth to do with the hunchbacks, or how they could be hidden. Now near the fireplace there was a large box bed, which could be moved around, and in it there were three compartments. What do you think happened next? Quite simple, really: she put one hunchback in each compartment. The husband came in and sat down beside his wife, whose favours he greatly appreciated. He didn't sit there for long, however, but soon went out again, down the stairs and away.

The wife didn't in the least mind when she saw her husband leave the house. She wanted to dismiss the hunchbacks whom she had hidden in the box bed, but, when she opened up the compartments again, she found all three of them had died of suffocation! Greatly alarmed, she ran to the door and, calling to a street porter whom she saw passing, asked him to come over. Hearing this, the young man hurried over to her without delay. 'My good fellow', she said, 'Listen to me! If you will solemnly promise that you will never inform against me for what I'm about to tell you, you shall be richly rewarded. I'll give you thirty pounds in hard cash when you've done this job for me.' When the porter heard that offer, he promised readily enough, for he coveted all that money, and besides, he didn't lack resolution. He fairly raced up the stairs. The lady threw open one of the compartments and said 'Don't be alarmed, my friend! Just throw this corpse into the river for me, and you will have done me a very great service.' She handed him a sack, and he took it and quickly stuffed the hunchback into it, then hoisted it onto his back and went down the stairs with it. He hurried straight on to the bridge over the river, hurled the hunchback into the water and, without pausing, went straight back to the house.

In the meantime, the lady had with great difficulty dragged another hunchback out of the box bed – a task which left her rather short of breath – and then moved away a little. The porter came hurrying back. 'I'll take the money now, lady,' he said. 'I've got rid of that dwarf for you.' 'You insolent lout!' she exclaimed, 'How dare you try to make a fool of me! The dwarf has just turned up again: you didn't throw him into the water at all – you brought him back with you. There he is, if you don't believe me.' 'How in the name of all the devils in hell did he get back into the house? I simply can't make it out. He was dead, wasn't he? He must be antichrist himself, but, by St Remy, it won't do him any good!' With that, he seized the other hunchback, stuffed him into the sack, slung him effortlessly over his shoulder and hurried out of the house.

The lady at once dragged the third hunchback out of the box bed, laid him down by the fire, and then made for the door. The porter flung the second hunchback head-first into the water. 'On your way!' he cried, 'I dare you to come back!' Then he hastened back to the house and told the lady to pay him off. She didn't argue, but, assuring him he would be paid, led him towards the hearth as though she knew nothing of the third hunchback lying there. 'Well, fancy that!' she exclaimed, 'Who ever heard of such a thing? Look! It's that hunchback lying there again!' When he saw the corpse lying there beside the fire, the young man was anything but amused. 'Look at that!' he cried, 'By the Sacred Heart! Who ever saw such a customer? Am I to do nothing else this blessed day but hump a beastly hunchback around? Every time I throw him into the water, I find him here when I come back!' With that, he put the third one into the sack and vigorously swung it over his shoulder, fairly seething with rage, vexation and annoyance. He angrily stumped off down the stairs, tipped the hunchback into the water and thus got rid of this third load. 'You can go the the devil,' he said. 'I'm fed up with humping you around all day. Just let me see you come back again after this, and it'll be too late for you to be sorry. You must have cast a spell on me, but by the God who gave me life, if you follow me once more and I can find a cudgel or an iron bar, I'll give you such a whack on the head that you'll have a bloody crown!'

With those words he turned away and went up the the house again, but before he reached the top of the staircase he looked back and saw the owner of the house returning. The good fellow took it very much to heart: with his hand he crossed himself three times. 'Lord God, deliver me,' he said – and he was really furious, 'Honestly! This fellow must be mad to follow so close on my heels that he's nearly overtaken me. By the bowels of St Morant, he must take me for an idiot, seeing that whenever I carry him away I can never stop him from following me all the way back.' With that, he ran and seized with both hands a club which he saw hanging by the door, and came running back to the staircase. By this time, the owner of the house had nearly reached the top of the stairs. 'What's this, Mr Hunchback, back again? Looks like sheer obsinacy to me! By the body of St Mary, you'll wish you had kept away! You must think I don't mean what I say!' With those words he raised the club and gave him such a blow with it on that huge head of his that he dashed his brains out and struck him down dead on the steps. Then he put him in the sack, tied up the neck with a rope, set off at a run and hurled him, still securely inside the sack, into the water – for he was still seriously worried lest the other follow him again. 'Down you go!' he said, 'and bad cess to you! This time I don't think it's likely you'll come back in a hurry.' He hastened back to the lady and asked to be paid for having done her bidding so thoroughly. The lady did not feel disposed to haggle, and paid the young man the full amount – thirty pounds and no less. She paid him to his complete satisfaction, for she was herself highly satisfied with the bargain. She said he had done an excellent day's work in ridding her of that hideous husband of hers. She felt sure all her troubles were over for life, now that she was free again.

Durand, in bringing his tale to a close, declares that God never created a girl whom money could not buy; and if the truth is to be told, God never made any possession, however excellent, however valuable, that hasn't got its price. It was because of his money that the hunchback won the fair lady. Shame on any man (it doesn't matter who he is) who cares too much for sinful money; and shame on the man who first invented the stuff!

4. The Housewife of Orleans

Now I will tell you a most pleasing tale about a housewife, born and bred in Orleans. Her husband came from Amiens, and was a very wealthy landowner indeed. He knew all the tricks and the finer points of trade and money-lending, and what he had, he held – very firmly, in both hands.

To the town had come four young students, carrying their bags like porters. They were big fat fellows, and I really mean it when I say they were hearty eaters. They lodged in the city, and were held in great esteem. One of them was particularly impressive, and he spent a lot of time at our goodman's house. He was considered quite a gentleman; there was no pride or arrogance in him at all, and truly, the lady of the house enjoyed his company very much. He was so frequent a visitor that the townsman resolved to teach him a lesson either by his conduct or by his words, if he could see his way to it. Now, there was a niece of his living in the house, to whom he had given a home a long time before. Well, he secretly called this girl to him, and promised her a new dress if she would act as a spy and tell him truthfully what happened.

The student made such amorous overtures to the goodman's wife that she agreed to do as he wished, and the girl, who was eavesdropping all the time,

8

eventually heard them come to an arrangement. She went at once to the master of the house and told him what the arrangement was, namely that the lady was to send for the student when her husband was away on his travels: the student was then to come to the two locked gates of the garden (she had shown him where) and she would be there to meet him when it was quite dark. Hearing this, the husband was delighted. He went to his wife at once and said 'Wife, I have to go away on business. Look after the house, my dear, as a good wife should. I've no idea when I shall be back.' 'Of course I will, husband,' she said. The husband made his carters get ready, and said he would be spending that night a full three leagues from the town, so as to give himself a good start on his journey.

The lady did not realize it was a trick, and duly told the student all about it. But the husband, in his scheme to deceive them, sent his servants off to take lodgings for the night, and then turned up himself at the garden gate, for by this time it was almost dark. The lady stealthily went to the spot, opened the gate for him, and clasped him in her arms, thinking it was her lover – but that was wishful thinking! 'Welcome,' she said. The other refrained from speaking out loud, and returned her greeting in a whisper. As they slowly crossed the garden, he kept his face bent low. Suspecting a trap, his wife stooped down a little and peered under his hood, and then clearly realized that it was her husband, trying to take her in. Having recognized him, she wondered how she might deceive him in her turn. Women have been known to outclass Argus himself: since the days of Abel, wise men have been taken in by their wiles. 'Sir,' she said, 'I'm so glad to have you close to me like this. I'll give you enough money to pay your debts, if you keep this affair secret. Now let's go quietly into the house. I will secretly let you into an upstairs room to which I have the key, and there you shall quietly wait for me until our servants have had their supper. Then, when they've all gone to bed, I'll guide you to my bedroom. No one will ever know about it.' 'Well said, lady,' he replied.

Oh God! Little did he know what she had in mind for him! 'What the donkey-driver thinks is one thing: the donkey has other ideas!' He was soon to come to a pretty pass, for when the lady had locked him into that upstairs room, from which he could not escape, she went back to the garden gate to receive her lover, whom she met there. How she hugged him, embraced him, and kissed him! The second comer was far better off than the first, I fancy. The lady let her clod of a husband cool his heels in that upstairs room for a long time. The lovers quickly crossed the garden and made for the room where the bed had been made ready. Yes, she took her lover into that room and stowed him under the coverlet, where he soon began the game which love enjoins – indeed, he wouldn't have cared a filbert for any other game, nor would she have thanked him for any other. For a long time they

9

thus made merry. Then with a hug and a kiss, she said 'Darling, now you must stay here for a while and wait for me while I go and give the staff their meal. Afterwards, this very night, you and I will have supper together, all on our own.' 'Just as you say, lady.'

She stole away and joined the rest of the household in the hall and made them as merry as she could. Then, when their meal was ready, they all ate and drank their fill. When the meal was over, but before the company broke up, she addressed them all in her subtle way. There were two of her husband's nephews there, plus a kitchen-boy who used to fetch water, her husband's niece, two man-servants and an odd-job man. 'Now listen to me, all of you, in God's name,' she said. 'You've seen coming to this house a certain student who simply won't leave me alone. He's been asking me for my love for a long time now, and I've refused him any number of times. When I saw there was nothing else for it, I promised him I would do whatever he asked, as soon as my husband was away. Well, now he *is* away, and may God keep him safe! I've been as good as my word to this fellow who pesters me every day. Now his hour of reckoning has come! He's waiting for me in the room upstairs. I'll give you a generous measure of the best wine in the house on condition that you pay him out for me. Go upstairs to him in that room and beat him soundly with sticks, whether he's standing up or lying down. Give him such a thrashing that he'll never come here again and make suggestions to a respectable woman.'

When the household heard what was afoot, none lagged behind: they all jumped to their feet. One seized a stick, another a club, another a stout and sturdy cudgel. The goodwife gave them the key. Now if anyone could keep a tally of all the blows that were to be struck, I'd consider him a first-class reckoner! 'Don't let him get out: lay hold of him in the room upstairs!' 'By God!' they said, 'Master Student, now you're going to get it!' One of them forced him to bend down and, seizing him by the throat, pulled his hood so tightly round his neck that he couldn't utter a word. Then they began to pitch into him, and they were anything but grudging with their blows. If he had paid a thousand marks for it, he couldn't have had his coat dusted more thoroughly! Several times over, his own two nephews took pains to let him have it, both above and below the belt. His yells for mercy didn't help him a bit. At last they dragged him out like a dead dog, flung him on a dung-heap, and went back into the house. They were given generous measures of the best wines in the house – white wines and Auvergne wines – just as if they had been royalty. As for the lady, she and her lover had cakes and wine on a fine white linen table-cloth, by the light of a big wax candle, and they held converse all night, in fact until daybreak. When they parted, out of love for him she gave him ten marks in cash, and begged him to come back whenever he could.

10

The husband, lying on the dung-heap, bestirred himself as best he could and made for the house. When his servants saw him so badly knocked about, they were amazed and horrified, and asked him how he felt. 'Awful!' he answered. 'Carry me into the house, and don't ask me any more questions.' They lost no time in lifting him up. Yet one thing was a great consolation to him, and quite banished evil thoughts from his mind, and that was that he now thought his wife was quite devoted to him. He cared nothing for all his aches and pains, and mentally resolved that, when he got better, he would always cherish her. Thus he re-entered his house. When his wife saw him, she gave him a bath with healing herbs, and completely healed all his injuries. She asked him what had happened. 'I was involved in a nasty accident,' he said, 'and some of my bones got broken.'

The servants told him how they had dealt with the student, whom the mistess had handed over to them. 'Upon my soul, she disposed of him like a virtuous and sensible wife.' Never again, for the rest of his life, did he criticize her conduct or mistrust her, and she – well, *she* never tired of steadfastly loving her lover, until he went back to his own district.

5. Brownie, the Priest's Cow

My tale is of a peasant and his wife, who on a feast-day of Our Lady went to church to pray. Before the service, the priest preached a sermon in which he said that it was a good and sensible attitude to give for God's sake, 'for God restores twofold a gift sincerely given'.

'Do you hear what the priest is promising us, my dear?' said the peasant. 'He says that if you give something for God's sake, and really mean it, God allows you to thrive and prosper. So if it's all right with you, we can do nothing better with our cow than give it to the priest. Besides, she isn't a very good milker.'

'In view of what you say, husband,' the wife said, 'he can have her so far as I'm concerned.'

Then they went home, and there was no further discussion. The peasant went into the cow-shed, led the cow out by its halter, and went and presented it to the dean, who was a wise and clever priest. With his hands respectfully clasped, the peasant said 'Reverend, I'm giving Blanche to you, for God's sake'; then, placing the halter-rope in his hand, he swore that he had nothing else to give. The Rev. Mr Constant, the priest (always keen on snapping things up) replied 'That's very sensible of you, my friend. Off you

11

go now, your mission's well accomplished. I only wish all my parishioners were as intelligent as you – then I'd have a lot of cattle.'

When the peasant had taken his leave, the priest at once gave orders that Blanche was to be tethered to Brownie, his own big cow, so as to accustom them to each other. His clerk led her into the paddock and there, I fancy, he found their own cow and tied the one to the other. Then he went away and left them. Now the priest's cow, wishing to graze, tried to put her head down, but Blanche would have none of this, and pulled so hard on the rope that she dragged Brownie right out of the paddock. Down the road, past houses, hempfields and meadows, all the way back to her own home, Blanche led the priest's cow – no easy task!

When the peasant looked out and saw them coming, his heart was filled with joy. 'Hurrah, my dear,' he said, 'God certainly gives increase, for here's Blanche back again, bringing us another cow, a big brown one. Now we've got two of them for one. Our shed will hardly be big enough!'

This tale tells us, by means of an illustration, that it's foolish not to give freely. It's the man who gives his worldly goods to God who really possesses them, not the man who hides them or buries them. If he is to thrive and prosper, a man has to be very lucky, that's obvious. And it was precisely because he was very lucky that the peasant had two cows in the end, and the priest none. He who thinks he's doing well may fare badly!

6. The Donkey's Last Will and Testament

He who tries to live his life in comfortable circumstances and to follow the example of those who aim at amassing wealth, meets with a great deal of trouble in this world, for there are many slanderers about, ever ready to harm him, and there are also large numbers of envious people in our midst. However handsome or gracious a man may be, if there are ten people sitting in his house, six of them will be slanderers, and nine of them envious. Behind his back, they care nothing for him, but to his face they are all smiles and nods. When those who share his very table are envious of him, unreliable and disloyal, it is obvious that those who get nothing from his way of life will be envious of him too. And so they are, without a doubt.

I'm telling you this because of a certain priest who had a good living. Now, he had concentrated all his endeavour on making money and getting rich: on this he brought all his ingenuity to bear. That priest had plenty of clothes and money, and his barns were full of corn, for he knew just when to sell, and when to hold over a sale from Easter to Michaelmas. Why, even his best friend could get nothing from him, unless he was absolutely forced to hand over. His domestic establishment included a donkey, the like of which was never seen. I don't think I've ever known so good a servant – why, it worked for him for twenty years! Now that donkey, which had contributed a great deal to his prosperity, died of old age. The priest so valued it that he would now allow the corpse to be skinned, and he went and buried it in the churchyard. Now I will speak of something else for a while.

His bishop was a very different proposition. He was neither covetous nor miserly, but courteous and kindly: even when he was very ill, if he saw a worthy man coming to his house, no one could have kept him in bed. The best possible physic for him was the company of good Christians. His hall was always full, and his staff good-natured. Anything the master wanted was no trouble to his servants. Such furniture as he had was not paid for, for he who overspends, gets into debt.

One day the worthy bishop, that authority on goodness, had a large company in his house, and the conversation happened to fall upon those wealthy clerics, those mean and miserly priests who do no favours for a bishop or a lord, and bring no honour upon them. Our extremely rich and wealthy priest came in for some slander on that occasion: his life was as fully described as if they had read a book about him, and he was credited with having more money than three men could have had, for people always make much more of such things than is found to be justified in the end. 'And what's more, he has done something which could cost him a great deal of money, if all the facts were made public,' said one who wished to curry favour, 'and there would be a big reward in it for someone.'

'Well, what has he done?' asked the worthy bishop.

'Worse than any heathen Arab would have done – he's gone and buried Baldwin, his donkey, in consecrated ground!'

'Damnation take the fellow!' exclaimed the bishop. 'If that's true, shame on him and all his money! Walter, summon him to our presence: we'll see what he has to say to the accusation Robert has just made. And I'll tell you this – so help me God! – if it's true, he shall pay for it.'

'I give you leave to hang me if what I've told you isn't true. Besides, he's never done anything for you.'

The priest was summoned, and he came, for he must give an account of himself before the bishop in this matter, which was serious enough to ruin him. 'You false and faithless enemy of God,' the bishop began. 'What have you done with your donkey? You have grievously wronged the Holy Church. I never heard of a more flagrant case! Why, you've buried your donkey where Christian folk are laid to rest! By St Mary the Egyptian, if this can be proved, and found to be true by honest folk, I'll have you put in prison. I

13

never heard of such an outrage.' The priest replied 'My dear good lord, I could make a statement here and now, but I ask for a day for deliberation, for it is only right (if you don't mind) that I should think the matter over. Not that I want to make a lengthy affair of it.' 'All right, you may have time for deliberation, but if this business is true, I'll have satisfaction.' 'Don't jump to any conclusions, my lord.' The priest then took his leave of the bishop, who took a grave view of the affair. The priest, for his part, was not at all worried, for he knew full well that he had a reliable friend in his purse which never let him down in the matter of fines or misdeeds.

'While the fool sleeps, the appointed hour comes round.' Well, the appointed hour came round all right, and the priest came back, bringing with him twenty pounds in his money-belt, in cash, all good money – he was clearly not likely to starve! When the bishop saw him coming, he could not refrain from saying 'Well, priest, have you thought it over, and do you now realize the extent of your folly?'

'My Lord, I've certainly thought it over; but acrimony doesn't make for balanced judgements, and you will, I am sure, realize that some matters have to be discussed privately. I will reveal to you what is on my mind; and if atonement is called for, whether it be financial or corporal, by all means set me on the right path!'

The bishop moved closer to the priest, so that they could whisper to each other, and the priest, who for once did not reckon the cost, looked up at him, taking care to keep the money under his cloak, so that the others could not see it. In a whisper he told his tale. 'My Lord, it's a very simple story really. My donkey lived a long time and proved to be an excellent investment. So may God grant me absolution, he was a willing and faithful servant for a full twenty years. Every year he earned twenty shillings, and thus saved up twenty pounds. He has left you that sum in his will so that he may be saved from hell-fire.' Then the bishop said 'May God be with him and forgive him all his sins and trespasses.'

As you have heard, the bishop was delighted in the end with the rich priest's misdemeanour, and showed him the right thing to do in the circumstances. Rutebeuf's edifying message to us is this: 'He who has money for use in emergencies, need not fear unpleasant entanglements.' The donkey continued to enjoy Christian burial, for his bequest was paid off in full; and with that I end this poem.

7. The Peasant Doctor

There was once a wealthy peasant, a man of much property, though very mean. He had three ploughs and their oxen, all his very own, two mares and two horses, much wheat, plenty of meat and wine, in fact everything he needed. Yet all his friends and neighbours criticized him because he was unmarried, so in the end he said he would marry a suitable wife, if he could find one. They all said they would try to find one for him, the very best available. In the district there lived an elderly knight, a widower with one daughter, and a very charming and beautiful young lady she was. The peasant's friends approached the knight and asked him for his daughter, on behalf of this wealthy and prosperous peasant, who had so many jewels and so much linen. Well, the marriage was arranged. The young lady, a thoroughly sensible girl, had lost her mother and, not wishing to oppose her father's wishes, agreed to whatever he decided. As soon as it could be done, the wedding was held and the peasant married the girl, though she would much rather not have married him, had there been any alternative.

When the business of the wedding and other matters were over and done with, it wasn't long before the peasant, thinking it over, came to realize that he had made a mistake, and that it ill became a man in his position to be married to a knight's daughter. 'When I'm ploughing, the chaplain will come down the lane, for every day is a holiday for him; and when I'm away from the house, that priest will be there day after day, and in the end he'll seduce my wife, and she will never love me – why, she won't care a straw for me. What a wretched business!' said the peasant. 'I really don't know what to do, and just being sorry won't make things any better.' He began to rack his brains for a way to prevent his wife from being seduced. 'I know!' he said. 'If I beat her every morning when I get up to go to my work in the fields, she will cry all day long. Surely no-one will come courting as long as she is in tears. Then when I come home in the evening, I'll ask her to forgive me in God's name. I'll make her happy every evening, and miserable every morning.'

Having hit upon this idea, the peasant asked for a meal. No fish or partridge for them: they had good cheeses, and fried eggs, and bread and wine in plenty, all from his ample supplies. Then, when the table-cloth had been removed, he gave his wife such a blow on the face with the flat of his big broad hand that you could see the marks his fingers left. The brute then seized her by the hair and beat her just as if she had fully deserved it! After that, he went off to plough his land.

'Oh dear!' she cried. 'What shall I do? How can I help myself? Oh dear! I'm so unhappy,' she went on. 'Oh dear! I wish I had never been born! Oh God, what a mess my life is in! Oh God, how my father let me down by

15

marrying me to this peasant! Was I afraid I might starve? Really, I must have been out of my mind when I agreed to it!' And she added, in her distress, 'Oh God, why did my mother have to die?' So she wept all day long, until the peasant came home from the fields. He fell at his wife's feet and begged her, in God's name, to forgive him. 'Wife,' he cried, 'for God's sake have pity on me! It was the Devil who made me do it! I'm really and truly sorry for beating you and ill-treating you like that.' That vile peasant talked her into forgiving him, and then asked for his supper, and she gave him a generous helping of what she had prepared. They went to bed on good terms. In the morning, however, the loathsome fellow ill-treated her so badly that he nearly maimed her for life, and then went off to plough his fields. She began to cry. 'Oh dear,' she said, 'how unhappy I am! Oh dear, I wish I had never been born! What a wretched fate is mine! Oh God, has that husband of mine ever been beaten? No – he doesn't know what it's like. If he did, he wouldn't beat me like that, for all the world.'

While she was thus lamenting her fate, along came two of the king's servants, riding on two large palfreys. They came into the house and asked for dinner, and she readily provided it, and then asked them 'Where have you gentlemen come from, and what are you looking for? I hope you don't mind telling me.' One of them answered 'Lady, believe me, we are the king's messengers. We have been sent to fetch a doctor, and have to cross over to England.'

'A doctor? What for?'

'The king's daughter, Princess Ada, is in such a bad way that she hasn't eaten or drunk for a whole week, for a fish-bone has lodged in her throat. The king will be deeply distressed if he loses her: he'll never smile again.'

'Gentlemen,' she said, 'listen to me. You won't have to go as far as you think. Take my word for it when I tell you that my husband is an excellent doctor. Indeed, he knows more about medicine and physic and diagnosis than Hippocrates ever did.'

'Do you really mean it, lady?'

'I'm perfectly serious,' she said, 'but he has this odd quirk of character, that he won't agree to do anything unless he's given a good beating first.'

'We'll soon see about that,' they replied. 'If we fail, it won't be for lack of beating. Where shall we find him, lady?'

'You'll find him as soon as you ride out of the courtyard. You see that stream over there, beside the lane where the old houses are? The very first strip of plough-land you come to after that is ours: that's where you must go – and may St Peter the Apostle guide you.'

So they galloped off, and soon found the peasant. They greeted him in the king's name and then told him he must come without delay to the king. 'What for?' the peasant asked.

'Because of your great skill: there isn't so good a doctor anywhere else. We've come a long way looking for you.' When the peasant heard them calling him a doctor, he stared at the ground for a moment and said it was the first he had heard of it. 'Well, what are we waiting for?' said the one to the other. 'You know he won't cooperate unless he's beaten.' One of them hit him behind the ear, while the other struck him on the back with a big thick stick. Between them they so knocked him about that they felled him to the ground. Feeling those blows land on his shoulders and back, the peasant soon realized he couldn't win, and cried 'I'm a first-rate doctor! Now stop, for heaven's sake!'

'Just get on a horse, then,' they said, 'and come along with us to the king.' They did not try to get another palfry for him, but quickly put him on the first mare available. When they reached the court, the king came hurrying to meet him, for he was anxious for his daughter's recovery. He asked who it was they had found, and one of the servants told him: 'The man we've brought you is a thoroughly base-born fellow, but he's a good doctor.' Then they told him about the peasant's peculiarity, and how he wouldn't cooperate unless he was beaten first. The king's comment was 'A poor sort of doctor! I never heard of one like that. Well, if that's the way it is, let him be soundly beaten.'

'We're ready to start,' they said. 'We'll give him his due before you've even said the word!'

The king turned to the peasant and said 'Doctor, sit down here, and I'll send for my daughter, who needs urgent treatment.'

'But honestly, Sire, I assure you I know nothing about medicine and never had anything to do with it in my life!'

The King said 'This is incredible! Beat him for me!' They jumped to it and did so, readily enough. The peasant, feeling those blows on his back and shoulders, cried out to the king 'Have mercy, Sire! I'll cure her, I promise you.'

'Let him be,' said the king. 'Don't beat him any more now.' The girl was present in the hall, looking very wan and pale, with her throat all swollen on account of the fish-bone. The peasant wondered how he might cure her, for now he knew she must get better or die.

'I'm sure that if she were to laugh, the effort would make the fish-bone fly out, for it isn't embedded in the flesh. I must do or say something to make her laugh.' Then he said to the king 'Sire, by your leave, hear what I have to say. Make them light a big fire for me in a private room where there is no one but myself and your daughter. Then you shall see what I will do, for, if it be God's will, I will cure her.'

'Certainly,' the king replied.

Servants and squires promptly came forward and lit the fire where the

17

king directed. Then, I'm told, the 'doctor' and the girl were alone in the room. The young lady sat down by the fire on a chair placed there for her, and the peasant took off all his clothes – yes, even his breeches, and sat himself down by the fire and scratched himself and toasted himself all over. He had long nails and his hide was tough: there is no man, from here to Saumur, who wouldn't be in prime condition if he were scratched as thoroughly as that! And when the girl saw this, for all her suffering, she couldn't help laughing, and so strained herself that the fish-bone flew out of her mouth and landed on the hearth. The peasant promptly put his clothes on again and picked up the fish-bone. Very pleased with himself, he went out of the room and called out as soon as he saw the king: 'Sire, your daughter is cured; here, thank God, is the fish-bone.' The king was overjoyed.

'Truly, doctor,' he said, 'I can tell you there is no man I love better than you. You've saved my daughter's life: your coming was a blessing. You shall have jewels and clothes in abundance.'

'Thank you, Sire, but I don't want them. I cannot stay with you: I must go back to my farm.'

'By God!' exclaimed the king. 'You'll do nothing of the kind! You shall stay here with me as my doctor.'

'But Sire,' the peasant protested, 'there's no bread in my house. When I left home yesterday morning we were due to visit the miller.'

'We'll see about that!' was the king's comment. 'Beat him – then he'll stay!' Men at once sprang forward and lost no time in beating him. The peasant began to yell 'Stop it! I'll stay!'

And so he stayed on at the court. They cut his hair, and shaved him properly too, and he was given a fine gown to wear. He thought his troubles were over, but then all the sick people in the district – and there were, I believe, some thirty or forty of them – came as one man to see the king, and each of them told him of his symptoms. The king turned to the peasant and said 'Doctor, attend to these people, and cure them for me, quickly.'

The peasant said 'Spare me, for heaven's sake, there are too many of them, really there are!' The king called to his servants, and each of them took up a big stick, for they all knew very well what they had been summoned for. The peasant was greatly alarmed when he saw them coming for him, and said to the king 'Have mercy, Sire, I'll cure them!'

'Let me see, then,' said the king. The peasant asked for some firewood. He soon had an ample supply, whatever its use was to be. Expertly, he himself lit a huge fire in the hall, and then made all the sick line up.

To the king he said 'May I ask all those who are not ill to leave the hall?' The king readily agreed to this, and he and his retinue went downstairs. Turning to the sick, the peasant said 'Gentlemen, by the God who made me, curing you is going to be a very difficult business. There is only one way in which I

18

can manage it, and I'll tell you what it is. I'm going to pick out the sickest man and burn him in that fire. The rest of you will then benefit enormously from drinking a medicine made from his ashes: you will be cured instantly.'

They all looked at each other. There was none so crippled or so dropsi-cal that he could bring himself to admit – no, not even in exchange for Normandy – that he was the most seriously ill. The peasant said to the first man in the queue 'You look very frail: you must be the weakest of the lot.'

'No, Doctor,' he cried 'I feel perfectly all right.'

'Off you go then. What did you come in here for?' The fellow was out through the door in one bound.

The king asked him 'Are you cured?'

'Yes, Sire, thank God, I am. I'm as fit as a fiddle. That doctor's a real gentleman!' Need I say any more? Not a single one, big or little, could be induced to let the doctor throw him into the fire: no, they all walked away as if they had completely recovered.

When the king saw this, he was beside himself with joy. He strode into the hall and said 'My dear Doctor, I can't imagine how on earth you cured them all so quickly.'

'Sire,' he replied, 'I cast a spell on them: I know one stronger than ginger or zedoary.'

'Doctor,' said the king, 'Now you can go home when you like. You shall have clothes, money, palfreys, fine chargers – and you shan't be beaten any more. I'm ashamed at the way you've been treated.'

'I thank you, Sire,' said the peasant. 'I'm your loyal subject, entirely at your service.' He promptly left the king's hall and went home and lived in style in his own district. He never went ploughing again, and he never beat his wife again either, but loved and cherished her.

It all happened just as I have told you. Through his wife and by his own cunning, the peasant became a good doctor, and all without studying!

8. St Peter and the Minstrel

It is only to be expected that the man whose job it is to tell stories will tell as good a yarn as his wit allows.

There once lived a minstrel in Sens, a man of very lowly estate, whose clothes were seldom without patches. I don't know what his name was: anyway, he often lost all he had at dice. He often had to pawn his harp, or his boots, or his tunic, so that when the cold winds blew he often had nothing to wear but his shirt. Don't think I'm exaggerating: he often even went barefoot. Footwear meant a great deal to him: his clothes might hang in tatters from his body, but on those rare occasions when he happened to own a pair of shoes, full of holes and with no nails, he was tremendously proud of them: they were for him the last word in elegance. The tavern was his favourite haunt – the tavern and then the brothel: he was a pillar of both establishments. What more can I say about him than that he loved drinking and wenching, and drinking and gambling? He would spend whatever he had, for he always wanted to be living it up in tavern or brothel, with a green garland round his head. He would have liked every day to be a holiday: he couldn't wait for Sunday to come round. He wasn't a man for rowdiness or squabbling – he was just totally immoral.

Now you shall hear what became of him. He made sin and folly his way of life, but when he had lived out his mortal span he must needs pass away and die. The Devil, always seeking to ensnare people and catch them out, came at the moment of death to carry off his soul; and because the man had died in a state of sin, no one disputed the Devil's rights. He promptly slung him over his shoulder and made off with him, straight to Hell. In the meantime the Devil's henchmen had collected a large number of other souls from a wide catchment area: some of them brought in prize-fighters, others brought in money-lenders, or thieves, or bishops, priests, monks, abbots, knights – any number of folk who had been leading base and sinful lives, and who were thus caught up with in the end. The devils took them straight to Hell, where they found their leader Lucifer. He, seeing them coming in with their loads, exclaimed 'By my faith, a welcome sight! And about time too! These fellows are in for a rough time.' He had them thrown into the great cauldron. 'Gentlemen,' he then said to his devils, 'I rather think you're not all here yet, to judge from what I've seen.'

'Yes, we are, Master, all but one – a miserable wretch who's no good at all at ensnaring people, a dead loss when it comes to soul-snatching.' Just then they saw the straggler coming in at a leisurely pace, with that ragged minstrel slung over his shoulder. Ragged? Why, he was half-naked when he entered Hell. The minstrel was thrown down, and the Master addressed thim thus:

'Now then!' he said, 'How goes it with you? Are you a rogue? A traitor? A thief?'

'No, Sir, I'm a minstrel. I've brought with me no more than my body had in life, when it often suffered bitter cold and any number of harsh and cruel words. Now that this is my home, I'll sing for you, if you like.'

'Friend, I've no use for songs, you'll have to turn your hand to something else. And since you're so destitute and so poorly clad, you shall look after the fire beneath the cauldron.'

'Gladly,' he said, 'for by St Peter, I could do with some warmth.'

Then he sat down near the fireplace, quickly lit the fire, and soon had as warm a blaze as he wanted.

It happened one day that the devils got together and sallied forth from Hell for a world-wide round-up of souls. Their leader came to the minstrel, who kept the fire going night and day, and said to him:

'Now listen to me, minstrel. I'm going to entrust all my souls to you. Guard my flock, if you value your eyes – for I'll put both of them out if you lose a single one; in fact, I'll hang you by the neck!'

'Master,' said the minstrel, 'You can safely go. I'll do my utmost to guard them faithfully: you'll get them all back.'

'On that understanding, I'm handing them over to you, my friend, but let me tell you this. If you lose a single one, I swear I'll eat you alive on the spot. On the other hand, I can also honestly assure you that when in our own good time we get back, you shall have a nice fat monk served up on a griddle for your dinner, with money-lender sauce, or with lecher sauce.'

Then off they went, leaving the minstrel behind busily stoking the fire. There he was, all by himself in Hell.

Gentlemen, let me tell you briefly what St Peter did. He went straight off to Hell, looking most distinguished with his long beard and well-combed whiskers. Carrying a gaming-board and three dice, he slipped secretly into Hell, and very quietly went and sat down beside the minstrel and asked him:

'Do you fancy a game, my friend? Just look what a fine gaming-board I've brought, and three well-shaped dice to go with it! You might win some ready cash from me, on the quiet.' (With this, he gave him a quick glimpse of his purse with the money in it.)

'Sir,' the minstrel answered, 'leave me alone and go away! I haven't any money, so there! I swear by God, without a word of a lie, that all I have in the world is the shirt on my back!'

Then St Peter said 'In that case, my dear fellow, stake five or six souls.'

'I wouldn't dare,' the minstrel said, 'for if I were to lose a single one, my master would beat me, or eat me alive.'

To this St Peter said 'Who's going to tell him? Why, even twenty souls would never be missed. Look, here's the money, all bright and new. Go on, win these coins, fresh from the mint. I propose an initial stake of a hundred shillings.'

When the minstrel saw how much money St Peter had, I can tell you the idea greatly appealed to him. He took the dice and weighed them in his hand. How he longed for that money!

'Let's play, then,' he blurted out, 'with just one soul as the stake for the throw, and no more.'

'Make it two,' said the other. 'You're no sportsman. Why not increase the stake by one soul – it can be any colour you like.'

'All right then,' said the minstrel, and St Peter said:

'I'm raising the stake.'

'Damn you!' said the minstrel. 'Lay the money on the board before we throw!'

'Of course I will, in God's name,' said the other. Then he staked the money, and the pair of them sat down to a game of hazard[1] right there beside the furnace.

'You take first throw, minstrel,' said St Peter, 'since you're an old hand at the game.'

Right or wrong, the minstrel threw.

'That's eight,' said St Peter 'If you now throw a hazard, it will mean three souls for me.'

The minstrel threw a three, a two, and a one.

'You've lost the throw,' St Peter said.

'Yes,' said the other, 'I'm in disgrace. That last stake was three: let's make it six this time.'

'You're on!' said St Peter, and promptly scored a winning seventeen with his throw. 'You owe me nine souls: I'm beginning to enjoy this!'

'No doubt about it,' the other said, 'I've lost all along the line. If I increase the stake, will you match it?'

'Yes,' said St Peter, 'that's a promise.'

'I owe you nine from last time: let's make it twelve for the winner this time.'

'A curse on all quitters!' said St Peter.

'It's your throw,' said the minstrel.

---

[1] *Hazard.* This game was played with three dice. There is only one thrower per round, chosen in the first instance by agreement or by a simple throw of the dice by all the players. If with his first throw he scores 3, 4, 5, 6, 15, 16, 17 or 18, these scores are 'hazards', and he wins. If he scores them with his second throw, however, he loses. If neither his first nor his second throw is a 'hazard', but a 'chance', i.e. 7 to 14 inclusive, he goes on playing until either his first score or his second comes up again. If the first, he wins; if the second, he loses.

'Right you are,' said St Peter. 'There now, it's a hazard, and I fancy you owe me three plus ten plus eight.'

'Now really,' the other exclaimed, 'by God's eyes, it can't have happened fair and square. Tell me on your word of honour, are you playing with four dice instead of three? Or have the dice been tampered with? From now on I want to play "highest points"[2].'

'By the Holy Ghost, I'll be glad to accommodate you, my friend: it shall be just as you wish. Is it to be one throw or two?'

'Let's make it one throw from now on. It's twenty-one so far, and the same again.'

Then St Peter said 'May God be on my side!' and threw without further ado. He scored fifteen, and felt confident that he could make it worth sixty.

'All right,' said the minstrel. 'Now it's my throw.' Then he threw beside the gaming-board.

'That throw's a dead loss,' said St Peter. 'You've lost the trick, for I can see six on two of them. From now on my luck is in. You owe me sixty-three souls.'

'Well, really!' the other said. 'So help me, this game is ruining me. By all the saints in Rome, I won't believe you or any man who tells me you're not fixing the dice at every throw!'

'Get on with the game! Are you out of your mind?'

'I reckon you must have been a pretty good thief, if you're still such a slippery customer! You still can't resist fixing the dice and fiddling the score!'

When he heard that, St Peter was furious, and he at once retorted angrily 'That's a lie, as I hope to be saved! But it's typical of a twister like you to say a man's cheating when things aren't going your way. A curse on the one who accused me of that, and a curse on the one who cheated, if anyone did! You're a rogue and a scoundrel, to call me a thief. Why, by St Michael, for two pins I'd punch your head for you!'

'Oh yes you are,' the other cried, beside himself with rage. 'You are a thief, old'un, to try to get our souls by cheating. You shan't take a single penny-worth with you, so there! Oh no, I'm not parting with them. Come on, try and get them, and see if you can keep them! By this head of mine, you won't get away with it!'

With that, the minstrel sprang forward and grabbed the money, but in a trice St Peter seized him round the waist. In a fury, the minstrel then let go the money, seized St Peter by his beard and pulled him violently towards

2 *Highest Points.* This is a very simple and basic game of dice. Each player throws three dice and the highest score wins. If there is a tie, the first thrower in the round is given a deciding throw.

him. Then St Peter ripped his shirt for him, right down to the waist. The minstrel had never been so upset as he was when he saw the neck of his shirt brought so low – below the belt, in fact! The two of them tussled violently: how they pushed, pulled and punched each other! One tugged, the other tore: the minstrel's shirt was badly ripped. Then the minstrel realized that he was beaten: he simply wasn't as big or strong or powerfully built as St Peter was, and he could see that if he went on fighting any longer, his shirt would be in such a state that he would never be able to wear it again.

'Sir,' he said. 'Let's call a truce. We've had a good trial of strength, now let's play again on friendly terms, if that's all right with you.'

'I'm all for it,' said St Peter, 'for just now you criticized my play, and called me a thief.'

'That was very rude of me, Sir. I'm sorry now that I was so foolish. But you did worse than that to me when you tore my shirt: that's going to mean great hardship for me. Now let's call it quits.'

'All right,' said St Peter. So they were reconciled.

'Now listen to me,' St Peter said. 'You owe me sixty-three souls.'

'By St Germanus, that's true,' said the other. 'I began the game too early in the day. Now, if you'll agree, Sir, let's go on playing, for six score souls this time, or nothing!'

'I'll do it, on condition that you do the same for me.'

'Don't worry,' said the minstrel, 'I won't say no to that.'

'So you'll pay up willingly then, will you, my dear fellow?'

'Yes,' the other said, 'and with no hard feelings. Take whatever souls you want: knights, ladies, canons. What's your fancy? Prize-fighters? Thieves? Monks? How do you like them, nice or nasty? D'you want princes or castellans?'

'Now you're talking,' said St Peter.

'Don't worry about payment, just go ahead and throw.'

That time St Peter scored only a five and a four and a three.

'That makes twelve,' the minstrel said.

'Oh dear!' said St Peter. 'Unless God takes pity on me, this last throw spells ruin.'

The minstrel threw two fives and a two, that's all.

'My God!' said St Peter. 'What luck! It's a tie, but it may yet prove to have been worth it. Let's make it twelve score, win or lose.'

'By all means,' said the minstrel. 'Twelve score it is, and no less. Throw then, in St Julian's name!'

St Peter promptly threw two sixes and a one.

'My friend,' he said, 'that was a good throw – I've beaten yours by one point.'

'Look at that! Just see what a close-run thing it was,' cried the minstrel.

'He's outdone me by a single point. Oh God! How unlucky I am! I've never had any luck – always dogged by ill-fortune, both here and in the land of the living!'

When the souls in the furnace heard clearly that St Peter had won, they called out to him from all sides 'Sir, by the God of glory, we're all counting on you.'

'Fair enough,' said St Peter, 'I'm counting on you and you're counting on me. I staked all my money to get you out of this torment. If I had lost my money, you would have had to whistle for your freedom. If I can manage it, you shall all be in my company by nightfall.'

Then the minstrel was troubled. 'Sir,' he said, 'there's nothing else for it. Either I shall completely free myself from obligation, or I shall lose every single soul, and my shirt too.' What more can I tell you? St Peter went on dicing so long, and led the minstrel such a dance, that he won every single soul. He let them all out of Hell in great crowds, and went back to Paradise. The minstrel remained behind deeply depressed, and very worried.

Then all the devils came back. Their leader entered his abode and looked all round about him – not a soul to be seen, neither in the furnace nor in the cauldron. He called the minstrel over:

'Hey you!' he said. 'What have you done with the souls I left you in charge of?'

'I'll tell you, Sir,' he said, 'only, for God's sake, have mercy on me! An old man came in here to see me, bringing a large sum of money. I thought I could easily get my hands on it, and the two of us gambled, and it all went wrong for me. The faithless trickster used loaded dice! I never had a chance to win, honest I didn't, and I've gone and lost all your souls!'

When the Master heard that, he nearly threw him into the furnace. 'Why, you misbegotten, thieving twister! We can't afford your sort of minstrel's tricks here. To blazes with your minstrelsy, it's cost me my whole establishment! And as for the devil who brought you here, by St Paul, he's going to pay for it!' The devils rushed at the one who had brought in the minstrel, and how they beat him, and thumped him, and knocked him about, and generally ill-treated him! What's more, they made him promise he would never bring into Hell any rogue, lecher, or minstrel, – nor any gambler either! They thrashed him and pulled his hair out until he agreed never to bring a minstrel into the place again. Then the Master turned to the minstrel and said:

'Get out of here, you! Just get out, that's an order! I can do without servants like you. I shall never go out looking for minstrels, or keep any of their kind here. I don't want any of them: they can go their way. Your fun-loving God is welcome to them! Now clear off, I don't want you!'

So the minstrel ran off as fast as his legs could carry him, chased out of

Hell by fiends; and he came rushing over to Paradise. When St Peter saw him coming, he ran to open the gate for him. In he came, and now he's safe! The fiends retreated.

Now cheer up, all you minstrels, rogues, lechers and gamblers, for the one who lost those souls at dice has set you all free![3]

9. The Knight who Won Back his Estranged Lady

Without further preamble, I must tell you what befell a knight and a lady. It happened not long ago in Normandy, so the written version says. The knight in question wanted to win the love of a lady, and for her sake went through a great deal in his endeavours to convince her that he loved her. He would do all the things he knew must surely please her. But I must be brief. So long did the knight woo the lady that one day she questioned him and demanded to know what right he had to woo her, when he had never in his life performed any knightly deed or prowess to please her and thus provide her with reasons for loving him. And so she told him with a smile, and certainly without resentment, that he would never command her love until she knew for certain whether he could carry a shield and a lance, and if so, with what success. 'Lady, do not concern yourself on that account. Just give me leave to organize a tournament against your husband, to take place right outside his door, so that you will be able to see all the jousting clearly. Then, if it pleases you, you will find out how handy I am with shield and lance.' The lady readily gave the knight leave to arrange the tournament, and he, thanking her warmly, hurried off at once to make the necessary arrangements.

And so the tourney was duly arranged. The two organizers not only informed all famous knights of the forthcoming event, and invited them to attend, they were so enthusiastic that they sent out invitations in all directions, right up to the last day. No time was lost in informing the knights of the exact day and time, and large numbers of them duly congregated, for such an occasion brought together the famous, the proud, and the mettlesome. When the time came for jousting, you should have seen them all putting on their hauberks and lacing on their helmets! Soon every man was

---

[3] For further information on medieval dicing see articles by C.A. Knudson in *Romania* 63 (1937) pp. 248–53 and by F. Semrau in *Beihefte zur Zeitschrift fur romanische Philologie* 23 (1910).

ready. The pair who had arranged the tourney were the first in the lists, in armour on their swift chargers, all ready to break a lance or two. They bounded forward without delay and, with their shields held in position, levelled their lances, slackened their reins and charged forward full tilt at each other. Firm and upright in the stirrups, they smashed and splintered their lances, and did not spare one another. Then they engaged in combat with their swords, each pitting his skill against the other's. The knight who had started the whole thing, and who had solemnly sworn that he would joust with the lady's husband as soon as possible, come what might, galloped towards him faster than a well-aimed arrow from a bow. With raised lance, he hurled him off his horse: neither breast-strap nor saddle-girth could hold him, and down he crashed in a heap on the ground. When the lady saw that her husband had come to grief, she was on the one hand distressed, but on the other delighted that her suitor had acquitted himself so well.

But I must get on with the story. All the participants in the tourney had made a very good beginning, when misfortune and tragedy struck, and a knight was killed. I cannot tell you the manner of his death, nor the cause of it, but the fact is that it cast a pall of gloom and depression over all those present. They buried the knight beneath an elm-tree. Then, since it was getting late, the tourney broke up, and they all dispersed to their homes. As for the lady, she hesitated no longer, but sent a messenger-boy to tell the knight that if he wanted her to cherish him and consider him her lover, he was to come and see her that very night. He was delighted with this summons, and replied that he would come most willingly. 'I won't fail, even if I were to be cut to pieces,' he said. Then the messenger-boy departed.

When night fell, he greatly longed to be at the tryst. A maid was on the look-out for him all the time, and when he arrived and greeted her she showed the anxious and trembling knight into a room where she told him to wait until the lady came to him. With that the maid went off and told her mistress that the knight had arrived and was in the room, waiting.

'Are you sure of that?'

'Yes, quite sure.'

'Then I'll go to him,' the lady said, 'when my husband has gone to bed.' The knight, finding the long wait irksome, could not help first lying down and then falling asleep, for he was very tired after wearing armour all day. The lady, worried at having delayed so long, hurried to the knight. When she saw that he was unmistakably asleep, she would not shake or push him, but immediately went away again and called her maid. 'Quick, go this very minute and tell that knight from me that he's to leave the house at once.' The girl was puzzled at this and asked why. 'I'll tell you why,' the lady answered. 'It's because he's asleep!'

'In God's name,' said the girl, 'I think you're wrong to do this to him.'

27

'Nonsense, girl! Why, he ought to stay up all night just for one kiss from a lady like me. I find his conduct offensive, for I'm sure that if he loved me, he wouldn't behave as he has done, no, not if you were to give him a hundred pounds. Go and send him packing this instant!'

Then the girl hurried off to the knight, who was fast asleep with his head on his arm. She stepped up to him and gave him a push. He sprang to his feet immediately. 'Why, hallo, lady, welcome to you! You've been an awfully long time!'

'There's no point in greeting *me*,' said the maid. 'Listen, I've got news for you. My mistress has gone to bed with her husband, and she has sent me to tell you that you must never on any account dare to show up in any place where she is.'

'Good heavens, Miss, why on earth not? Tell me!'

'All right, I will: it's because, whatever the circumstances, you shouldn't have fallen asleep while waiting for a lady so high-born, so fair, so white-skinned and so tender as my mistress is.'

'Upon my soul, Miss,' he said, 'I admit it was wrong of me but I beg you, for charity's sake, to let me go where my lady and her husband are in bed together. I tell you there's nothing in the world I've ever wanted so much as just that.'

'You may do that, I warrant you,' the maid replied. This was welcome news to the knight, and he immediately hurried off to the bedroom – there was nothing wrong with his legs! He walked straight towards the bed, but halted a little way off, with his drawn sword in his hand. The husband, awakened by the gleam, opened his eyes and caught sight of him.

'You there,' he said. 'Who are you?' The knight replied without hesitation 'I am the knight who was killed this very morning – surely you remember? That's who I am!'

'And what brings you here?'

'Sir, my soul is in grievous torment, nor will it ever find release, until it pleases that lady lying there beside you to forgive me for a single wrong I did her when I was alive. May God on high send you honour, joy and an abundance of his blessings! Ask her to forgive me, for I have told you exactly why I have come here.'

'My dear,' the husband said, 'If you feel any ill-will, or anger, or resentment towards this knight, forgive him, I beg of you.'

'I'll do nothing of the kind,' the lady replied. 'You're worrying yourself over nothing at all. It's just a will-o'-the-wisp or some such creature plaguing us all night long.'

'I certainly don't think it's that.'

'Nor do I, Sir, not for a moment,' said the knight, 'for I believe in the Lord God and in His Mother.'

'Tell me by the faith you owe to St Peter, Sir Knight,' said the husband, 'what's the source of this anger and resentment my wife feels towards you?'

'Nothing would induce me to tell you that, Sir,' said the knight, 'for if I'm in trouble now, I'd be in far worse trouble if I explained.'

'Now you shall certainly be forgiven, Sir Knight,' the lady said. 'I will torment you no longer.'

'I thank you, dear lady, for that is all I ask.'

The knight waited no longer, but went away, for he had acquitted himself of his errand; but if he had not acted as he did, he would never have won back the love he had so recently gained and lost.

Pierre d'Anfol, who first made up and composed this little tale, did so only that it might prove instructive to those who, if they had thought of it first, would certainly pass it on, for no one hears it without becoming a better man, unless he is too far gone in wickedness.

10. The Covetous Man and his Envious Companion

Gentlemen, I have just been telling you some tales, but now I will turn my hand to the truth, for a man who can relate only fiction, and cannot at times forsake falsehood for fact, is not a versatile story-teller fit for high society. If, on the other hand, he is skilled in his art, he will be well able to tell one ripe berry from two green ones.

The fact is that rather more than a hundred years ago there were two fellows leading sinful lives, for one of them was so consumed with envy that no one could compete with him in that respect, while the other, whose covetousness knew no bounds, was just as bad, or perhaps a shade worse, for his was a vice which is the high road to utter baseness. A covetous man will, for instance, lend money for gain, and give poor measure so as to enrich himself. But perhaps envy is worse after all, for it is the blight of all mankind.

This pair of whom I tell were one day riding along together through the countryside when, if I am not mistaken, they overtook St Martin.[1] Now, the saint was not long in their company before he was able to put to the test those vices which were so deeply rooted in their hearts. They came to a spot where, near a church, two well-frequented roads diverged. 'Gentlemen,' he

---

[1] St Martin was one of the most popular saints in Europe, but particularly so in France.

said, 'when we reach the church, I shall take that turning to the right; but first I must do something for your mutual benefit. One of you must make a wish, and he shall at once receive what he asks for, while the other must say nothing, though he will immediately receive twice as much.'

The covetous one promptly decided to let the other do the asking, for in that way he, for his part, stood to gain twice as much – and how he longed for that double portion! 'My good friend,' he said, 'make your wish known, in full confidence that you will get whatever you ask for. And when you ask, don't stint yourself, for if your wish does the trick, you'll be a rich man for life.'

But the other, eaten up with envy, was not going to make such a wish if he could help it, for he would be sure to die of envy if the other got more than *he* did. So they both stood their ground for a long time, and neither would make a wish. At last the covetous one said 'What are you waiting for? Do you think you stand to lose? I'll have twice as much as you in any case, and you can't stop me. Go on, make that wish, because if you don't I'll give you a bigger hiding than the proverbial donkey got when it wouldn't cross the bridge!'

'All right then,' the envious one replied. 'Rather than put up with any of your rough stuff, I'll go ahead and made a wish, so there! But because, if I wish for money and wealth, you will expect twice as much for yourself, I'll see to it that you get nothing!' He then turned to St Martin and said 'My wish is to lose one of my eyes, so that this fellow here loses *both* his. Then he will be twice as *badly* off!'

There and then, the other lost the sight of both eyes, for the saint's promise was fulfilled to the letter. And so, between them they lost three eyes out of four, and that was all they got out of it! St Martin made one of them one-eyed and the other blind – and their loss was entirely of their own making!

'Bad cess to anyone who feels sorry for them,' that's what I say, for both of them really were very nasty characters.

Spanish Tales

1. The Well

There was a young man who devoted all his energy and his thoughts and his time to learning every single one of the wiles of women, and when he had done this he decided to get married. But first he decided to take advice, and he asked the wisest man of that district how he could look after the woman he wanted to marry. The wise man advised him to build a house with high stone walls, and to keep his wife in it with enough to eat and enough to wear, but not too much; and the house should be so built that it had only one door and only one window, the window being placed so high and designed in such a way that nobody could get in or out by it.

Having heard the wise man's advice the youth followed it exactly. When he left the house in the morning, he locked the door after him, and locked it again when he came home in the evening. When he went to sleep, he hid the keys under his pillow. And he carried out this policy for a long time.

One day when he went off to business, his wife went to the window to watch the passers-by, just as she usually did. While at the window, she saw a young man with a handsome face and fine figure, and fell in love with him on the spot. Because she was passionately in love, she began, although she was so closely guarded, to work out methods of talking to her beloved youth. In her cunning and wickedness, she decided to steal the keys from her husband while he slept. And so she did. Each night she gave her husband wine and got him drunk, that she might more safely go out to meet her lover and gratify her desires.

The husband, however, having learned from the warnings of the philosophers that no actions of women are without guile, began to wonder why his wife plied him with drink every night. In order to keep an eye on her, he pretended to be drunk. His wife, not realizing what had happened, got out of bed, went to the door, opened it, and went out to her lover. The husband also got up quietly because the night was so still, went to the door, closed and locked it, and then went to the window, standing there until he saw his wife coming back, naked except for a nightdress. When she reached the house, she found the door closed, whereupon, with great pain in her heart, she began to knock on the door. The husband, hearing and seeing her, but pretending ignorance, asked who it was. She begged forgiveness for her sin, and promised never to do it again, but this did her no good, for her angry husband said he would not let her in, and would report her behaviour to her parents. She, crying louder and louder, said that unless he opened the door, she would jump into the well that was near the house and thus put an end to her life, so that he would have to account to friends and relations for her death.

33

The husband treated her threats with contempt, and still refused to let her in, so she, full of skill and cunning, took up a stone and hurled it into the well, so that he would think, hearing the noise, that she had fallen in. Then she hid behind the well. The poor simple fellow, not suspecting such a trick, heard the stone fall into the water and immediately rushed out of the house and ran to the well, thinking that he really had heard his wife falling in. As soon as the wife saw the door left open, she cunningly slipped into the house, locked the door and went to the window. Her husband, seeing how he had been fooled, said: 'Deceitful woman, you're full of the Devil's tricks! But if you let me in, I'll forgive you anything you've done to me.' She, however, hurling abuse at him, swore that she wouldn't let him in: 'You traitor, every night you creep out of here to leave me and go to the brothel, and now I'm going to denounce you and your evil deeds to your parents.' And that was what she did.

His parents, hearing what she said and thinking it was the truth, rebuked him bitterly. And so she was spared, because of her cunning, the punishment that she deserved, and it was inflicted on her husband instead. Thus he gained nothing by watching over his wife so carefully, but instead unhappiness was heaped on him, for many thought he had deserved what he had suffered. He lost much of his wealth and was left without honour, his reputation blackened by his wife's slander – in short, he suffered the punishment for gross immorality.

2. The Parrot

I heard of a man who was jealous of his wife, and so he bought a parrot and put it in a cage in his house, ordering it to report to him everything that it saw his wife do, and to suppress nothing. Having done this, the husband went away on business, and the wife's lover came to the house. The parrot saw all that they did, and when the husband returned from his business trip he entered the house quietly and sat down without his wife's knowing that he was there. Then he had the parrot brought to him, and asked it what it had seen. It told him everything it had seen the wife do with her lover, so the husband was very angry, and refused to have any contact with his wife. She was sure that her maid had given her away, and called her, saying, 'You've told my husband everything that I did.' The girl swore that she had said nothing, adding, 'But you ought to know that the parrot told him.'

When night fell, therefore, the wife got the parrot, put it on the floor, and began to pour water over it as if it were raining; she took a mirror in her hand and put it on the parrot's cage, and a candle in the other hand, putting it above the mirror, so that the parrot thought it was lightning; and then she began to turn a grindstone, so that the parrot thought it was thunder. She kept this up throughout the night, until daybreak.

In the morning, the husband came and asked the parrot: 'Did you see anything last night?'

'I couldn't see anything because of the heavy rain and the thunder and lightning.'

'Well, if what you told me about my wife was as true as what you've just told me, you're the biggest liar in the world, and I'll have you killed.' And he sent for his wife, and forgave her, and made his peace with her.

3. The Bathkeeper

A prince went to take a bath one day. Although he was young he was so fat that he could not see where his genitals were, and when he undressed the bathkeeper saw him and began to weep. 'Why are you weeping?' asked the prince.

'Because you are a king's son, the only one he has, and you can't make use of your private parts as other men can, for I really believe that you couldn't lie with a woman.'

The prince asked him: 'What shall I do? My father wants to marry me off, and I don't know whether I'll be able to make love to a woman.' Then he added, 'Take these ten pieces of silver, and go and find me a beautiful woman.' The bathkeeper thought to himself, 'I can keep the money and let my wife go to him, since I know very well that he won't be able to sleep with her.' Then he went to fetch his wife, and the prince went to bed with her, and the bathkeeper spied on them, and saw the prince making love to his wife.

The prince laughed, and the bathkeeper was sorely distressed, saying, 'I brought this on myself.' Then he called out to his wife, 'Go home at once.'

'How can I?' she replied, 'since I promised the prince that I'd sleep with him all night.' And when he heard this, with the grief and anguish that he felt he hanged himself, and so he died.

4. Book-Learning and Experience

There was a young man who did not want to marry until he had learned all the tricks and evil ways of women. He came to a village where, he was told, there were wise men who specialized in the knowledge of women's wiles, and the acquisition of that knowledge cost him a great deal.

The most learned of the wise men said to him: 'Do you want me to tell you something? You will never fully learn or understand women's tricks until you sit among ashes for three days, eating nothing but barley-bread and salt, and then you'll learn.'

The young man said that that was what he wanted to do, and he did it. He sat among the ashes and copied out many books on the wiles of women, and when he had done that he said he wanted to return to his own land. He lodged in the house of a good man who asked what he was carrying with him. The youth told his host where he had been, and how he had sat among the ashes while copying out those books, and how he had eaten only barley-bread, enduring great hardship and misery for the sake of the books. The host, when the young man had told him all this, took him by the hand and led him to his wife, saying, 'I've found this young fellow who is exhausted by the journey he's made.'

The host told his wife all about it and asked her to look after the young man until he recovered, for he was very weak. Then he went about his business, and the wife did what he had asked. She asked the young man who he was and what he was doing, and he told her everything. When she understood what he had done, she took him for a man of little sense or discretion, for she realized that he would never be able to accomplish what he had undertaken.

She said to him: 'I'm sure that no woman in the world will ever be able to deceive you or get the better of those books of yours.' But she added to herself, 'Let him be as learned as he likes now, I'll make him realize how little sense he's got and how he's gone astray. I'm the right person to do it!' Then she called to him, saying, 'Look, my friend, I'm a young, beautiful and lusty woman, and my husband's a tired old man. It's a very long time since he slept with me, so you can sleep with me if you like, since I see that you're a wise and understanding man who'll say nothing about it to anyone.'

The young man thought she was telling the truth, and he got up and tried to get hold of her. 'Wait a minute,' she said, 'let's get undressed first.' He undressed, whereupon she cried loudly for help, so that the neighbours came running. Before they came in, she said to him, 'Lie down on the floor, you're a dead man.' He did as she told him, and she put a large piece of bread in his mouth.

36

When the neighbours came in, they asked her what was up. 'This man is staying with us, and he's choked on a piece of bread, and only the whites of his eyes are showing.' She pointed him out to the neighbours, and threw water over him to bring him round. He did not come round, despite the cold water that was thrown over him, and the wiping of his face with a clean white cloth. Eventually the neighbours left and went about their business.

The wife said to the young man: 'Now, my friend, is there any trick in your books to equal that one?'

'My God, I've never found a trick like it.'

'Well,' she said, 'you had a wretched time while you were learning all that stuff, and you needn't expect that any good will come of it, for what you want can't be achieved by you or by any other man in the world.' And the young man took his books and threw them all in the fire, and admitted that he had been wasting his time.

5. The Debate of Greeks and Romans

The Romans had no laws, so went to the Greeks and asked to be given some, but the Greeks replied that they did not deserve them since, being so ignorant, they could not understand laws if they had them. However, if they really wanted to have laws and make use of them, the Greeks added, they should first debate with the wise men of Greece, in order to see whether they understood the laws and thus deserved them. This clever answer was simply an excuse for refusing.

The Romans replied that they liked the suggestion, and the arrangements for the debate were put in writing and signed. However, since they did not understand the strange language of the Greeks, they asked that the debate should be conducted in the sign-language used by learned men.

A date for the debate was fixed, but the Romans became very anxious, not knowing what to do, since, not being learned, they would not be able to understand the wise Greeks nor match their vast knowledge. In the midst of their anxiety, a Roman citizen suggested that they should select a lout, a Roman ruffian, who would make with his hand whatever gestures God put into his mind. It was a good idea.

They approached a ruffian, very big and cunning, saying: 'We're committed to a sign-language debate with the Greeks. Ask whatever you want and we'll give it to you, if you can get us out of this.' They dressed him up in valuable robes, as if he were a Ph.D., and he took a seat on the rostrum, saying boastfully: 'Now let the Greeks come and do their worst.' Then a Greek came along, a very learned doctor, carefully chosen from among his fellow-countrymen, and praised by all. He took the other seat, and began to make signs, as had been agreed.

The Greek got up, calmly and taking his time, held up his index finger and then resumed his seat. The Roman lout got up in his turn, fierce and ill-humoured, stretching out his thumb and his first two fingers towards the Greek like a trident, with the other two folded back; then he sat down again, admiring his clothes. The Greek got up, holding out his open palm, and then sat down with a calm mind. The ruffian arose, full of foolish presumption, showing his clenched fist, longing for a fight.

The wise Greek said to all his fellow-countrymen: 'The Romans deserve to have laws, and I can't deny them to them.' So the meeting broke up calmly and peaceably, and Rome gained great honour on account of a low tramp.

The Greeks asked their wise representative what he had said in his signs, and what the Roman's answers had been. 'I said there is only one God, and the Roman replied that God is three in one, making appropriate signs. I said that everything happens by God's will, and he answered truthfully that God has the whole world in His power. As soon as I saw that they understood and believed in the Trinity, I realized that they were undoubtedly worthy to have laws.'

The Romans asked their ruffian what had happened. 'He said he'd put my eye out with his finger. I was fed up about that and got really angry, so I told him in a rage that, right there in front of everyone, I'd put both his eyes out with my fingers and smash his teeth with my thumb. Then he told me to watch out, because he'd box my ears so that they rang, so I said I'd punch him so hard that he'd never get even with me. When he saw how badly things were going, he dropped his threats, since they weren't getting him anywhere.'

6. Pitas Payas, the Breton Painter

I'll tell you a story about a man who neglected his wife, and if you think it's a good joke you can tell me another as good. Pitas Payas, a Breton painter, married a young girl and enjoyed it, but in less than a month he said: 'Look, love, I've got to go to Flanders, but I'll bring you back lots of presents.' 'Right,' she said, 'off you go, but don't forget your home and don't forget me.' Then Pitas Payas said: 'Darling, I want to paint a pretty picture on you that will keep you from getting up to anything while I'm away.' 'If you want to, that's all right.' He painted a little lamb on her belly, and went off on his first business trip. He took a long time over it, and was away two years; each month of his absence seemed like a year to his wife.

Since the girl was newly married, and had only lived with her husband for a short time, she took a lover to fill the empty house. The lamb was rubbed away, and soon nothing was left of it. When she heard that her husband was coming back, she hastily sent for her lover and told him to paint a little lamb as best he could in that same place. In his haste, he painted a fully-endowed ram, with a fine head of horns. The same day a messenger announced that Pitas Payas was about to arrive.

When the painter, back from Flanders, reached home his wife greeted him coldly. Indoors, alone with her, he remembered the picture he had painted, saying: 'Now, love, show me that picture and we can have some fun.' 'See for yourself where it is,' his wife said, 'and do whatever you fancy there, but do it with a will.' Pitas Payas looked at her belly and saw a great horned ram. 'What's all this, love? How is it that I painted a lamb and find this plate of meat instead?'

Since women are always crafty and cunning in this kind of situation, she replied: 'What, love, you don't want a lamb to grow into a ram in two years? If you'd come home sooner you'd have found your lamb.'

7. The Youth and the Millstone

There was once a crazy boy, a really wild youth, who did not want to marry just one girl, but insisted on three. Everyone tried to reason with him. His father, mother and elder brother urged him, if only for their sake, to marry only two, and to start with the younger girl; then, when a full month had passed, he could marry the older one.

On that basis, he got married. When the first month was up, his family asked him what he thought of his elder brother's taking just one girl, no more, to be his lawful wedded wife. The youth replied that there was no need for that, since he had a wife who would more than suffice for both of them. The family should tell his brother that, and shouldn't bother about marrying him to another girl.

The father of this foolish youth, a worthy man, had a mill with a fine large millstone. Before the boy was married, he was so strong that he could easily stop the stone with his foot, even when it was revolving very quickly. His great strength and boldness, before his marriage, made the stone seem light; after a month of marriage, he wanted to try his strength as before, and went along to the mill one day. He tried to stop the stone, just as he had done in the past, but it knocked his legs from under him and threw him flat on the ground. The foolish youth picked himself up, cursing the wheel heartily: 'All right, my fine millstone, just wait till you're married!'

8. The Drunken Mouse

Once upon a time a mouse fell into a barrel of wine. A cat, passing by, heard the mouse making a great noise but unable to get out of the wine. The cat asked, 'Why are you shouting so much?'

'Because I can't get out.'

'What will you give me if I get you out?'

'I'll give you whatever you want.'

So the cat said, 'If I get you out, this is what I want: you must come to me whenever I call you.'

'Right, I promise that I'll do it.'

'I want you to swear to it.' And the mouse swore, so the cat took him out of the wine and let him scamper off to his hole.

One day the cat was very hungry, and went to the mousehole, telling the mouse to come to him. 'By God, I'll do nothing of the sort,' replied the mouse.

'But didn't you swear that you'd come out when I called you?'

'My dear chap,' said the mouse, 'I was drunk when I swore that oath.'

9. The Reluctant Monk

A woman was leading an unhappy life with her husband, and came to dislike him intensely. Therefore she thought up a wicked trick to play on him, putting into his wine the juice of certain herbs. He was not merely drunk, but lay there on his bed, acting like a madman, twisting and turning, foaming at the mouth, and unable to speak. His wife hurried off to the nearby monastery, weeping. She said to the monks: 'For the love of God, come to my house, for my husband seems to be dying. He can't speak, but before he lost the power of speech he told me that above all else he wanted to become a monk, or if, through this illness, God took him, he must be dressed in a monk's habit before he was buried. I don't want to stand in the way of his wishes, so I'll swear to give up sex for as long as I live, even if God restores him to health. But for God's sake hurry, and dress my poor husband in a monk's habit, for he's at the point of death.'

She pressed them so much that they had to go. They shaved her husband, gave him a large tonsure, and dressed him in the habit of their order. The next morning he got up, sober again, and was astonished to find himself with shaved head and dressed as a monk, so he asked his wife what had been happening and who had done that to him. She, pretending to weep, said: 'Oh, my dearly-beloved husband! Don't you remember that last night you were made a monk, and that when you were in agony from your illness that was the only thing you wanted? And for your soul's sake I promised perpetual chastity, so now I must live alone and like an inconsolable widow.'

Her husband protested that he certainly didn't want to become a monk, and that he wanted to live a normal married life with her, just as before, but she said that she couldn't go against the oath she had sworn, for he most assuredly was a monk, and God would never permit her to sleep with a monk. 'Oh, you wretch,' she added, 'wouldn't you even be ashamed if you broke your vow? If you became a layman again, everyone would call you an apostate, a renegade monk.'

She spoke so persuasively, and shed so many false tears, that the unhappy

41

man, through shame and because of all the things she had said to him, took holy orders. He became a monk, and entered the monastery, leaving her in possession of their house and of all the jewels and other goods.

10. The Timid Lover's Expedition

If a man is timid and lazy by nature, how can such a poor wretch love or be loved? If he is expected to go by night, or in the cold, or through mud to where his beloved lives, first he has to stretch, and then to yawn, and then to put his head out of the door to see if it's snowing or raining. After all this, he starts to think about it and dither: 'I'll go. No, I shan't. Yes, I'll go after all. But if I go someone will see me, I'll get wet, I'll get muddy. I'll run into the police and they'll confiscate my sword, and if the night watch find me they'll chase me round the streets. If I stumble I'll probably fall down, and my beautifully polished shoes will get all dirty in the mud: I'm not stirring out of this house without my overshoes. Oh dear, what if a dog bites me in the leg, or someone stabs me or hits me on the head with a stone? And if I'm caught in her house they'll cut off the best part of me. And what if they catch me at the door and beat me up? The hell with it, I'm not going! My God, I'm not setting foot outside this house tonight! I know when I'm well off. Let's go to bed. God help anyone who goes looking for trouble!'

And if a man like that does go out, spurred on by passion, and heads for his beloved's house, if he runs into anyone carrying sticks or wineskins on his back that make a noise, then his heart shrinks to the size of an ant, and he runs away, stumbles and falls; he gets up dazed and sets off again, looking round to see if anyone is following him, for he thinks that there are armed men at his heels, panting with eagerness to kill him, so he runs as fast and as far as he can.

If by any chance he actually reaches his mistress's house, he lacks the nerve to climb in at a window, or up a rope ladder, or to enter by the roof; he won't take the door off its hinges or jump from a high garden wall; and if the door is opened for him, he goes in very timorously, thinking he sees armed men in every corner. If a cat moves, he's more scared than a woman, and he faints. His mistress has to bring him round with a good stiff drink, and try to reassure him: 'Come on, love, cheer up, it was only a cat.' And the wretched man, sweat pouring off him, as white as a sheet, eyes starting out of his head, his heart pounding away, says: 'I'm as good as dead, dear! Just now I saw what looked like a hundred men or more, and from the noise they were making I was sure they were armed. I'm as good as dead, I tell you. Open the door, love, I'm off – I can feel the first pangs of death already.' And all the while, he is looking round for a way of escape.

'Now then, love, don't be afraid, it was only the cat, who ran away when he saw you', or 'It was the hen who's got the pip, and was making a noise', or 'It was the mule eating noisily', or 'It was a couple of ducklings splashing about in the farmyard', or 'It's the old woman, the one I work for, coughing', or 'It's my mother using the sieve', or 'My sister kneading dough', or 'It's our bitch scratching at her fleas and growling to herself. Stay where you are, love, calm down, you're as safe here as in your own home so don't you worry.'

'No, dear, I'm off. I'm too scared to stay here: my hair is standing on end. A fine state of affairs this is!'

When she sees him trembling like a leaf, more dead than alive, and sees that even if he stayed it would be no more good to her than having another woman with her, she says: 'Right, I don't need another woman here.' She opens the door and lets him out, and you'd scarcely credit the farewell she gives him: curses and insults in plenty, vulgar gestures, snorts and whistles. 'I hope your mother never gets any joy from you,' she cries, 'and I hope she never gives birth to another child. You call this behaving like a lover? Get out of here!'

ENGLISH TALES

1. Dame Sirith

As I came along the road I heard a story about a fine, lively man, who was clever, learned, handsome, and well-dressed. He began to love a married woman – he shouldn't have done that. His heart belonged entirely to her, so that he had no rest: the love was so severe.

He thought very hard about how he could get her. One day it happened that the husband went off on a business trip. The other man went to the house which she lived in, which was a fine place. He came into the hall where she was standing in her expensive clothes, and he began like this:

'May God Almighty be here!'

'Welcome, as ever I hope for joy,' said this wife. 'If you would like to, come in and sit down, my dear, and tell me what you want. By Our Lord, the King of Heaven, if I can do anything to please you, you could find me very generous. I'll very gladly do what I can for you, with no sorrow!'

'Lady, may God reward you. If you won't give me away, or be angry, I'll tell you my business. But I'd hate to make you angry for anything I did.'

'No, not at all, Willikin, not for anything that has ever been mine, though you want it ever so much, will I be rude. I don't know anything about meanness, and I don't intend to learn. You can say anything you like, and I shall listen and sit still while you tell it. And if you tell me what is right, I shall do what you want – you can be sure of that. And though you say anything shameful, I shan't blame you for what you say.'

'Now I have got permission, it would be wrong if I should be unhappy. Certainly, lady, you speak very graciously, and I shall come to the point and tell you everything I want, and why I have come. I am not one to tell lies, and I won't. I've loved you for many years – though I haven't been here to show my love. While your husband is at home nobody can have a quiet word with you with any grace. Yesterday, as I came along the road, I heard about your husband and heard that he'd gone to the fair at Boston in Lincolnshire. And because I knew he was out, I took the trouble to speak to you. His life must be very pleasant who could possess such a woman, in privacy. Lady, if you agree, I'll love you both quietly and secretly.'

'By our Lord, the King of Heaven, who is above us, I won't do that on any account! I have my lord, as my husband, who brought me with great honour to this house as a maiden. He loves me, and I love him well. Our love is as true as steel, without a doubt. Though he's away from home on business, I'd be a fool if I learned to be a whore. That will never happen, for me to do such a false thing, in bed or anywhere else in the house. Not while he's alive, though he's a hundred miles beyond Rome, not for anything would I take any man on earth as my mate, before he came home!'

47

'Lady, lady, change your attitude. You were always gracious, and will be still. For the Lord's sake who created us, alter your attitude, change your mind, and have pity on me.'

'Oh dear! Oh dear! Do you think I'm a fool? As sure as Christmas, you *are* silly. You'll never change my mind. My husband is a gracious courteous man, and a man of substance. And I am a good and faithful wife. No one can know a more faithful woman than I am. That time will never come when either by persuasion or through pride I shall do anything shameful.'

'Sweet darling, have mercy! I'm not offering you shame or disgrace, but secret love as a man who wants to do well in love and find happiness!'

'As ever I hope to eat or drink, you're losing all your labour here. You may just as well go home, dear brother, for I don't want your love or anyone else's, but my wedded husband's, and I don't hesitate to tell you so.'

'Certainly, lady, I'm sorry for that. And sad is the man who works hard and fails at last. He's no choice but to complain. That's certainly my situation, who love the love that I must lose. And lady, now, good-day! And may that Lord, that can rule all, grant that your mind may so change, that I may no longer mourn for you!'

He went away gloomily, and thought both night and day how he might change her. A friend advised him to leave his great sorrow, and go and see gracious Dame Sirith. Straight away he went there as fast as he could, meeting no one on the way. He was full of misery and grief. He greeted her politely with gentle and also cunning words.

'God bless you, Dame Sirith. I've come to speak with you from great need. If you can help me, you shall have, as you shall see, a great reward.'

'Welcome to you, dear son and if I know or am able to do something for you in any way I shall do my very best. So, dear son, tell me what you want me to do.'

'A cure, dear old lady. I'm getting on very badly I live a life of misery and care:

> With much unease I lead my life
> And all because of a sweet wife
> Whose name is Margery.
> I have loved her many a day
> And of her love she says me nay
> So here I come to thee.
> Unless she change and be more kind,
> For sorrow must I lose my mind,
> Or to my death to go.
> I had bethought myself to slay
> But then a friend showed me the way
> To you, my grief to show.

48

He told me that without fail you could help and assist and bring me out of my misery through your trickery and devices. And I will give you a rich reward when that is done.'

'God's blessing be here! In this, my son, you have great sin. Lord, for his sweet name, let there be no shame to you for it! You're going to earn God's anger when you put such blame on me, for I'm old and ill and crippled. Illness has made me quite tame. Bless you, bless you, dear boy! – that you may not get into trouble because of this lie that is invented about me, who am so hard pressed. I'm a holy woman, I know nothing about witchcraft, only about alms given by good men. I keep going day by day, and say my *pater-noster* and creed so that God may help them when they need it; God grant that they may succeed who have helped me to keep going. His life and soul deserve to be disgraced who sent you to me on this business. And may I be avenged on him who spoke this shame about me.'

'Dear old lady, leave all this: it seems to me you're being silly. The man who directed me to you knew that you could bring people together. Dame Sirith, help me if you can to be reconciled to my sweetheart, and I will give you a really big gift, lots of pounds and pence, warm clothes, warm shoes, if my business is well done. You will be able to boast of a regular fortune if you will help me!'

'Don't lie to me, Willikin. By your loyalty, are you really being sincere? Do you really love Dame Margery?'

'Yes, old lady, I really do. I love her. It could do me harm if I don't get her to do what I want.'

'Well, good Willikin, I'm sorry for your harm. May our Lord send you help soon. If I could be sure it wouldn't be known, it would seem a good thing if I could get you what you wanted on your own. Promise me for certain, with raised hand, that you'll keep it quiet, and I will see if I can tell her. I wouldn't want for all the world to be brought before the Chapter for any such affairs. I'd be straight away sentenced to ride shamefully on an ass, driven by priests and clerks.'

'Certainly, old lady, I don't want you to have any ill-treatment or shame for doing me a good turn. I promise you my truth here that I shall do everything I can to keep it quiet, by the holy cross.'

'You're very welcome here, Willikin! Here you've made a promise that may please you very well. You can bless this moment, for you can make yourself very happy. There's no need to sigh any more. It's your good fortune that you ever came here, for I'll go there straight away and make her understand. I'll teach her such a lesson that she shall love you much more than any man in the country.'

'As I hope to have the peace of God, you've said well, Dame Sirith, and you shall have good fortune. Here is twenty shillings. I give it to you as a reward, to buy sheep and pigs for yourself.'

'As ever I hope to enjoy a roof over my head or a floor under my feet, pennies were never better laid out than these shall be, for I'll do the business, and a wonderful trick, as you shall see very well.

[*To the dog*] Now I'm going to make you eat pepper and mustard – that will make your eyes run! I know very well where and when I shall tell a lie about your running eyes'

'What on earth are you up to now? You must have gone mad! Are you giving the dog mustard?'

'Be quiet you fool! With this trick I'll get her love to be all yours. I shall get no rest nor peace till I have told how you will do. Wait for me here till I come back home.'

'Right, by the summer flower, nothing will take me from here, till you come back.'

Dame Sirith went off, like a miserable wretch, until she came to the house where this wife lived. When she came to the door, she began very pitifully.

'Lord,' she said, 'how miserable these old women are who always live in poverty. No man knows so much trouble as a poor woman who falls into want. Any man can tell that by me, for I can't either walk or sit. I wish I were dead. Hunger and thirst have already killed me. I can hardly stir a limb for great hunger and thirst and cold. What can such a wretch live for? Why won't God fetch my soul?'

'Good woman, may God release you! I'll find you food today, for the love of God. I am so sorry for your misery, for I see how badly clothed and shod you are. Come in here. I'll feed you.'

'God Almighty reward you, and the lord who was set on the cross, and fasted forty days to noon, and has power over heaven and earth. May that lord repay you.'

'Have this meat and bread too, and cheer up, I tell you; and have this cup of drink.'

'May God reward you for your efforts,' then said the old woman – God curse her life. 'Alas, alas, that I'm still alive! I'd forgive all the sin to the man who'd cut off my head! I wish someone would take my life!'

'What's the matter, good woman?'

'But I can easily be sorry. I had a lovely noble daughter – you couldn't ever see a more beautiful girl. She had a courteous husband – you couldn't find a more generous man. My daughter loved him all too well, which is why I'm so heartbroken. He went out one day, and that's the reason that my daughter was disgraced. He made a trip out of town, and a fine scholar in orders came and offered his love to my daughter and she wouldn't do what he wanted. He couldn't get his way for anything he asked for. So he began to do magic and he turned my daughter into a bitch. This bitch here is my daughter I'm telling you about. My heart is breaking for sorrow about her. See how her

50

eyes run, the tears run together on her cheek. So it's no wonder, lady, if my heart's breaking. And any young housewife there may be has very little liking for her life, if any scholar offers her his love, unless she gives way and lets him succeed.'

'O Lord Christ, what can I do! Only the other day a scholar came to me and offered me his love after his own fashion, and I wouldn't pay any attention to him. I think he'll transform me. How do you think, old woman, that I can escape?'

'God Almighty help you that you don't become bitch or pup! Dear lady, if any scholar offers you that love-business, I advise you to give him what he wants, and become his lover straight away. And if you don't do that, you're taking up a worse plan.'

'Lord Christ, how sorry I am that the scholar went away before he had taken me. I'd give anything for him to have once slept with me and done it immediately. I'll be yours for evermore, old woman, if you'll fetch me Willikin, the scholar I've told you about. I'll give you presents you'll always be better off for, by God's own bell!'

'For sure, my sweet lady, if I can do it without being blamed I'll be glad to try. If I can meet him anywhere, I'll not hesitate. Good day, lady. I'm off!'

'See you do what I asked you, at all events. Unless you bring me Willikin, I'll never be able to laugh or sing or be glad!'

'Certainly, lady, I'll bring him even today if I can by my efforts.'

She went home and found Willikin, by our Lord!

'Sweet Willikin, don't worry, I've done very well with her. Come on quickly with me there, for she's sent for you. You can be glad now for sure!'

'May God who rules heaven and earth reward you, dear old woman!'

This fine man immediately went with Sirith to his sweetheart that very minute.

Dame Sirith began to tell [the girl] and swore by God's own bell she had found him. 'Lady, I've so looked for Willikin that now I've brought him to you.'

'Welcome, Willikin, sweet man, you're more welcome than the king! Sweet Willikin, I promise you my love, to do all you want to. I've changed my mind, for I don't want at all that you should die!'

'Lady, as sure as I expect noon, so I'm ready and eager to do everything you say. Old woman, by God, you must go away, while she and I amuse ourselves.'

'God knows, so I will. And see you plough her and stretch out her thighs! God give you sorrow if you spare her while you're with her. And if there's anyone who is foolish and can't get his sweetheart for any price, I'll make him succeed – if he will pay me – for I know very well how!'

51

2. The Lady Prioress

O glorious Lord, our governor, make all delight in this telling, and give joy to those who will hear what I say or sing.

I should be sorry to be blamed by those who are ignorant; there are kinds of men who will interfere in everything. Plenty of men for a dozen reasons will find fault. They know no more than my heel, yet they think nothing is well done unless they do it themselves. Unless they do it themselves they think nothing of it. Many men are like this. Their limits are soon reached. Their idea is simple when it is produced.

As for me, I have it in mind to tell you something, declare a case to you, to make every one of you merry, and I'll tell about a nun, the loveliest creature alive, who was prioress of a nunnery.

This beautiful lady was a lord's daughter, and in every respect pure and precious. Lords and laymen and clergy pursued her to win her love, because her beauty offered great temptation. They brought great gifts to her and many men loved her to distraction. She looked for means to keep herself from shame, but didn't know how to begin.

A young knight, being a fresh handsome lord; and a parish parson, an unparalleled priest; and a citizen of a borough, wooed her. Listen and you will hear how they set their love on that dear lady, and none knew about the others. They called continuously, and wanted her love immediately, and swore by sun and moon to have their desire.

The young knight tossed and turned for the lady's love, and sent many bucks and does. The parson, to help his situation, secretly gave her beads, brooches and bottles of wine. The citizen gave from his store of gold and his rents. Thus they pestered her. She did not know how to keep her soul pure, until she had an idea.

The young knight thought it would be marvellous to have to do with her. He flattered her with many a tale and chattered away. Lies jumped out and rang like a bell. 'Madam,' he said, 'unless I have my desire of you I shall kill myself. Grant your love to me. I endure a bloody side bravely in battle to make the Jews hide their heads from my great strokes and I kill many a huge giant.

'All is for love of you, Madam. I would risk my life if you will give me what I've wanted for many a year, to do what I want under your lovely cowl.' 'Sir,' she said, 'you are our lord, our patron, our president; your will shall be done, provided you will now go down to the chapel by the wood and do as I shall tell you'. 'All ready,' he said then.

'Down in the wood there is a chapel. I order you, if you want to get my love, to lie there all night like a dead body, sewn in a sheet until daylight tomorrow. Then you will have my love, my own sweet honey.' 'Madam,' he said, 'for your love, by God above, it shall be done. If anyone should say "no", here is my glove as pledge that I will fight him in that quarrel.'

The knight kissed the nice lady: the bargain was made. He was never half so glad of any bargain made in his life. He went to the chapel as the lady told him. He sewed himself into a sheet. He wasn't at all afraid, he didn't think about sorrow. When he came there he lay flat on his back with two candles burning bright. He meant to lie there all night and kiss the lady next day.

When the knight was gone she sent for Parson John. I'm sure he wasn't long; he came straight away. 'Madam,' he said, 'what shall I do?' She answered then, 'Sir,' she said, 'I shall tell you what should be a private matter, but it's already well known. I have a cousin who lies dead in the chapel by the wood. His burial is forbidden because he owes a sum of money.

We cannot pay the sum men want, so we send for you to preserve our honour. Say his dirge and mass and lay him in his grave, and soon you shall have my love – keep this truly secret.' His heart leapt, his lust stirred. He promised to do all this. He swore by Heaven and Hell to say his service upon a book.

'Do what you have promised,' said the lady, 'as far as you can, then you can do what you want with me.' And I can certainly tell you that Parson John was as glad of this as ever bird was of the daylight. He made his way with a mattock and a shovel to the chapel where the knight lay in his sheet. When he came there he dug his pit and said his dirge at the knight's feet. The knight lay still and dreamed that his sweetheart had become his love.

As soon as the priest was gone to bury the young knight, the lady sent for the merchant. He came very cheerfully to her. She said, 'Down in the wood there is a fine chapel under a pear-tree, where there lies a dead body. You must bestir yourself to help us about that to get our rights. He owes us a sum of gold. I intend to forbid his burial. I am told that a priest is on his way there to bury him this night.

'It will be a foul shame for us to be betrayed by the corpse being buried and our money not paid. If you will do what I tell you the priest will be terrified. You must dress up in devil's clothes and go there very quietly. When you see the priest go to bury him who lies on the bier, jump in at the door of the choir like a devil from hell.'

'Madam, for your love I shall soon get dressed, provided you will grant me what I have so often asked you for.' 'Sir,' she said, 'you shall have it, but first I need to be certain that you will keep our secrets so that they will not be discovered. If you avoid the place, or run away before daylight tomorrow you lose my love for ever.' 'I agree, Madam,' he said, and put on the clothes.

He put on a devil's garment, went out, and as the dirge was finishing came running in at the church door, roaring and rattling with his chains as it seems that devils do. The priest started up like a deer, his heart almost stopped. He reckoned he would die, he was so frightened he would be killed. He didn't know how he sprang up; he broke out of a window and badly hurt his head.

But he that bore all the brunt of this, was so sorely provoked, to hear his dirge sung and see his grave dug, that he said to himself, 'I think I was cursed from birth. I could have been comfortably at home, but now I'm done for unless I'm the quicker off the mark.' Then he jumped up. The 'devil' saw the body rise. That made his heart begin to race – I reckon we're not all sensible – and he began to run.

He had clean forgotten his rags and his chains. So had the young knight that he was sewn in the sheet. The priest thought them both devils – he didn't want to meet them. He spared neither hill, wood, bush, plant, or grit. Lord, he was badly scratched. The other two were terribly frightened. They spared neither stile nor gap. They would rather have escaped from each other than win the earth.

The priest took a by-path – he didn't want to meet them. His head was badly cut, the blood ran down to his feet. He ran in a furred gown. His body began to stink. He threw off all his clothes down to his underpants because he wanted to travel light. He thought he heard the devil rushing along. He jumped into a bramble bush, that scraped all the skin right off his body.

The knight ran into a wood as fast as he could go. He fell on to a stake and badly tore his leg. He didn't care about that, he was frightened of the devil. He thought it was a long way to the end of the path. But then his real trouble began. As he dodged into a gap he was caught by the middle. He shot up into a treetop, caught in a deer-snare.

The merchant ran into a meadow, where there were no thorns. He fell onto the back of a bull. The bull caught him up on his horns. 'Out, alas that I was ever born,' he said, 'for I'm now going to the devil, to the pit of hell, because I insulted him.' The bull ran into a bog. There he laid our fine gentleman. He did not dare stir until he heard a bell.

In the morning he was glad he had escaped so far. So was the priest also, though he was naked. The knight was in the treetop, shaking for fear. He would gladly have given the best jewel he had to come down. He caught hold of the top of the tree, yes, and he broke the trap. He fell and cut his forehead on the bare ground.

So they gave up the game, tricked and deceived. Neither knew about the others. They went home badly used. The Parson told the lady in the morning what danger had appeared there, how he had run for her love. His pleasures had been slight, he was so afraid of death. 'When I should have buried the corpse, the devil came in, the body rose. To see all this made my heart fail. I hardly escaped with my life.'

'Remember,' said the lady, 'what evil follows from this. I never yet had a lover who died a good death.' 'By that Lord,' said the priest 'who created both ale and mead, you'll never be wooed as far as I'm concerned while I have speech or breath, while I can see or hear.' So they vowed to each other. He went out without the corpse. Then the knight came for his purpose and told her how he had got on.

'Now I hope to have your love that I have served so long for – for I have never bought love so dear in all my life.' 'Keep quiet,' said the lady, 'say no more about it, for you have lost my love for a hundred years by the new bargain.' She answered him, he went on his way. The merchant came the same day. He told her of his great battle and his high adventure.

'I stood by the bargain until the corpse was about to be buried. When the dead body rose, a grim spirit glided up; then it was time for me to stir myself. I jumped many a stile. No hedge was too high, no water was too wide to stop me having my will of you.' The lady at once said 'Quiet. Never in your life, for I shall tell your wife and everyone around, and to make it worse for you I'll proclaim it in the market-place.' At that he gave her twenty marks to keep quiet. So the citizen of the borough, after his death, endowed the nunnery with legal deeds to hold property for evermore.

Thus the lady behaved honourably; she kept her virginity; and endowed the nunnery with property; and cured her lovers of their pains.

3. The Tale of the Pot

Many people tell stories and idle tales, some true and some otherwise. One can spend the whole live-long day with joy and sport in harping and piping and other merry tales. You may like to hear (and possibly the story may be true) about a parson and a brother he was very fond of – they loved each other dearly.

One of them was the heir to his father's house and lands, and the other was a parson, as I understand. He was a good manager and became rich. He was known for a good clergyman by God's ordinance, and regarded as a wise man. The other was thoughtless, knew nothing of good management, but did just what his wife wanted and whatever she told him.

Like many others he was a feeble husband, and did what his wife told him to immediately. It's an old proverb, I swear by St Ives, that it is due to the wife if a husband prosper both at home and outside. If a wife have a bad fault the husband shall have something of it, unless he looks carefully to it.

That young man became very uneasy. After a year or two he could not please his wife. Much of the income of his land went to the comfort of a priest. She taught her husband how the cat sneezed, just at her own will. He who had been a lord was neither, at bed or board. When she told him to be silent he dare not speak a word.

The husband paid no attention to management, and his wife was very keen on good food and drink. She would neither work nor toil for it, but when her belly was full she lay down and slept and rested her bottom. They led this life so long that everything they had was spent. The wife told her husband to go out straight away

'To your brother the parson who's such a rich rotter, and ask him to ease some of your sorrow. Make sure you get forty or fifty pounds from him. So long as you get it I don't care a bit about repaying.' He went to his brother, who lent him lots of money. Soon that was spent, and they had hardly anything left.

He fetched a lot of money from his brother, and for all that he took he was no better off. The parson got tired of this and thought he would stop him. 'If he goes on like this he will get into debt to me and yet be never the better off. The game is going wrong between his wife and him. I'll find out, as I hope for Heaven, how it is.'

Some time later he came again one day to the parson to borrow money, but he didn't succeed. 'Brother,' said the parson, 'you don't bother at all about how you fall into debt to me, which worries me very much, and still you're no better off. By God, you were the heir of my father's fine house and land, and yet you're always in despair. How the devil can this be?'

'I don't know how it happens, but I'm always behind. It's natural for me to be generous. I'll tell you truly what's on my mind.' The parson said, 'Tell me,' 'Brother,' he said, 'by St Alban, it's a priest called Parson John. I never knew such a fellow. He's the best of good chaps.'

'He's always good and polite. He plays the harp and the guitar and sings to them; he wrestles and jumps and puts the shot too.' 'Brother,' said the parson, 'I tell you, go home straight away, and see if you can by any trick get out of the bedroom the pot that they make water in and please bring it to me.'

'Brother,' he said cheerfully, 'your will shall be done. It's a round pot, I know it well.' 'Bring it here as secretly as you can and hurry up. Don't delay. Come back immediately.' He went home, he didn't wait a moment. And then his wife began to tell him off because he'd come back so soon.

He took up the pot and went out and didn't waste a moment until he came to his brother. The parson took the pot and carried it to his room, and there did a secret experiment. And he said very cheerfully to his brother, 'See where you took the pot from and put it back in the same place, and then come right back again without delay.'

He took the pot and went back; when his wife saw him she raised her eyebrows. 'Why has your brother sent you back home so soon? It can't be for good, I know for sure, that you came home so quick.' 'No, sweetheart,' he said, 'I must just get a little thing and take it to my brother, to please some people.'

Then he secretly went into his bedroom and put the pot down by the side of the bed. He said goodbye to his wife and rode off. She was glad he went and told him not to stay. She began to feel cheerful. Immediately she killed a capon or two and quickly cooked with them some other good food.

When everything was ready she secretly sent for Parson John to come in at the postern gate as quiet as a mouse. They ate and drank as usual until they felt like going to bed on the quiet. After a little while Parson John woke up and had to make water. He knew where to find the pot in the usual place.

He took the pot to make water in it. He couldn't for the world get his hands away from it. 'Alas,' he said 'what shall I do now? This is some witchcraft.' He held the pot tight, and his whole body shivered with cold. He would rather than a hundred pound that it could be taken from him.

He carried the pot between his hands in the bedroom just like a pedlar selling his wares. The wife was annoyed that he stood there so long and asked him what he was doing, standing there like a fool. 'What, woman,' he said, 'for heaven's sake you must help if you can to get this pot off. It won't come away from my hand.'

The good woman sprang up, stopped for nothing, and put both her hands on the pot. Thus they were both stuck fast, and he never got the better for it. It was an awkward situation for a man to get into, day or night. They began to call out and shout to a maid that slept near them for her to come quickly to see if she could help them.

The girl jumped up half awake and ran naked to her mistress. 'Alas,' said her mistress, 'who has made this grief? Help to get this pot away and get rid of our trouble. This is terrible bad luck.' The girl grabbed the pot, intending to help, and so they were all three stuck fast. It was a fine dance.

They danced all night till the sun rose. The parish clerk rang the daybell as usual. He knew his master's private affairs and when he had to get up. He thought he was too late in saying his service, his morning matins. Very quietly he went to him. When he got there he saw clearly that his master was in great fear and brought to great sorrow.

As soon as he could see Parson John he began to call him. When they heard they all came down into the hall. 'Why are you behaving like that?' said the clerk. 'It's a shame to you all. Why are you naked? May evil take you. That pot must be taken away.' He made a snatch at the pot, and put both his hands on it. The first word that he then said was, 'Alas, what shall I do?'

57

The carter was shovelling earth from the hall door, to make it clean, I suppose. When he saw them go round in a row, he thought, as he said later, that they were fools from the fair. He said he'd have a try, as well. He hardly dare go in for fear. All except the clerk were naked. When he saw the girl there it seemed to him all wrong.

The girl who was hopping in the crowd was his special girl-friend. 'Let go the pot or I'll give you a clout!' He hit the girl a blow on the bottom with a shovel. The shovel stuck fast with no mistake, and he hung on to the end. The carter, with bad luck to him, led the dance of the whole lot. One couldn't find such another business in England, Scotland or France.

The husband and the parson came in at that moment and found all that fair company dancing. The husband said to Parson John, 'By the Lord's sweet wound, you'll lose your balls or a hundred pound, you have no other choice.' Parson John said, 'I swear to you, help to get rid of this pot and I'll pay the money rather than lose my balls.'

The parson charmed the pot so that it fell away from them. Everyone then quickly went away. The priest left the district for the shame of it, and he and the wife left off their lewdness and did it no more. So the husband and his wife lived in peace together. May Mary for the sake of her Five Joys keep us all from care.

4. The Friar and the Boy

God who died for all of us, and drank gall and vinegar, bring us from evil, and grant a good and long life to those who will listen to my song and attend to my story.

A man lived in my part of the country who in course of time had three wives. By the first wife he had a fine and cheerful lad.

His father loved him dearly, but his stepmother not at all, as I think. By the Cross, any food or drink that did the boy any good she thought utterly wasted.

He had not half enough to eat, and that was rotten, but still she thought it wasted. May she come to a bad end for that because as far as she dared she made him thoroughly miserable. The wife said to her husband, 'Sir, you must get rid of this boy quickly. I tell you he's a bad boy. I wish some other man had him who would punish him more.'

The husband answered back and said, 'Dame, I tell you he's only young. He will stay with me for this year until he is stronger, to earn a better wage.

We have a man, a strong fellow, who looks after our cattle in the field and sleeps half the day. By Mary mild, he shall come back to the house, and the boy shall go into the field to see if he can look after them.'

The wife was truly glad and immediately agreed and said, 'That's best.' In the morning, at dawn, the little boy hurried out into the field. He carried his stock on his back and cared nothing for anyone. He was very cheerful. He went out until he came to the field and got out his dinner. When he saw the food was rotten, he didn't want to eat it, and put it away again immediately. By Christ, he was not to blame. He said, 'I'll eat very little until I get home at night.'

As he sat on a hill he met an old man who came walking along, who said, 'God give you success, good son.' The boy said, 'Sir, you are welcome, truly.'

The old man was terribly hungry and said, 'Have you any food put away that you can give to me?' The boy said, 'As God may save me, you can see what I have, and welcome.'

He offered him such as he had and told him to eat and be cheerful, and said, 'You are truly welcome.' The old man was easy to please. He ate, and made himself easy and said, 'Son, thank you very much. For this food that you have given me I shall give you three gifts that will not be forgotten.' The boy said, 'I think it would be best if I had a bow to shoot birds.'

'You shall have bow and arrows straight away that shall last you all your life and will always be suitable. Wherever you shoot, you'll never miss but always hit the target.'

Immediately he felt the bow in his hand, and he put the arrows under his belt. He laughed aloud and said, 'Now if I had a pipe, even a very little one, I would be happy enough.'

'You shall have a pipe too, which will always keep time, and everyone who hears this pipe won't be able to help themselves, but will dance and jump about.

'Let's see, what shall the other be – for you shall have three gifts, as I promised before.' The little boy then laughed aloud. 'By my truth, I have enough. I want no more.'

The old man said, 'I promised you; you shall have as I promised. So tell me; let's see.' The little boy said, 'By Saint James, I have a stepmother at home; she is very unkind to me. When my father gives me food she wishes that the devil would choke me, she glares at me so. When she looks at me like that I wish that she may let go a noise that will make the whole place echo.'

Then the old man said to him, 'If she looks at you like that she shall begin to blow off so that everyone can hear her and be unable to stop themselves all laughing.'

'Goodbye,' said the old man, and 'Goodbye, sir,' said the boy. 'I take my leave of you, and may God almighty prosper you day and night.' 'Thank you, son,' he said.

Then afterwards when it was night the boy went straight home as he was supposed to. He took his pipe and began to play on it, and all the animals began to dance around him. The boy went piping through the village and the animals followed him by the sound to his father's yard. When he had shut them all up, he immediately went home and into the hall.

His father sat at his supper, and as soon as he saw the little boy he spoke to him and said 'Welcome, Jack. Where are my animals, good son? Have you brought them home?'

'Yes, father, certainly. I have looked after them all today, and now they are shut up.' His father gave him a capon's leg and said, 'Jack, that's well done, boy, and you'll do the better for it.'

That sorely grieved the wife's heart. She felt more and more angry. Then she glared full in his face. And immediately she let go such a blast that everyone in the room was appalled. They all laughed and made sport of it. The wife became red for shame. She wished she were anywhere else. Jack said, 'You should know that this gun was as well loaded as if it had had a cannon-ball.'

Then she looked furiously at him. She let go another rouser, her arse was almost split. Jack said, 'Do you see? My lady can let a bullet go before she will finish.'

They laughed all the time and made good sport of it. The wife went away for shame. She was full of sorrow. The husband said, 'Go away, it's high time, for sure; you needn't leave your arse behind, either.'

Afterwards, as you will hear, a friar came to the house, and stayed all night. Our dame thought him a saint. Immediately she complained to him and told her story.

'We have a boy living in this house who is an absolute rascal. He upsets me terribly. I dare not look at him at all. I am ashamed to tell you what happens to me. Meet him in the field tomorrow and see that you beat him and make him lame and miserable. He certainly is a nasty piece of work. I think he must be a wizard. He greatly shames me.'

The friar said, 'I'll find out if he's a wizard.' She said, 'Don't forget. I'll be furious if you do.' The friar said, 'Believe you me, if I don't give that boy a good thrashing, never trust me again.'

The next morning the boy got up and went to the field, driving the animals. The friar left by the gate and ran at full speed because he thought he was behind time. When he came into the field he found the little boy looking after his animals. He said, 'Boy, God shame you; what have you done to your dame? Tell me straight away. Unless you can excuse yourself completely you'll pay for it; your arse shall be beaten, and I won't wait a moment.' The boy said, 'Friar, what's worrying you? My dame is as well as you are. What do you mean by telling me off? Would you like to know how many birds and other things I can shoot? I bet that though I'm only small I can hit that bird over there, and I'll give it to you.'

A bird was sitting on a branch. 'Go on, shoot,' said the friar, 'I'd like to see it.' The boy hit it on the head; it could fly no more but fell down dead. The friar went into the hedge, as he had to, to pick up the bird. The boy put down his bow and quickly took his pipe and began to blow lustily. When the friar heard the pipe he went on like a madman and began to leap about. He jumped at speed between the big and little branches but he couldn't find his way out. Brambles so scratched his face and many other parts that his sides began to bleed. Soon he tore his clothes, his tunic and his cloak and all the rest of what he wore.

The boy blew and laughed. How the friar jumped and twisted. He hopped marvellously high. The boy swore, 'By my truth, here is a royal sport for a lord to see.'

And always the friar held up his hand and cried out to the boy and pleaded with him to be still. 'And I promise you will get no harm from me. I will do nothing wrong to you.'

At that the boy said, 'Crawl out on the other side, and hurry off to where you were going. My dame complained to you and there's nothing else for it but for you also to go and complain to her.'

The friar went out of the hedge ragged and scratched and torn on every side. He had hardly a rag to wrap round his body to hide his balls. His fingers and his face were scratched everywhere and smeared with blood. Everyone who saw him wanted to run away. They thought he was mad.

When he came back to his host he didn't brag about his journey. He was meek and humble. When he came into the hall he was very sad, because everyone was frightened of him.

The wife said, 'Where ever have you been? By your dress you seem to have been in a rough place.' He said, 'Dame, I have been with your son. The devil of hell may overcome him, but certainly I cannot.'

Then the husband came in. 'See, sir,' the wife said then, 'here's a dreadful state of affairs. Your son, who is so beloved and dear to you, has almost killed the holy friar; oh dear, alas, alas.'

The husband said, 'Bless us, whatever has the boy done to you? Tell me straight away.' 'Sir,' said the friar, 'by Saint James, I have danced in the devil's name until I have almost lost my life.'

The husband said to him then, 'If you had lost your life in that way you would have died in deadly sin.' 'No,' said the friar, 'and I'll tell you why. It seemed to me that the pipe went so merrily that I could never stop.'

The husband said, 'As I hope to thrive then, that's a fine sport, unless you're to blame yourself. I'll listen to that pipe.' 'By God and Saint James, that will not I,' said the friar.

That night the boy came straight home as he should do. When he came into the hall his father immediately called him and said, 'Come here, son. Listen, boy, now you're here, what have you done to this friar? Don't tell me any lies.' 'Father,' he said, 'honestly, I didn't do anything to him today but just piped a dance for him.'

'I want to hear that pipe,' said the husband. 'No, for God's sake', said the friar, 'that would be a terrible thing.' The husband said, 'Yes, by God's grace.' The friar screamed, and said 'Alas.' He wrung his hands.

'For the love of God,' said the friar, 'if you're going to hear the pipe, tie me to a post; I can't think of any better plan. I know I shall die, I'm nearly dead already.'

They immediately got some ropes and bound him to a post that stood in the middle of the hall. All those sitting at supper were amused and laughed at him, and said, 'The friar won't fall over.'

Then the husband spoke up, and said to his son, 'Pipe on when you want to.' 'All ready, father,' he said, 'I'll show you my sport; I'll give you a tune.'

As soon as ever the pipe sounded no one could stop himself but began to dance and jump. All that heard the pipe could not contain themselves but tumbled into a heap. Those who sat at supper then jumped over the table and pranced about. Those who sat on the bench had no time to turn but were thrown on to the ground.

The husband was in despair. Immediately he started up out of the chair with a gloomy look. Some jumped over the furniture and some broke their shins against it, and some fell in the fire.

The wife came in behind and began to jump and wriggle and swiftly shake. But when she looked at little Jack immediately her arse began to speak and gave a loud report.

The friar was almost a lost man. He beat his head against the post, and had no better fortune but the rope to rub off his skin so that the blood ran down all over him.

The boy went piping in the street, and the whole crowd tumbled after him. They couldn't stop. They went out of the door in such a crush that everyone fell on the other's neck, so strongly did they struggle to get out.

Those who lived nearby who heard the pipe as they sat in their houses jumped over the half-doors, they had no time to undo the latch, they were so loth to linger. Those who lay in their beds, big and small, immediately raised their heads and dashed straight into the street, as I heard say, as naked as when they were born. When they were all gathered together there was a great crowd in the middle of the street. Some were lame and couldn't walk, yet they also hopped about on hands and feet.

The boy said, 'Father, would you like to rest?' 'In faith,' he said, with a cheerful look, 'I think it would be best. Finish when you like. Surely this is the merriest music that I have heard this seven years.'

When the pipe sounded no more, they were all astonished by their behaviour. 'Ah, by Saint Mary, what has happened to all this jolly music that made us dance?'

Everybody was in a good humour, except the wife and the friar. They were utterly dismayed. As the proverb says, 'He who doesn't get all he wants, whether good or bad, is not well pleased.'

5. Dom Hugh of Leicester

Once upon a time there was a very famous abbey of monks in the town of Leicester, as you will now hear. Amongst all the monks one was outstanding. His name was Dom Hugh, as I hope for heaven. He was a young and lusty monk, with a great fancy for beautiful women, and he spent a lot of time going after them.

I read that there was a tailor in Leicester who had married a good and beautiful woman. They had loved each other for seven years or more. Dom Hugh loved this tailor's wife passionately and was always thinking how he might find her on her own, and try her out, and see if she would say 'No' to him.

One day he said to her, 'Beautiful, generous woman, unless I can have my pleasure of you I shall go out of my mind.' 'Sir,' she said, 'I have many a vigorous turn with my husband every day.' 'Dame,' he said, 'do not say no. I must have my pleasure of you whatever it cost me.' She answered and said, 'If it must needs be, come to me tomorrow, for my husband rides out of town then. And then we can do what you want, and we can have good fun. And if you do not come, you are to blame. But first, Dom Hugh, tell me what my reward shall be.' 'Dame,' he said, 'On my word, twenty nobles of good money, for we will have a fine time this day.' And so they kissed and parted.

The tailor came home at evening as usual, and his wife told him the whole story of how Dom Hugh would come in the morning, and what her reward from him would be. 'What, Dame, as I hope to thrive, are you mad? Are you going to make me a cuckold? That would make me feel terrible.' 'No, sir,' she said, 'by sweet Saint John, I will keep myself a good woman, and get you some money also, for sure. For he has promised to be here tomorrow early. I know very well he will not fail. And I shall lock you in the

63

chest, so that you will be missed and thought to be out of the way. And when Dom Hugh comes here early, about five o'clock as arranged, without any difficulty, then I shall call you quickly, and see that you come to me without delay.'

And when the dawn began to appear in the morning, Dom Hugh came running there – he thought he had missed his time. Then he knocked softly on the tailor's door. She got up and invited him in and said, 'Sir, you're very welcome.' 'Good morning, gentle mistress,' he said. 'Now tell me where your husband is, so that we can be sure we are safe.' 'Sir,' she said, 'so help me God, he has gone out of town and won't come home till afternoon.'

Dom Hugh was very pleased about that, and quickly took her in his arms and thought to have some fun. 'Sir,' she said, 'wait a moment, for shame. I want to know first what I shall have. For when I have it I won't be longing for it. Give me twenty nobles first, and then do with me what you please.' 'By my priesthood,' he said then, 'you shall have it in gold and silver straight away. You shan't long for them any more. See, my mistress, here they are, and he threw the money in her lap. 'Thank you,' she said.

Dom Hugh thought to make love to this wife. 'Wait, sir,' she said, 'till I have put it away,' for she thought that would be the best thing to do, and with these words she opened a chest. Then Dom Hugh thought to have had her alone, but the tailor jumped out of the chest straight away, and said, 'Sir monk, if you will stand I will give you such a stroke with my sword that you will have little lust for my wife.' And promptly, with no more argument, he hit Dom Hugh on the head so that he fell down stark dead. That was the first time that he was really killed.

'Alas,' his wife said then, 'have you killed this monk so soon? What bad luck. Wherever shall we run or go to?' 'There's no remedy for it,' he said, 'unless you give me good advice how to carry this false priest out of the way, so that no one shall speak about it or say that I have killed him. Otherwise, we've done it in vain.' 'Yes, sir,' she said, 'let him stay until early evening. Then we can easily deal with him, for you must carry him directly to the abbey and prop him up straight by the wall, and then you must quickly get away.'

The abbot looked for the monk everywhere, for he had heard said that he was missing. The abbot was very angry with him indeed, and would not rest, as God's my witness, until he had found Dom Hugh. He told his man to look for him around the place and tell him to come 'and speak with me straight away.' The man went out and looked around, until at last he saw Dom Hugh, and went straight up to him, thinking him to be alive, and said, 'Dom Hugh, as I hope to thrive, I've been looking for you everywhere, and I'm astonished that I couldn't find you till now.'

Dom Hugh stood as still as one who couldn't tell what he should say, and no more could he, for good or ill. With that the abbot's man, thinking all for the best, said, 'Sir, you must come to my lord, or else you'll be in trouble.' When Dom Hugh answered not a word the man thought he'd better get some advice and hurried off to the abbot. 'Please, my lord, come quick and see where Dom Hugh stands up straight by the wall, and won't answer me, whatever I say.' 'Get me a staff,' said the abbot, 'and I'll see if he won't answer me.'

Then when the abbot came there and saw him standing upright against the wall, he began to shout at him, and said, 'You false vagabond, you'll pay for this. Why don't you perform your services properly? Come here and jump to it.' But Dom Hugh answered not a word. 'You bastard,' said the abbot, 'why don't you speak? Speak! Or I vow to God I'll give you such a bang on the head that I'll make you drop dead.' And with that he gave him such a clout that he fell down at the blow. And that's how he was killed the second time. And yet he made much more trouble for them as you will hear fully in a moment.

'Sir,' said the abbot's man, 'you've done an evil thing, for you've killed Dom Hugh, and I vow to God you've profaned this place.' 'Is there a remedy?' said the abbot. 'Yes,' said his man, 'by sweet Saint John, if you will give me such a good reward that I shall be the better for it during my life.' 'Yes,' said the abbot, 'I'll give you forty shillings if you can save my honour.' 'My lord, I tell you, as I hope to thrive, he used to go to a tailor's house to woo his pretty wife, and without anybody knowing anything of it I'll take him back there, and set him upright. Then everybody will say that the tailor has killed him, for he was very angry with him for coming to his wife so often.'

The abbot was well pleased with his advice, and his man took up Dom Hugh in a moment and quickly set him up at the tailor's door, and ran home as fast as he could. The tailor and his wife were in bed and were very much afraid that Dom Hugh would give them away. The tailor said to his wife, 'I've dreamt all night of how this false scoundrel came to our door.' 'Jesus,' said his wife, 'what sort of a man are you that you're so much afraid of a dead man? I thought you'd killed him.'

With that the tailor took a poleaxe in his hand and went to the door, and saw the monk stand by the door, which made him terribly afraid. He stood still and said nothing until he spoke to his wife. 'Dame, now my life is lost unless I kill him first.' He brought out his poleaxe or mace, and hit Dom Hugh on the head, so that he fell down stark dead. And so Dom Hugh was killed three times; and yet he played another trick. 'Alas,' said the tailor's wife, 'this wretch causes us a lot of trouble.' 'Dame,' said the tailor, 'what shall we do now?' 'Sir,' she said 'as I'm alive, you must lay the monk in the corner till tomorrow before dawn. Then you must put him in a sack and throw him in the millpond. That's the best plan, surely.'

So the tailor thought he would indeed do it. In the morning he put Dom Hugh in a sack and quickly got him on to his back and hurried off to the millpond. There he saw two thieves coming as fast as they could from the mill. But when they saw the tailor they were very much taken aback, for they thought it was the miller, whom they were so much afraid of that they dropped their sack and went a little way aside, I don't know where. When the tailor saw the sack lie there he looked into it and saw that it was full of bacon. He laid Dom Hugh there and carried the bacon off home, and that is true.

The thieves took up the sack with Dom Hugh in it and went on their way home. Then one of the thieves said to his wife, 'Dame, do take a look in that sack, for I'm sure there's good bacon in it. So let's have a good time now.' The wife quickly ran to the sack, and when she had untied it she found the dead monk in it. Then she screamed and said, 'Alas, I see you've done a crazy thing, to have killed Dom Hugh. If it comes to be known, you'll be hanged.' 'No, good dame,' he replied. 'It must have been the false miller.'

Then they took up Dom Hugh again and actually brought him to the mill where they had stolen the bacon before. And there they hung up Dom Hugh in storage. Thus he was once indeed hanged. And the thieves ran home as fast as they could. The miller's wife got up early in the morning and quickly made herself ready to go and fetch some bacon. But when she looked up she was aghast to see the monk hanging there. She cried out and frightened everybody and said, 'There's a strange thing, now, for here, by God, hangs the false monk Dom Hugh, who has been so lecherous so long and used to sport with men's wives. Now someone has paid him out – I think it must have been the devil from Hell – and our bacon is stolen. This is a rotten trick. I don't know what we shall eat this winter.'

'What, wife! Forget all this fuss. Give me some good advice how we can take this monk away and get rid of him secretly.' 'Sir,' she said, 'you can easily know that. Lay him in a corner until it is night, and we shall carry him away before daylight. The abbot has a yard near here where he keeps a good horse loose. Go and fetch the horse at night and bring him straight to me, and we'll put the monk on him and tie him tight, as God's my help, and put a long pole in his hand, as if he were going to attack his enemies, and we will push it under his arm as if he were going to make a fierce joust. For as you know well, the abbot has a gentle, meek mare which only ambles and never trots. But in the morning when the abbot gets up, he orders his mare to be brought to him so he can see his workmen, if they're short of anything. And as I'm telling you, he rides on the mare to see if everything's all right. When this horse sees this mare he will immediately rush after her.'

When the miller understood this he thought his wife's advice was good, and was very pleased with it, and absolutely ran for the horse. When he had at last fetched the horse he threw Dom Hugh on to the horse's back and fixed him very firmly so that he could the better manage to ride as fast as it could run. Now you shall know what the miller did then. He immediately took the horse, with Dom Hugh sitting on it, by the bridle, and led him so that he could see the mare. Then the horse ran all right.

The abbot glanced aside and saw that Dom Hugh was riding towards him. He was almost out of his mind for fear when he saw Dom Hugh coming so close. He shouted out, 'Help, for the love of the Trinity, for I can see that Dom Hugh is out for revenge. Alas, I'm a dead man.' And with that he ran away from his mare.

The abbot's men quickly ran against Dom Hugh, and with clubs and staves rapidly gave him many a blow, then they threw him down on the ground. So they killed him once again. Thus he was hanged once and killed four times, and in the end, he was buried, as the best thing to do. I pray God send us all good rest.

6. About a Man who Acted in a Play as a Devil

It happened that in a market town in the county of Suffolk there was a stage play in which a man called John Adroyns who lived in another village a couple of miles away acted as the devil. And when the play was over he left the aforesaid market town to go home to his own house. Because he had no change of clothing he went out in the devil's costume. On the way home he went through a rabbit-warren belonging to a gentleman of the village where he himself lived. At this time it happened that a priest, who was vicar of a nearby church, with two or three other useless companions, had brought with them a horse and a net and a ferret in order to catch rabbits. When the ferret was in the earth and the net was set over the pathway along which John Adroyns had to come, this priest and these other fellows saw him coming wearing the devil's clothing. Thinking that they were in the devil's service since they were stealing rabbits, they thought it was indeed the devil, and they ran away for fear. This John Adroyns in devil's clothing, because it was dark didn't see the net, but hurrying along stumbled over it and with the fall almost broke his neck. But when he had revived a bit he looked around and saw that it was a net to catch rabbits with, and looking further he saw that they were running away for fear of him. And he saw a horse tied to a bush loaded with rabbits which they had caught. He took the horse and the net, jumped on to the horse, and rode to the house of the gentleman who owned the warren, in order to get some thanks for catching such a prize.

When he arrived he knocked at the gates. One of the gentleman's servants asked who was there, and immediately opened the gate. But as soon as he saw him in the devil's clothing he was immediately taken aback, and barred the door again, and went in to his master and swore to him that the devil was at the gate and wanted to come in.

Hearing this, the gentleman called another of his servants and told him to go to the gate to find out who was there. This second servant when he came to the gate dared not open it, but asked in a loud voice who was there. This John Adroyns in the devil's clothing answered at the top of his voice and said,

'Tell your master I must speak with him before I go.' This second servant when he heard that answer also thought that it was the devil. He went in again to his master and said,

'Master, it is indeed the devil that is at the gate, and he says that he must speak with you before he goes away.'

The gentleman then began to be a little nervous, and he called the steward of his house, who was the most sensible servant that he had, and told him to go to the gate and tell him for certain who was there. This steward, because he thought he would make sure who was there went to the gate and looked through the gaps in the gate in various places. He saw clearly that it was the devil, and how he sat upon a horse, and around the saddle on every side he saw the rabbits' heads hanging down. In great fear he rushed back to his master, and said,

'By God's body it is indeed the devil that is at the gate, sitting on a horse loaded with souls, and in all probability he has come purposely for your soul, and he's only short of your soul, and if he had your soul I expect he would go away.'

Then this gentleman, remarkably frightened, called his chaplain, and had the holy candle lighted, and got holy water, and went to the gate with as many of his servants as dare go with him. There the chaplain with holy words of incantation said,

'In the name of the Father, Son and Holy Ghost, I exhort and charge you in the holy name of God to tell me why and wherefore you come here.'

This John Adroyns in the devil's clothing, when he heard them begin to exorcise in such a way said,

'No, no! Don't be frightened of me – I'm a good devil! I'm John Adroyns your neighbour. I live in this village and acted as the devil today in the play. I've brought my master a dozen or two of his own rabbits, that were stolen in his warren – and their horse, and their net – and made them run away for fear!'

And when they heard him speak so, they knew him very well by his voice, and they opened the gate and let him come in. And so all the fear and dread just mentioned was turned into laughter and amusement.

By this tale you can see that on many occasions men fear more than they need, which has caused men to believe that spirits and devils have been seen in various places, when there has been nothing of the kind.

7. About the Miller who Stole the Nuts

There was a certain rich farmer in a village who had an extraordinary love of nuts, and who planted trees of filberts and other nut trees in his orchard, and looked after them well all his life. When he died he made his executors promise to bury a bag of nuts with him in his grave, or otherwise they could not be his executors; and for fear of losing their appointment they carried out his intention and did so.

The same night after the day that he was buried there was a miller in a white coat who came to this man's garden in order to steal a bag of nuts. On the way he met a tailor in a black coat, who was one of his shiftless friends, and told him what he was up to. The tailor revealed to him in return that he intended at the same time to steal a sheep, and so they both agreed then each to carry on with his own project, and afterwards to celebrate with each other and to meet again in the church porch, and he who came first would wait for the other.

This miller, when he had got his nuts, was the first to get to the church porch, and he waited there for his companion, and meanwhile sat still and cracked nuts.

It happened that the sexton of the church, because it was about nine o'clock, came to ring the curfew evening bell. When he looked into the porch and saw someone all in white cracking nuts he thought it was the dead man risen out of his grave cracking the nuts that were buried with him, and he rushed home again and told a cripple who was in his house what he had seen. This cripple when he heard it scolded the sexton, and said that if he could walk he would go there and exhort the spirit.

'By my truth,' said the sexton, 'if you dare do it, I'll carry you on my shoulders.' So they both agreed. The sexton took the cripple on his shoulders and came into the churchyard again. The miller in the porch saw someone coming carrying something on his back and thought it was the tailor coming with the sheep. He got up to meet them, and as he came toward them he asked and said,

'Is he fat? Is he fat?'

When the sexton heard him speak so, in a fright he threw the cripple down and said,

'Fat or lean, take him there for me!' and he ran away, and the cripple by a miracle was cured and ran away as fast as the sexton, or faster.

This miller, when he saw that they were two and not one, thought that someone had seen the tailor stealing the sheep, and was running after him to catch him. He was also afraid that someone had seen him stealing nuts. In a fright he left his nuts behind him and as secretly as he could ran home to his mill.

Just after he had gone the tailor came with the stolen sheep on his shoulders to the church porch to look for the miller. And when he found there the nutshells, he supposed that his friend had been there and gone home, as he had indeed. So he took up the sheep again on his shoulders and went towards the mill. But while this was going on the sexton who had run away did not go to his own house but went to the room of the parish priest and explained to him how the spirit of the man had risen out of his grave, and was cracking nuts, as you have heard before. So the priest said that he would go and exorcise him if the sexton would go with him. And so they both agreed. The priest put on his surplice and a stole about his neck, and took holy water with him, and went with the sexton toward the church. As soon as he entered the churchyard, the tailor with the white sheep on his shoulders intending, as I have told you before, to go down to the mill, met them and thought that the priest in his surplice was the miller in his white coat. And he said to him,

'By God, I have him! I have him!' meaning the sheep that he had stolen.

The priest, seeing the tailor all in black, and a white thing on his shoulders, thought it was the devil carrying away the spirit of the dead man that was buried, and ran away as fast as he could, taking the way down to the mill, and the sexton running after him. This tailor, seeing the man following thought that someone was following the miller to do him some harm, and thought he would follow in case there was any need to help the miller; and he carried on until he came to the mill and knocked at its door. The miller, who was inside, asked who was there. The tailor answered and said,

'By God, I have caught one of them, and made sure of him, and tied him fast by the legs', meaning the sheep that he had stolen and at that moment had on his shoulders tied fast by the legs. But the miller hearing him say that he had him tied fast by the legs, thought it was the constable who had caught the tailor for stealing the sheep, and had tied him fast by the legs, and the miller was afraid that the constable had come to take him also for stealing the nuts. So he opened the back door and ran away as fast as he could.

When the tailor heard the back door opened he went round to the other side of the mill and there he saw the miller running away. He stood there for a little while puzzled, with the sheep on his shoulders. The parish priest and the sexton who were standing near, just by the millhouse, hiding themselves for fear, saw the tailor again with the sheep on his shoulders, and still thought it was the devil with the spirit of the dead man on his shoulders, and they ran away for fear. But because they did not know the ground well, the priest jumped into a ditch, and was in almost over the head, and was almost drowned, so that he shouted at the top of his voice, 'Help! Help!' Then the tailor looked around and saw the miller run one way and the sexton another way, and heard the priest shout for help, and thought it was the constable with a lot of people shouting for help to catch him and take him to prison for stealing the sheep. So he threw down the sheep and ran away in another direction as fast as he could. And so everyone was frightened of the other for no reason.

By this you can easily see that it is ridiculous for anybody to be too frightened of a thing before he sees some proof or cause.

8. About the Married Man who Came to Heaven

There was a certain married man who when he was dead came to the gates of heaven to Saint Peter and said he came to claim his inheritance, which he had deserved. Saint Peter asked him what he was. He said, 'A married man.' Immediately Saint Peter opened the gates and asked him to come in, and said he was worthy to have his inheritance because he had had much trouble and was worthy to have a crown of glory.

Immediately after, another man came who claimed heaven. He told Saint Peter that he had had two wives, and Saint Peter answered him and said,

'Come in! You are worthy to have a double crown of glory, for you have had double trouble'.

Finally there came a third man claiming heaven, and he told Saint Peter that he had had three wives, and he asked to come in.

'What?' said Saint Peter, 'You were once in trouble, and were freed from it, and deliberately wished to be troubled again, and were again set free; and for all that you couldn't beware the third time, but you willingly entered trouble again? You go to hell – you'll never get into heaven; you aren't worthy.'

This tale is a warning to those who have been twice in danger to be careful how they come into it the third time.

9. Of the Three Wise Men of Gotham

A certain man who was living in a town called Gotham went to a fair four miles away to buy sheep. And as he came over a bridge he met one of his neighbours and told him where he was going. And the neighbour asked him which way he meant to bring them back. He said he would bring them over the same bridge.

'No,' said the other man, 'but you won't.'

'By God,' said he, 'but I will.'

The other again said he would not. And he again said he would bring them over in spite of him, and so they fell to words, and at last to blows, so that each one knocked the other badly about the head with his fists.

A third man came up to them, a miller, with a sack of meal upon a horse. He was a neighbour of theirs, and parted them, and asked them the cause of their quarrel, which they made clear to him, as you have heard. This third man, the miller, thought he would rebuke their foolishness with a familiar example, and took his sack of flour from his horse's back and opened it and poured all the flour in the sack over the bridge into the running river, so all the flour was lost. And he said as follows: 'By my truth, neighbours, because you fight about driving over the bridge sheep which haven't yet been bought, and you don't know where they are, it seems to me that there is as much sense in your heads as there is flour in my sack.'

This tales shows you that some men take it upon themselves to point out good sense to other men, while they are but fools themselves.

10. About the Yeoman of the Guard who Said he would Beat the Carter

A Yeoman of the King's Guard living in a village near London had a very pretty young wife. A carter of the village, a big fellow, visited her and slept with her at various times when her husband was away from home, and this was so openly known that it was common gossip. So a young man of the village, who knew this Yeoman of the Guard very well, told him that such and such a carter had slept with his wife. In reply, this Yeoman of the Guard said and swore by God's body that if he met the carter it would cost him his life.

'By Mary,' said the young man, 'if you go straight away even now by the high way, you will overtake him, driving a cart carrying hay towards

London.' So this Yeoman of the Guard without a moment's pause rode after this carter and within a short space overtook him. He knew him well enough, and he abruptly called the carter to him and said as follows,

'Hey you! I understand you sleep every night with my wife when I'm away from home.'

This carter, not being afraid of the other answered,

'Yes, by Mary! What then?'

'What then?' said the Yeoman of the Guard, 'by God's heart if you hadn't told me the truth I'd have cracked your skull.' And so the Yeoman of the Guard returned, and no harm was done, nor any blow struck or offered.

By this you can see that the biggest boasters sometimes when it comes to proof are the biggest cowards.

11. About the Man who Meant to have the Pot Stand where he Wanted

A young man recently married thought that it would be a good policy to get control over his wife from the beginning. He came to her when the pot was boiling on the fire, and although the meat in it was not cooked he suddenly commanded her to take the pot off the fire. She answered and said that the meat was not ready to eat. And he said in return,

'I will have it taken off for my pleasure.' This good woman was still reluctant to offend him, so she set the pot beside the fire as he required. Immediately afterwards he commanded her to set the pot behind the door, and she answered back and said in reply,

'You are not sensible to do that.'

But he strictly said that it must be as he required, and she mildly again did what he commanded.

This man, still not satisfied, commanded her to set the pot high up on the hen-roost.

'What?' she said again, 'I'm sure that you must be mad.' And then he fiercely commanded her to set it there, or else, he said, she would be sorry for it. She was rather frightened of upsetting him, so she took a ladder and put it up against the roost. Taking the pot in her hand she herself went up the ladder, asking the husband to hold the ladder firm to stop it slipping, which he did.

And when the husband looked up and saw the pot standing there high up, he said,

'Right! Now the pot is standing where I want it!'

'Right! Now the pot is standing where I want it!'

And when the wife heard him say that, she suddenly poured the hot stew onto his head and said,

'And now the stew is there where *I* want it!'

By this tale one can see that there's no sense in trying a mild woman's patience too far, lest it turn to his own hurt and damage.

12. Why there are no Welshmen in Heaven

I find written among old stories how God made Saint Peter porter of Heaven, and how God, in his goodness soon after his suffering on the cross allowed many men to come to the kingdom of heaven who very little deserved it. So at this time there were in heaven a lot of Welshmen, who troubled all the rest with their boasting and chatter. So God said to Saint Peter that he was fed up with them, and that he'd be very glad to have them out of heaven. Saint Peter replied to him,

'Good Lord, I guarantee that it will be done in no time.' So Saint Peter went outside the gates of heaven and shouted in a loud voice,

'Cause bobe!' which is as much as to say, 'Roasted cheese.' When they heard this the Welshmen ran out of heaven at great speed. And when Saint Peter saw that they were all outside, he quickly went in to heaven and locked the door, and so he barred all the Welshmen out.

By this you can see that there is no sense in a man loving or setting his mind too much upon any dainty or worldly pleasure whereby he may lose heavenly and eternal joy.

13. About the Friar who Preached against People who Ride on Sundays

A friar was preaching in a certain parish and in his sermon he rebuked those who rode on Sundays, all the time looking at one man who was booted and spurred ready to ride. When this man saw that all the people looked at him, half in anger he answered the friar,

'Why do you preach so much against those who ride on Sundays, since Christ himself rode on Palm Sunday, as you well know is written in Holy Scripture?'

And immediately the friar answered him and said,

'But I ask you, what came of it? Wasn't he hanged on the Friday after?', and when they heard that all the people in church burst out laughing.

ITALIAN TALES

1. Sir Bernabò Commands an Abbot to Tell him Four Impossible Things

Sir Bernabò, Lord of Milan, foiled by the excellent reasoning of a miller, gave him a very great benefice. This lord in his time was feared more than other lords, and though he was cruel, there was a good deal of justice even in his cruelty. Among many instances which arose was this. A rich abbot having been negligent in properly looking after two mastiffs which belonged to the said lord, and which had become scabby, was ordered to pay four florins, for which the abbot began to ask mercy. And the said lord, seeing him beg for mercy, said to him:

'If you can explain to me four things, I will forgive you the whole fine. And what I want you to explain to me are these things. How far is it from here to heaven; how much water is in the sea; what does one do in Hell; and how much am I worth?'

The abbot, hearing this, began to sigh, and it seemed to him a worse business than before. Nevertheless to calm the lord's anger and to gain time, he asked that it might please him to set a date for answering such difficult questions. And the lord granted him all next day, and wanting to hear the conclusion made him give security against his return. The abbot went back to the monastery wracking his brains and very gloomy, panting like a startled horse. When he got there he met his miller, who seeing him so distressed said,

'My lord, what's wrong to make you pant so heavily?'

The abbot said, 'I've very good reason, for the lord Bernabò will do me a bad turn, if I don't explain to him four things which neither Solomon nor Aristotle could tell him.'

The miller said, 'And what are they?'

The abbot told him.

Then the miller, thinking about it, said to the abbot, 'I'll relieve you of this labour, if you like.'

The abbot said, 'May God grant it!'

Said the miller, 'I believe that God and his saints wish it.'

The abbot, who didn't know where he was, said 'If you do it, take from me anything you want – you won't be able to ask me anything within my power that I won't give you.'

Said the miller, 'I will leave that to your judgment.'

'O what way will you do it?' asked the abbot.

Then the miller replied, 'I want to dress myself in your habit and cowl, and shave my beard, and tomorrow morning I shall go into him early, saying that I am the abbot: and I shall decide the four questions in such a way that I think he'll be pleased.'

It seemed a thousand years to the abbot before he could put the miller in his place. The miller being turned abbot, he set out early in the morning, and when he arrived at the door of the place where the lord lived, he knocked, saying that such and such an abbot wanted to answer to the lord certain questions that he had set him. The lord, wishing to hear what the abbot would say, and surprised that he had come back so soon, had him called in. And being come into the darkest part of the room, making a bow, and often putting his hand in front of his face so as not to be known, the miller was asked by the lord if he had brought answers to the four questions he had been asked.

He answered, 'Yes, my lord. You asked me, how far is it from here to heaven. Taking everything into account, it is from here to there thirty-six million, eight hundred and fifty-four thousand and seventy-two miles and twenty-two and a half paces.'

Said the lord, 'You've measured it very exactly. How do you prove it?'

He answered, 'Have it measured, and if it isn't so, hang me by the neck. Secondly, you asked, how much water is there in the sea. This has been very difficult for me to find out, because it doesn't stay still and there's always more coming in. All the same, I have measured in the sea twenty-five thousand, nine hundred and eighty-two million hogsheads, seven barrels, twelve gallons and two cups.'

Said the lord, 'How do you know?'

He answered, 'I measured it as best I could. If you don't believe me, have the barrels found and measure it yourself. If you don't find it so, have me quartered. Thirdly you asked me what they do in Hell. In Hell they cut up, quarter, tear to pieces, and hang, neither more nor less than you do here.'

'What proof do you give of this?'

He answered, 'I once talked to someone who had been there, and it was from him that Dante the Florentine learnt what he wrote about the things in Hell. But he is dead. If you don't believe him, send someone else to see. Fourthly you asked me what you are worth – and I say you're worth twenty-nine pence.'

When Sir Bernabò heard this he turned to him in a rage, saying, 'The Devil take you! Am I so valueless that I am worth no more than a cooking-pot?'

He answered, not without great nervousness, 'My lord, listen to the reason. You know that our lord Jesus Christ was sold for thirty pence. I reckon that you're worth a penny less than he.'

When he heard this the lord realised only too well that it wasn't the abbot, and looking at him very intently, seeing that he was a man of much greater learning than the abbot, he said 'You are not the abbot.'

The miller's fear can be imagined by anyone. Falling to his knees with his hands clasped he implored mercy, telling the lord that he was the abbot's miller and how and why he had come into his palace disguised, and how he had taken the habit, and all this more to please him than through ill-will. When Sir Bernabò heard this he said,

'It doesn't matter. Since he made you abbot, and you're worth more than him, in the name of God I confirm you in his place, and I want you to be abbot from now on, and him to be the miller, and you to have all the income of the monastery, and him to have the income of the miller.'

And the lord kept it so all the time he lived, that the abbot was the miller, and the miller the abbot.

2. Lapaccio di Geri Sleeps with a Corpse

Lapaccio di Geri from Monteluppo lived in my time, and I knew him, and often sought his company, because he was a pleasant and rather silly man. When somebody said to him, 'So-and-so is dead' and had touched him with his hand, immediately he tried to touch him back; and if the first one got away and Lapaccio couldn't touch him again, he went out to someone else passing in the street, and if he hadn't been able to touch anybody, he would touch a dog or a cat. And if one of those couldn't be found, at last he touched the blade of a knife. And he was so superstitious, that if, having been touched, he had not immediately touched someone else, as has been described, he thought that for certain he would die the same death as the one on whose account he had been touched, and that soon. And because of this, if a criminal was led to execution, or a bier or a cross was carried past, the thing was so well known that everybody ran to touch him, and he ran about now after this one now after that like someone beside himself; and so those who had touched him were highly amused.

It happened on one occasion that Lapaccio was sent during Lent by the Commune of Florence to tell someone he had been elected Chief of Police. He left Florence and went to Bologna and then Ferrara, and then, going further, arrived late one evening at a nasty boggy place called C'a Salvadega. Having dismounted at the inn, he could hardly get his horses and baggage looked after, because there were lots of Hungarians and pilgrims going to Rome, who had already gone to bed. Having found something to eat, when he had finished supper he asked the innkeeper where he should sleep. The innkeeper replied,

'Go where you can, come in here where all the beds I have are, and lots of pilgrims; look around. If there's a spare inch fix yourself up the best you can, because I haven't got any other beds or rooms.'

Lapaccio went into the said room, looking from bed to bed in the dim light, and found them all full except one, in which on one side lay a Hungarian, who the day before had died. Lapaccio, not knowing this (or he would have lain down in a fire before he lay down in *that* bed) and seeing that there was no one on the other side, got in to sleep there. And as often happens as a man turns over to get comfortable, it seemed to him that his companion occupied too much of Lapaccio's own terrain, and he said 'Move over a bit, there's a good chap.' His friend stayed silent and unmoving, being gone to the other world. After waiting a bit, Lapaccio touched him and said, 'O you sleep heavily. Give me a bit of room, please.' And the good man was silent. Seeing he didn't move, Lapaccio punched him.

'Damn you, get over!'

He might have been speaking to a stone, because he couldn't move. So Lapaccio began to get into a rage, and said,

'Damn you, I wish you'd drop dead – you're a scoundrel!'

And placing himself across the bed with his legs towards the other man, and taking a firm grip on the bedstead, he gave him a couple of great kicks, and hit him so full that the dead body fell from the bed to the ground so heavily and with such a crash, that Lapaccio began to say to himself,

'Oh dear, what have I done?'

And fumbling over the coverlet he leaned over the side of the bed under which his friend had fallen to the ground, and began to say gently,

'Are you all right? Have you hurt yourself? Come back into bed!'

But he remained as still as a stone, and let Lapaccio say whatever he wanted, for he was in no condition to reply, or to get back into bed. Since Lapaccio had heard him fall like a dead weight, seeing that he did not complain, or get up from the ground, he began to say to himself,

'Oh dear, what bad luck! I must have killed him.'

And he looked and looked again, and the more he looked, the more it seemed to him that he had killed him, and he said,

'O miserable Lapaccio, what shall I do? Where shall I go? At least, if I only could get away. But I don't know where, because I've never been here before. I'd rather have died at Florence than still be here. And if I stay, I'll be sent to Ferrara or somewhere else and have my head cut off. If I tell the innkeeper, he'll rather I die than he lose anything.'

And remaining the whole night in this suffering and distress, like one who has been condemned to death, he expected to die when morning came. At first light the pilgrims going to Rome began to get up and go out. Lapaccio, who seemed more dead than the corpse, began to get up also, and hurried out as quick as he could for two causes. And I don't know which of them gave him the greater misery. The first was to escape the danger and get away before the innkeeper should know of it. The second was to get away from the corpse and escape from the superstitious terror that he always felt for the dead. Once outside Lapaccio hurried the servant who was saddling the animals, and found the innkeeper, reckoned the bill, and paid him. While counting out the money his hands shook like aspen leaves.

The innkeeper said, 'O, are you cold?' Lapaccio with great difficulty said that he thought it might be because of the fog which had arisen over the marshes. While the innkeeper and Lapaccio were at this point, a pilgrim came up who said to the innkeeper that he couldn't find a bag of his in the place where he had slept. So the innkeeper with a light that he had burning in his hand immediately went into the room, hunting here and there, Lapaccio staying at a distance with fearful eyes. As the innkeeper bent down by the bed where Lapaccio had slept, looking on the ground with his light, he saw the dead Hungarian at the foot of the bed.

When he saw that, he began to say, 'What the devil's this? Who slept in this bed?'

Lapaccio, listening all of a tremble, didn't know whether he was alive or dead. A pilgrim, perhaps the one who had lost the bag, said,

'He slept there' – nodding towards Lapaccio. Lapaccio seeing that, like one who seemed already to have the axe on his neck, called the innkeeper aside, and said

'I put myself in your hands, for the love of God, for I slept in that bed, and I couldn't in any way make him give me room and stay on his own side, so I gave him a kick and he fell to the ground. I didn't mean to kill him. It was an accident, not done on purpose.'

The innkeeper said, 'What's your name?' and he told him. So the innkeeper continued,

'What's it worth to you, to get out of this?'

Lapaccio said, 'Brother, set any price you like and get me away from here. I've got property in Florence – I'll write you a promise to pay.'

The innkeeper, seeing what a silly man he was, said, 'What you unfortunate man! May God make you miserable! Were you blind last night? Ha! You lay down with a Hungarian who died yesterday after vespers!'

When Lapaccio heard this, it seemed to him he was in a situation a little different, but not much, because he made little difference between having his head cut off and having slept with a dead body. When he had recovered a bit of nerve and confidence, he began to say to the innkeeper,

'Good God, you're a strange man. Why didn't you tell me last night, there's a corpse in one of those beds? If you had told me that, not only would I not have stayed here, but I'd have gone further for ever so many miles, if I had had to stay in the valley among the reeds. You've given me such a shock that I'll never be happy again, and perhaps I'll die of it.'

The innkeeper, who had asked for a reward as if he had saved him, when he heard Lapaccio's words, was afraid he might be accused by him, and with the best words he could he made peace with Lapaccio. And the said Lapaccio departed, going as fast as he could, often looking back for fear that the C'a Salvadega might be following him, with a face a good deal paler than that of the dead Hungarian whom he'd thrown out of bed on to the ground. And with this anguish, which was not small, in his mind, he went for a certain gentleman, Andresagio Rosso, of Parma, who had only one eye, who came as Chief of Police to Florence. And Lapaccio returned, reporting that he had offered the post to the said Chief of Police, and he had accepted it. When Lapaccio got back to Florence he had an illness of which he almost died.

I believe that Fortune, hearing how superstitious he was in considering touching the dead as bad luck, wanted to amuse herself with him as told above, since it was certainly an extraordinary case, as happening to him; if it had happened to another it would not have been so extraordinary.

But how different are men's natures!

For there are many who not only do not fear omens, but would not care a thing if they laid or stayed with dead bodies. And there are others who would not care if they laid in bed with snakes or toads, scorpions, and all sorts of poison and filth. And there are others who will not dress themselves in green, which is the prettiest colour there is. Others would never begin anything on Friday, which is the day on which was our salvation; and so it is with many other things which are fantastic and with no sense, which are so numerous that they could not be contained in this book.

3. Benghi goes to Joust

It is not long since there was in Florence a silly fool called Agnolo di ser Gherado, a sort of jester, who imitated everything. He used to consort with a number of townspeople who were very much amused by him. There was a fad for jousting, and since he was going to Peretola with some who were going there for that purpose, he also jousted. And he had begged the loan of one of the horses from the Dyeworks, in the Borg'Ognissanti, a miserable nag, high and thin, which was the very image of hunger. Once arrived at Peretola, the fine fellow had himself armed, and he was on the further side of the square, so that it happened that he would gallop towards Florence. And to put the helmet on his head, give him the lance, and place a thistle under the horse's tail, was the work of a moment. The saddle was very high: nothing was to be seen but the helmet on the saddle, so that he looked just like someone whom he himself had often mocked amongst his friends. As soon as the nag moved, with Agnolo on top, and felt the thistle, he began to buck, and battered Agnolo back and forward between the saddle-bows, so that the lance fell to the ground, and the horse, leaping and jumping, began to run towards Florence. Everyone around was ready to burst with laughing. Agnolo didn't laugh, because he was feeling the hardest knocks in the world from the saddle-bows. And so, bruised and battered at every step be came to the Prato gate, and went through, galloping and shaken to pieces (which made the toll-collectors forget their duty), and along the Prato, so that every man and woman said in astonishment, 'What does this mean?' and entered the Borg'Ognissanti. Oh, here was a running and shying and kicking of horses, everyone scattering and yelling 'Who's this?' 'What's happened?' And the horse never stopped until he reached the Dyeworks, where his stable was, where he was caught by the bridle and led inside. When Agnolo was asked 'Who are you?' he panted and moaned. They unlaced the helmet, and he screamed and groaned, 'Hey! gently!' And when the helmet was drawn off, Agnolo's head looked like a skull, or a man dead for many days. He was lifted from the saddle with difficulty by others and pain to himself; and groaning all the time, he couldn't for a moment stand on his feet. So he was carried to a bed; and when the man who owned both the house and the horse, came outside and found out all about it, he nearly burst with laughing. He came to where Agnolo was and said,

'O, I didn't think, Agnolo, that you were John of Grana and could joust. At least, you should have told me when you borrowed my horse, which you must have spoilt, since he wasn't meant for jousting!'

Agnolo said, 'He has spoiled me, he was so headstrong. If I'd had a good horse I'd have given my opponent a great wound, and I should have had honour, where I am disgraced. I beg you, for the love of God, send to Peretola for my clothes, and tell those young men that I've done myself no damage, because the good armour saved me.'

And so his clothes were sent for, and with them came all the people who had been so amused by him. They came to Agnolo and said, 'Dear me, Mr Benghi (for so he was called), are you alive?'

'O my brothers,' he said, 'I thought I'd never see you again. I'm bruised all over. That cursed horse has killed me. I've never tried a worse animal. When I was on him I was hammered like a kettle at the kettle-makers. I must have broken all the saddle and the breast-plate. I say nothing of the helmet, for at times it was banged against the saddle so much that it must be completely broken.'

No need to ask if the group laughed.

In the end, late in the evening, they dressed him, and carried him in their arms to his house. There his wife rushed out and began to wail as if he were dead, saying 'Oh dear, my husband! Who has beaten you?'

Agnolo said nothing, but his wife kept on asking 'What's happened?' The men said, 'Nothing you need cry for', and left him, and went off. His wife embraced him and began to ask 'Husband, tell me what's the matter?' And Agnolo asked to go to bed. When his wife undressed him and saw him all black and blue, she said, 'Who has beaten you up so?' His body was so battered that it looked like porphyry or marble. In the end, when Agnolo had got his breath back, he said,

'Wife, I went with some people to Peretola, and it was agreed that everyone should joust. So as not to be behind the others, and remembering my ancestors from Cerretomaggio, I also wanted to joust. And if the horse, which was headstrong, and which fixed me up as you see, had been any good, today I should have had more honour than any man who has carried a lance this many a year.'

His wife, who was a sensible woman and knew Agnolo's vanities, began to say,

'Surely, you're out of your mind, you dissolute old man! Cursed be the day I was given to you as your wife. Here am I wearing my fingers to the bone to bring up your children, and you, you worthless thing, at seventy years old go jousting! And what could you do, who in the natural way of things don't weigh ten ounces! Get away with you – you'll be thinking that you can be elected Governor. And what's worse, because you're called Mr Benghi, do you think you're a solicitor? You idiot, don't you know who you are? And even if you were one, how many solicitors have you seen jousting? Are you out of your mind? Don't you realise that you're a wool-worker? And that you've got nothing but what you earn? Are you mad? Get away with you! Lie down, you wretch. The boys in the street will run behind you in future and throw stones at you!'

Agnolo said faintly, 'Wife, you tell me to lie down. I'm sorry I've got to go to bed. I beg you to keep quiet, if you don't want me to die altogether.'

And she said, 'You'd be better dead than live with such shame.'

Said Agnolo, 'Am I the first to meet disaster in deeds of arms?'

'Oh, go to the devil,' said his wife. 'Go and beat wool as you're used to, and leave fighting to those who know how to do it.'

And the quarrel went on till night, but at night they made it up as best they could. Agnolo never jousted again.

This woman had much more sense than her husband, because she recognised her own and her husband's condition in life. And he did not even know himself, until his wife told him much that improved him.

4. Matteo and the Mouse

Not many years ago there was in the Cavalcanti family a gentleman called Matteo di Cantine, whom I, the writer, and many others, used to see. The said Matteo di Cantino had been in his time a jouster and fencer and everything else of that kind that a gentleman knows about. He was as skilful and experienced and as well-bred as any of his equals.

When he was seventy years old, very prosperous, during July when the heat was very great, he was standing in the New Market exchanging news with a group of gentlemen and merchants, and wearing short socks and breeches of the old fashion which were very baggy in the legs. And as Matteo stood with this group, it happened that a gang of those boys who serve the bankers in that place, came with their brooms in their hand, and a trap in which they had caught a mouse, and stopped in the middle of the square. They put the trap on the ground and when that was done they opened the door. Once the door was opened, the mouse escaped and ran about the square. The boys beating with their brooms ran about after it to kill it. The mouse, looking for a hole to run into, and not seeing where one was, ran into the group where this Matteo di Cantino stood, and coming to his legs instantly ran up his shanks and entered his breeches. Anyone may realise what it was like for Matteo when he felt that. He was beside himself. The boys had lost sight of the mouse. 'Where is it?' Someone said, 'He's got it in his breeches!' People gathered round. The laughter was enormous. Matteo, like one out of his mind, went into a bank. The boys ran after him with their brooms, shouting, 'Chase it out! He's got it in his breeches!'

Matteo hid himself behind the counter of the bank and let down his breeches, the boys who were within with their brooms shouting 'Chase it out! Chase it out!' The breeches fallen to the ground, the mouse shot out. The boys shouted, 'There it is! There it is! After it! After it! He had it in his breeches, by the Gospels! And he took his breeches down!'

The boys killed the mouse. Matteo stayed there like a dead man, and several days passed when he didn't know where he was. And there wasn't a man who would not have nearly burst with laughter if he had seen it, like me, the writer, who did. Immediately after, Matteo made a vow to the Virgin in the church of the Servi, never again to wear in his life short socks, and this he kept.

What shall we say of different things that happen? Certainly I don't think anything has happened more strange or comical than this. A man will stand there with great state and pride, and a little thing will throw him down. He will go with short socks because of fleas, and a mouse so attacks him that he loses his sense. There is not creature so small that it cannot hurt man; and man can overcome them all, when he sets his mind to it.

5. A Windy Night

An amusing trick was played on someone by Agnolo Moronti of the Casentino, a pleasant jester, who has been mentioned in a story before. This Agnolo left his house and went to a fair to pick up some money, as those of his sort do, and coming back he took the road to Pontassieve, where another fair was being held. As he approached, he drove his donkey in front of him, to whose saddle he had tied a cymbal, and under whose tail he had placed a thistle. So that the donkey, as it went along twisting and jumping because of the thistle, made the cymbal clang, and Agnolo arrived at the fair dancing behind this donkey and this instrument. When he arrived everyone ran laughing to see this amusement, because of its novelty. Having been all day at the fair, he did not continue his journey, but was kept in the evening at the house of one of the townspeople, and given both board and lodging. Seeing that amongst the company was a silly man called Golfo, Agnolo asked the master of the house, as a kindness, if he might sleep with that Golfo, and he was promised he should. After they had eaten, Agnolo and Golfo were shown to their room. Wherever Agnolo had got it from, either his own or someone else's, he lay down at the foot of the bed with a pair of bellows, secretly, and Golfo lay down at the head, covering himself up well because he was elderly. When Agnolo saw that Golfo was about to fall asleep, he began to blow the bellows underneath the coverlet towards Golfo. He, when he felt the draught, began to say, 'Oh, dear! there must be some windows open in here, which a great draught blows through.'

Said Agnolo, 'I can't feel a draught. I don't know what you're talking about' – and after waiting a bit, he blew again with the bellows. Golfo began to cry out and said,

'Oh dear! and you say you can't feel it? I'm freezing,' and he drew the coverlet up, wrapping it round and round himself.

Said Agnolo, 'I don't know what you're doing. You pull the coverlet off me and say you're freezing. I think you're dreaming. I don't feel cold. Do let me go to sleep, if you don't mind.' And when he saw that Golfo had settled down a bit and was just falling asleep, Agnolo blew again. Golfo sat up in bed and shouted. 'I won't stay here! The doors and windows must be wide open' – and he looked all round and then glared up at the rafters.

Said Agnolo, 'Golfo, if you don't want to sleep, at least let me.'

Said Golfo, 'By the Gospels, you're quite wrong. It's like being in a field, there's such a wind comes on this bed. Don't you feel it?'

'I don't feel it,' said Agnolo, 'neither draught nor cold. I think you're delirious.' Golfo lay down again, while Agnolo let a little time pass without blowing. Then Golfo said,

'It doesn't seem to be so cold now as it was before.' And Agnolo waited until he heard him begin to snore, then began to operate the bellows again. Golfo called up the master of the house, who slept in a nearby bedroom, and said,

'I wish you'd drop dead for bringing me here, and the house fall to pieces. It's like being naked on Monte al Prino in the Alps.'

Agnolo, blowing with the bellows at the other end of the bed, said,

'If God gives me grace to get through this night, you'll never drag me here again! Surely, Golfo you must be bewitched. I know perfectly well that I'm flesh and bones like you, and I don't feel this cold.'

Said Golfo, 'Good! Good! So I'm out of my mind! So I don't feel the draught here!' and he began to shout. He got out of bed and put on his clothes, and went to the room where the others were sleeping, and shouted,

'Open up, for God's sake! I'm dead with cold.' The company were crowded into the bed. After a while, very reluctantly, they opened the door, and made a bit of room for Golfo, who almost had the death tremors. Now one said something to him and now another, that he was almost mad. At last one of them got out of the bed because it was so crammed, and went to sleep with Agnolo Moronti, where Golfo had come from, and he said to Agnolo,

'What's the matter with Golfo tonight? Have you done anything to him?'

Agnolo, ready to burst with laughter, told him the story from beginning to end. When the man had seen and heard how it was, they laughed together the greater part of the night.

In the morning, when he got up, Agnolo said,

'It's clear that Golfo was brought up in the town. I was born and grew old in the mountains, so that I don't care about either cold or wind, and Golfo shouted last night when a moth flew around the room, because of the little breeze which he made with his wings.'

Said Golfo, 'Some wings! They weren't wings, unless they were a vulture's! It seems a thousand years to me until I get into my own room at Florence.'

And so he returned with the rest of the company, saying that he would never come back again to that fair or that place. And Agnolo went to the Casentino, having done what he intended to.

Amusing men have strange qualities and ideas, especially jesters. This one saw the silliest man present in a whole company, and asked the favour of sleeping with him, in order to play this trick, which gave great pleasure to all. And the entertainment which they had over Golfo, when they heard about it, how he spoke of the great cold he had felt in the room, and how windy it had been, lasted them almost a year after they had returned to Florence. And perhaps this was the reason Golfo went to the Baths of Ponetta, and did not live eighteen months after this episode took place.

6. Thrown into the Drink

And there was a great war between the Catalans and the Genoese, and as often happens, the fighting was often so cruel and treacherous that one man killed another in all sorts of violent ways, without any discrimination or humanity, and that was very much the way with the Catalans. At this time a Genoese galley, or one of the other nations who were allied with them, fell into the hands of a Catalan warship, whose captain was a man entirely without pity. He intended to avenge himself for some offence which he had received from the Genoese, and being cruel and angry he prepared to have all those in the galley thrown into the sea, one by one. And in order to show greater contempt he first gave each one a bit of bread and biscuit, and after that had been eaten he said – 'Go and drink', and threw him into the sea. When he had committed this cruelty on thirty, it was the next man's turn to come to execution. This man, while he ate the bread fell on his knees to the captain, and with clasped hands said,

'O my lord, this is a very small amount of food to so much drink!'

When the captain heard him, either these words pacified him, or he had pity on the submissiveness with which the man behaved, and he pardoned both him and all the rest, who were more than a hundred, who would have met such a cruel death. And when he found time and opportunity he put them ashore and let them go and kept the galley itself.

In this little story one can see how powerful words are, when a witticism by a common sailor may be said to have had so much power, that it made such a cruel captain merciful. It can easily be understood how much power must be in prayer, when it is made to Him who is the supreme mercy. There is nothing so useful to the soul as prayer, when it is said in such a way as comes from the heart. And nothing ever moves Our Lord so much as prayer to grant salvation to the soul of him who has spoken it with a pure heart. There are plenty of examples of this, which would take long to tell, as the Gospels and Holy Scripture show us.

GERMAN TALES

1. The Judge and the Devil

In a certain town there was once a man whose sins were such that I am neither able to nor know how to nor ought to tell them all. He was so utterly given up to all kinds of sins that people considered it fortunate that the earth did not swallow him up. Two things made him well-known: he had no equal either in sinfulness or in wealth. He was a judge in that town, and his way of life was known far and wide.

One market-day he declared he was going to ride out and have a look at his favourite vineyard. That selfsame morning, very early, the devil began to look out for him. He approached him on the road as he was riding away from the vineyard. The devil was wearing magnificent, very well-cut clothes. The judge came riding along, and as he supposed him to be an ordinary man, he greeted him and asked where he came from and who he was, saying: 'That is something to which I should very much like to know the right answer.'

'It will be just as well to keep that from you,' replied the devil.

'I must have an answer,' retorted the judge angrily, 'or you will suffer for it. I have so much power in this district that whatever injury I wish to inflict on you, no one will prevent me.' He began to swear angrily that if he did not inform him where he came from and who he was, he would take his life and confiscate his possessions. 'Before you do me such great damage, I will tell you my proper name and lineage,' said the accursed one straight away. 'I am the devil.'

The judge then enquired what his job was. 'I will tell you. I am going into the town. Today is the time that I take away everything that is in all seriousness given to me.' The judge replied: 'Now be so kind as to allow me to see whatever you get to take for as long as the market goes on.'

'No, I won't do that,' he said. The judge declared: 'Then I command you not to leave my presence and to allow me to see everything that you do here today. I command you by God to do this, and by the same command by which you were all laid low I command you by the power of God and by God's wrath, however many commands it may be necessary to make, which you cannot withstand, neither you nor your fellows. Therefore, be commanded. I command you on pain of God's judgement that you take everything that anyone may give you today in my sight.'

'Alas that I should be alive!' exclaimed the devil. 'You have caught and bound me with such strong bonds that I have never experienced such torment in many an hour. However much I think about it, I know no trick anywhere against which you could do anything. As it will bring you no profit, release me from these things.' The judge said: 'No, I won't do that. Whatever happens to me as a result, let it happen. I want to see you take

95

whatever comes your way today.' The devil said: 'All right then. The fact that you will spare me nothing causes me great sorrow. If you had any understanding, you would stop forcing this on me. Both your fellows and mine hate each other greatly and will never cease from doing so. You ought to let me go if you want to maintain your position.'

The judge then replied: 'Don't be so upset about the fact that I want to go with you. Whether it is much or little, whatever is given you willingly, without constraint, today, I want to see you take it, even if it goes against me. I won't spare you from it. If you have anything to object, you might as well stop doing so.'

'Now, stop being so angry,' said the accursed spirit. 'Before the day is out you'll learn a bit about what you know next to nothing of.' At this the judge became merry and cheerful. He was pleased that he was about to see some marvellous things.

Thereupon they went into the town. The market was in full swing there, and there were plenty of people around. Lots of people offered the judge a drink. No one knew who his companion was. The judge offered him a drink, but the devil refused. Then it happened that a woman got into some trouble with a pig, which she quickly drove out of her door. 'Be off to the devil!' shouted the angry woman. 'I hope he kills you today.' The judge said: 'My friend, take the pig quickly now! I can hear her saying it's yours.'

'No, that isn't so, unfortunately,' the devil answered him. 'I'd gladly take it, if she were genuinely giving it to me. But if I were to take it, she would be sorry.'

Then they went further into the market. I don't know what happened to make another woman say to an ox: 'To the devil with you, may he kill you today!' Then the judge said: 'Now, do you hear, someone has given you the ox.' But the devil again said: 'That's a mean trick misleading you. She would be upset for a whole year if she thought I would take it from her. I don't care what she actually said; she didn't mean it seriously. I haven't any claim to the ox!'

Then a woman shouted at her child: 'You won't do anything for me, the wicked devil take you!'

'Now take the child!' said the judge.

'I have no right to it,' answered the devil straight away. 'She wouldn't take two thousand pounds to allow me to get hold of it. I'd gladly take it, if I could.'

They then proceeded into the middle of the market. It was so busy as a result of everybody being there who wanted to go that day. They were standing there quietly when a widow came up to them. She was both old and ill and suffered from all kinds of disabilities, as a result of which she was in great pain. She could scarcely walk, even with a stick. When she saw the judge, she burst into tears and said: 'How did it come about, judge, that you should be so rich and I so poor and that you thought you could not survive without depriving me, without justification or God's favour, of my little cow, which was my only means of livelihood in my poverty? I haven't been given the strength to be important enough to try any way of getting it back out of Christian charity. You have gained nothing from this but scorn. Now I beg God, for the sake of His death and the grim torment that He suffered in the flesh for all us poor people, to grant me, poor woman that I am, that the devil take you off, body and soul!'

At this the devil said to him: 'Listen to that, she's serious!' He seized the judge firmly by the hair and began to rise into the air so that everyone who was at the market could see him. The going must have given him much trouble. It was more awkward for him than it would have been for a hen with an eagle. The devil rushed away with everybody looking after him. I don't know what happened afterwards as he was seen from afar. That is where the story ends.

Thus with his victory the judge was vanquished. He imagined that he would get something, and he lost. It is an unwise business to have anything to do with the devil. Whoever enjoys going around with him will be given a sorry reward. He knows so many grim tricks that it is best to fear him.

2. The Three Monks of Colmar

A story I was once told as being absolutely true actually did happen at Colmar. Now listen to this strange tale that a man told us who rode here from Colmar. In that town there lived a man who was wealthy and jovial, apart from the fact that luck had it that he made countless losses every day. Now at that time he had a lovely wife, who was abundantly happy and provided with everything that one looks for in a beautiful woman. She had a shapely figure and was twenty years old. She was devout and fulfilled God's commands; she loved God as much as she did herself.

Just before one Easter-time she decided to make her confession, as she was supposed to, at a monastery where there were Dominicans. She got herself ready and went to the monastery that she intended to. When she arrived there and the confessor took a look at her, he said: 'God welcome you, beautiful lady!' She replied: 'God have mercy on you, dear sir!' He took a particular liking to the lady, as she displayed so many good qualities. She knelt down and fully prepared herself to make her confession. When it was over and she had told him everything that she had done and was about to depart, he said: 'My dear lady, for your sins I instruct you now to allow me straight away to come to you and to do my will. Struggle no more against it: I will give you thirty marks.' The lady was taken aback that he should speak to her about such things. She began to feel faint and became worried and upset and thought to herself: 'How can I get away from this good man?' She said: 'Dear sir, I don't know whether that will be possible. I will find out at home and let you know later how it can be arranged. Just wait a while!' The monk was very pleased at this, and his heart was gladdened. Yet she little intended to comply with his request. She took her leave, went away and left him.

On leaving the monastery she was very upset that the monk had acted like this towards her. She then considered where she could go to make a proper confession and eventually went off to another monastery, at which there were Franciscans, who have to sing mass frequently, read a lot and remain enclosed. When she arrived there a monk received and welcomed her. 'Thank you, dear sir!' the virtuous good woman replied, for her mind was full of serious thoughts. He quickly heard her confession and when she had finished speaking and had told him everything, the monk behaved in exactly the same way as the Dominican. 'I will give you sixty marks if you will allow me to enjoy your love in secret. This I faithfully promise you.' The estimable lady reacted as she had done to the Dominican, then took her leave and departed. Once she was on her way, she pondered to herself: 'Oh, dear Lord, what shall I do to make a proper confession?'

Then, as I heard, she went to another monastery and entered inside. They were Augustinians there and served God sensibly. When she went into the monastery, she was immediately greeted by a monk. She thanked him and said: 'Tell me whether you will hear my confession!'

'Yes, certainly!' he replied. She made her confession again on the spot. This monk also made a request to the woman and promised her a hundred marks. Their orders were not so miserable that they could not have given her the money, but she wanted none of them. She answered him exactly as she had done the others and took her leave of him. She went away and left him behind.

Back home she immediately went into her room, took off her cloak and wept copiously and was very upset. The monks had tried to win her over with false teaching, but she wanted no man other than her own husband and did not want to deceive him or commit any crime. Meanwhile her husband came in and found her weeping. 'My dear good wife,' he said, 'what has upset you for you to cry so much?' She wiped away her tears, but he had already seen her distress. 'What has happened to you?' he asked and enquired what had occurred. At first she tried not to tell him. He said: 'No one can deny what I have seen with my own eyes.' Then she could keep silent about it no longer. She gave rein to her heartfelt suffering and told him of the whole tale of what the monks had done to her and how she had taken leave of them, saying she would see whether she could do as the monks wanted.

The husband immediately thought: 'Unfortunately I have made plenty of losses. If I want to get some back, I had better start today.' He said to her: 'We'll make something out of this. Tell the first one straight away to come here when he hears the bell ringing for the taverns to close, and to bring his silver with him. Tell the second to come secretly at midnight and to bring his silver as well, the third to come at matins and to bring the hundred marks with him, as is fitting, and tell them all also that I have gone off on a long journey!' On hearing the husband say this, his good and lively wife immediately did as he had told her. She sent messengers to all three monks telling them to come that night. When the monks heard the news, they were all on top of the world.

Once evening came, the husband and his wife busied themselves with fetching water in, as it was very late. They decided to fill the cauldron and a big tub as well. All of this was done in secret, as the husband filled the tub with hot water and placed it against the wall inside.

When this was completed and they were expecting the arrival of the first monk, they were all set. The husband ran behind the door to one of the walls, taking a club with him in his hand. The monk came walking up to the door. When the wife heard him, she said quickly: 'Who's there?'

'It's me, brother Tecia.' The lady let the monk in. 'Dearest lady,' he said, 'the reason I have come is to be granted your love, so put your mind to it. No man on earth was ever happier.'

'Of course I'll do that,' she said. 'Give me what you promised and I'll do what you want.'

He handed over the silver. When this was plain to the husband and he could hear from what his wife said that she had received the silver, he came along with the club in his hand and knocked about all over the wall as if he were out of his mind. The virtuous woman heard this, as had been arranged. The lively lady then said: 'Oh dear, sir, that's my husband coming. You must jump into the tub. Because he is tired I'll go to bed so that he will lie down soon and then leave us here in peace.' The husband approached noisily. The monk couldn't get into the tub fast enough and was immediately scalded alive. They took him out straight away and leant him against a wall. Water had got right inside him. When the husband and wife heard it striking midnight, they were careful to listen for the others coming.

Shortly afterwards the second monk arrived at the door of the house. The lady said: 'Who is there? Is it you, my dear sir?'

'Yes,' he said, 'let me in!' The lady let him in and took the silver from him. When the husband heard her take the silver, he took the club in his hand and beat it once more against the wall. The monk was not able to escape, but took refuge in the tub and was scalded alive there too. They placed him also against the wall.

When that had happened, the bell went for matins and the third monk came running up. On hearing him, the wife went to the door and let him in. She received the silver from him, and the husband repeated what he had previously done. The monk was unable to escape. He quickly fell into the tub and the boiling water put an end to him.

When that was all done and they were scalded to death, the husband seized one by the hair and dragged him outside the house-door. A wandering scholar was passing by, completely drunk. The husband asked him: 'Tell me, would you like to earn four pence?'

'Yes,' said the student quickly, 'what have I to do, sir?'

'Take the monk and dump him in the Rhine!' He took the monk immediately, as the husband had asked him, and carried him away.

Thereupon the husband took the second monk and carried him out and placed him outside the house. No sooner had he done that than the student was back demanding his pence. 'Don't I still see the monk here?' retorted the husband. When the student saw that this was the case, he took him by the hair and said: 'A bad year upon you!'

Once the husband saw the second monk being carried away, he brought out the third as he had done with the other two. The student came running back again, ready for his money. 'Have you come back again?' said the husband. 'He's still standing against that wall.' The student began to complain. 'I have carried him to the Rhine. He's lying there now at the bottom, unless the devil has brought him back again.'

The husband replied, 'But look at him still standing there!'

'May God never help you!' said the student to the monk. 'Have you run back again now?' He took the third monk as he had the other two and did the same with him.

Very soon he came running back for his pence, but on the way he came across a friar who was going to matins. The student did not hesitate, but seized him by the hair and clothes and dragged him roughly off with him. The friar protested: 'Why are you dragging me off like this?' The student replied: 'You've been running after me all night, and I can't get rid of you. I wish the devil had taken you!'

'It wasn't me, sire, God help me! I tell you truthfully: I was just on my way to matins to make amends for my sins.' The student nonetheless dragged him off a long way. The friar tried to escape, but the young fellow ran after him and caught him by the hood: 'Stay here, Brother Madcap!' He hit him and knocked him about badly and dragged him still further. The friar then began to shout out, but the student paid not the slightest attention to him in his intention of getting to the Rhine. The friar felt this was no joke any more. He thought: 'Dear Lord, what does this man want to do to me that I have done no harm to?' The student was exhausted and didn't know what to do. But when he got to the Rhine, he did with the friar just what he had done with the others.

Then, to the best of my knowledge, he returned to the man's house and received the pence. The husband paid very little for the job – the student got a penny for each monk. The student started to complain to the husband how he had met the monk and seized him and carried him off again and how he had given him a good beating. When the husband heard this news, he thought: 'Alas, that's a bad thing you've done. May God take care of his body and soul!'

This tale that I have told you has its message confirmed every day, since it frequently happens that the innocent have to pay for the misdeeds of the guilty. This is the end of the story. Let both rich and poor alike guard against such misdeeds, for things don't go well for people who try out unwonted tricks and will not abandon them, as these monks did. But they deserved what happened to them, as they perverted the confessional. God takes His revenge on such things. That is what Niemand says.

3. The Lover in the Tree

I am going to tell you a true story that I heard over ten years ago about a blind man who had a beautiful wife. She was as dear to him as himself. She was pretty, had a nice figure and also was very young. In fact, anyone who had seen her would agree with me that she was pretty and light-hearted. Now this good blind man was afraid of any other man getting too near his wife. He pondered to himself: 'I will keep a good guard over her so that nobody can take her from me, and I will keep her in a bridle.' At night, when he went to bed, he took an iron halter and locked both her legs in it. This was how she was taken care of. Early in the morning, at daybreak (now pay attention to what I say), he would release her from her bonds. His anxiety was very great and he thought: 'Alas, Lord God, for your goodness' sake, if I were to lose my beautiful wife, I should never recover from it.'

He said to her: 'Wife, we must leave here. I won't stay here any longer, for we can manage our life better somewhere else.' Now there was a student in the same town whom the wife was in love with. This the blind man got wind of, and this was why she had to leave the place. The student was out one day and came across the blind man, who was holding his darling mistress by the hand. Now the jaunty student thought to himself: 'Oh, God, if I could only do something with the good woman.' He bowed to her and said: 'I'm sorry about your trouble.' He pushed a note into her hand, by means of which he revealed his stratagem and his feelings. This pleased the beautiful woman very much. When she had read the little note, she said: 'Oh, my dear master, there's a tree over there. Let's go underneath it to see if we can get some fruit. There's nothing on earth I should like more than that.' He said: 'I don't know what to embark on with you that won't be risky. From your behaviour I don't think you're going to do right by me. I'll prevent it if I can. But I'll go with you myself to see whether I can get some of the fruit that you have praised so highly and so much want to go for.'

They went there together. This the student observed, having written his stratagem on the note. In his cap he had quite a quantity of lovely apples. With them he began to climb up into a lime-tree. The woman took the blind man to where she had observed the student climb the tree. She said to her blind husband: 'Now what shall I do so as to get some fruit, since the tree is so tall?' The blind man quickly took his stick and hit the branches so that an apple fell down, which the student dropped. He thus imagined he was hitting them down with his stick. The woman quickly picked up the apple. She put it into the blind man's hand. He cut the apple in two and offered his wife half. She said: 'I must have more than that or I shall feel worse for it.' He took out his stick again, swiftly knocked on the branches and listened to hear whether any apples fell down. She said: 'It's no use. I wouldn't give a hazel nut for what you can knock down, unless you had a long fork. Let me climb up into the tree so that I can fill my bag. I will get as many as I can.'

He said: 'Wife, I'm afraid somebody else might come to you.'

'Don't be afraid about that. You can go to the tree and hold it with your arms. Then you will know whether another man could climb up the tree to me. He would gain very little for the effort except for some hard blows.'

The blind man thought: 'Yes, you're right', and helped her up into the tree. When she got up there, he put his arms round the trunk and listened very carefully. The student began to move towards the woman. He wanted to have his fill of pleasure with her beautiful, shapely body. The blind man started to shout: 'Shake the tree at the top to knock something down.' The student was a clever lad. He and the woman began to shake about and at the same time he let the apples fall out of his cap. The blind man was satisfied.

Now our Lord and his servant St Peter happened to be going past, and the nice blind man heard them. He said: 'Who is that going past? Stop, if you are a friend.' St Peter said: 'Master, look! Do you see that disgraceful trick that the woman is playing her blind husband. I wish he could see that great crime.'

Our Lord replied: 'She would still find an answer, even if her husband could see it.'

'Lord,' said St Peter, 'I'd like to hear how that could be done.'

Our Lord said: 'Well, if you must, I'll let you see what the woman will say.' He then gave the blind man his sight (he was a strong giant of a man). When he looked up, you would obviously like to hear what he said. 'Look there, you whore, what an evil thing you have done to me! You will both pay with your lives for this love-making.'

St Peter said: 'Master, look and prevent this evil deed. Don't let this crime take place. Take away the blind man's sight again.'

The wife started to answer from up in the tree. She said: 'My dear husband, this love-making was designed as a cure for your blindness. I was assisted in this today by the Heavenly Child and by the student. He taught me this way of getting back your eyesight. You ought to go down on your knees for it and thank us both, the good student and myself, and pray God to keep the eyes that you now have. Oh, you idiot, how much longer are you going to stand there!'

The blind man fell on his knees and said: 'Wife, you have never deserted me. You have been kind to me. I shall reward you today and every minute for finding a cure for my eyes. So come down, and the student too. We must reward him on the spot for helping me.' The woman climbed down, followed by the handsome lad. The blind man fell at his feet and said warmly: 'May God in heaven reward you mercifully. Let us be joyful and give the student something for his trouble.' The wife had no objection, so he quickly weighed out ten pounds of pence and handed them to the student.

This St Peter observed and said: 'Lord, shall I tell the blind man to give his wife a beating?'

'Yes, Peter you may do that.' Immediately he went up to her and said: 'Good day. I want you to know that what you have done to the blind man has greatly distressed me.'

She replied: 'Look, husband, that's the man who ran after me and wanted to prevent the cure that I have got you, because he would rather have you blind so that I could do his will. I tell you in all honesty he carried on with me for a whole year. You ought to avenge that and put your knife through him.' The blind man drew out his knife, at which St Peter fled to where he found his Master and complained to him about what had happened. He answered: 'Peter, that was what you wanted. That's what happens to people who tell wicked tales. But you were so foolish as not to imagine that this woman could talk herself out of having deceived her husband, although he witnessed it all for himself.'

'Lord, if I had the power and were not to grow old, I would take revenge on this wicked old bag for proclaiming that I had been running after her. And she also said, "Stab him!" but I will forget that and take my revenge as you command.'

'No, Peter, I tell you, one has to forgive the sinner a great deal. Don't you know that I gave my life for sinners and want no reward for it. I want to have them under my protection. Before leaving them in distress, I would rather be killed again. Whoever confesses and is sorry and trusts in me, I forgive his guilt and allow him to gain my favour.'

This is the end of the story. May God be merciful to us.

4. Returning the Payment for Love

He is a very happy man to whom God grants an honest wife with no deceitfulness about her, who loves him with total fidelity and so unites herself with him that both his reputation and his possessions are well looked after and cared for. I have undertaken to tell a story I came across which happened some time ago. It is that that I shall now tell.

There was a debonair young knight who had a fine castle. He was noble, virtuous, handsome in physique, but had very little money, as his forbears had used it up. Now he was an extremely honourable man and would have liked to go off to tournaments to show off his strength. But he lacked the wealth to do so and consequently was sad and very low-spirited.

Not far away there lived an old knight who was stout-hearted and generous. In his younger days he had frequently broken a lance and charged through a shield in chivalric fashion. He began to get very worried that the fine young knight with the manly spirit was forced to be indolent and do penance for his sins with poverty and misery. The old knight, who was generous and wealthy, was sorry for him. He acted like a good friend and lessened his misery for him. He sent for him and said: 'My dear fellow, I'm sorry about your trouble and the fact that you are so indolent and don't go to tournaments as your forbears used to. You're a young man, strong and bold; your background and upbringing are such that you ought to be doing this. Now tell me what I need to do in order to help you.'

The young knight bucked up at this and replied, speaking frankly: 'Unfortunately I just don't have the wherewithal to carry out what I would dearly love to do.'

The old knight answered civilly: 'I'll remove that obstacle. If you set your mind to going off looking for adventure, I will lend you the money for it. I'll buy you two good horses, lance and shield and whatever else you need. Give it back to me when you can, and don't worry about me – I can well afford it. In addition, if God grants you good fortune, then I shall be well repaid. If it goes differently from what it should – which God forbid – rest assured that neither I nor my heirs will call upon you for money.'

The young man was very grateful to him for this. The estimable old knight made no more ado, but immediately brought him two horses for sixty *gulden* or more, also armour, shield and lance and the rest of what a knight requires he was well provided with for riding off to amusement and serious undertakings. Without any delay he pressed sixty *gulden* into his hands for his use. He also sent him an honest servant, a completely trustworthy man.

When the knight was ready, the old man told him that at that very time a festival had been advertised far and wide at a certain town. A great crowd of knights would be going there from all areas to be ready with all their physical strength to display their courtly skills in jousting and tourneying for charming and attractive ladies. He told him to ride there.

He delayed no longer, but took his leave straight away. He rode over the hills and various territories in the direction of the town. One evening they were overtaken by the dark night falling. The master and his servant dismounted in the fields and rested under a tree. The master said to his servant: 'Stay here with my horses and look after them while I go looking for adventure in the forest.' He must have gone about half a mile when he came to a thorn-hedge where there was a high fence. He went further and further round it. He saw a light shining through the fence, at which he was happy. Afterwards he saw in addition a beautiful, fine and splendid castle, from which the light shone down. Up in the castle, underneath a narrow little door, the lord of the castle stood, well protected. Indeed, it was he who was carrying the light in his hand. His wife was walking in the orchard down below. She was making a terrible noise because she had toothache. The lord was showing the light from a little door to see if he could alleviate matters for her. 'My dear,' he said, 'isn't your pain getting any better down there by the fence?' The beautiful lady replied: 'No, my toothache is getting worse. It's a horrible pain I'm suffering.'

The young knight heard all that was said down by the corner of the fence. He went further round by a way that was sharp and twisting until finally he found a little door. It stood open, so he went in. There he found the pretty lady standing in the orchard, waiting for her dear lover to come any minute. She quickly realized the knight had come in and stepped up to him. She imagined it was the person she was expecting and said very quietly: 'Is that you, my darling?'

He replied: 'Yes, sweet lady.' The knight uttered nothing more, fearing that the lady would recognize that he was not the right person. He laid her down on the grass and had his will with her to his heart's desire. The lady soon noticed that he was not the dear lover that she had been waiting for a long time. She became extremely distressed and said: 'Oh, what a poor woman I am! You have made love to me and I don't even know who you are! At least tell me now whether you come from a good family. It was a noble and tender knight who was to have slept with me here. Oh dear, what shall I do! It's you who have been given everything.'

The honourable knight answered her: 'Take heart, dear lady! I am also a good knight. I have always been on the look-out for adventure, and here I have found it. Chivalry has brought me this way, and I have always intended to expend my physical prowess in the service of every virtuous lady.'

She said: 'If only that were so, I should feel much better. If you are such a man, leave me something as a parting gift so that I can tell that you are of noble birth and good breeding.'

He replied: 'Actually, at present I have only sixty *gulden* with me, and that is what I have to pay my way with.'

She said straight away: 'Give it to me! I shall never forget you.' He gave her the money and said: 'Now, my lady, you ought to give me something so that I may also remember you.' The noble, beautiful lady gave him a gold ring that was fine and precious, but the exchange was an unequal one since it was only worth eight *gulden*.

The knight then went away. The good man under the little door continued holding the light to see if his wife's situation was any better. He thought she was in great pain with her bad teeth. She began to long for another man. He spoke to her again: 'Is it any less now, dear wife?' Straight away she answered the fool: 'Yes, my pain is less.' She returned to the castle, and there I will leave the matter.

The fine young knight went back to his servant under the tree where he had left him with the horses. The master informed him how things had gone. He also told him fully that he had given the pretty lady the sixty *gulden* for which she had offered a gold ring in return. This he showed the servant, who was very pleased at it. He said: 'Dear master, you must feel very happy. Don't worry about the *gulden*! God will take care of us; He will supply our needs. Indeed, for an honourable knight to have an adventure in the game of love is much better than keeping all his wealth and whatever else he has.'

After this conversation they rested and slept until the gleam of day and the bright sun appeared. The servant awoke, jumped up, caught the horses and saddled them. After this he went over to his master and quietly woke him up. The master seemed to be sad, at which the servant was very troubled. He said: 'Sir, you seem unhappy. What is the matter? Tell me!' His master answered: 'I am a stranger and unknown here. How can I travel without any money. That's what is worrying me a lot.' The servant was quite confident. 'God will look after us,' he said to his master. 'I have enough money in my purse for today. God will see to it that we get on all right afterwards. Stop being so timorous!'

This being said, they soon got through a thick forest, four miles long and wide. By then it was time to eat. Close by on the other side of the forest they saw a pretty village and rode up to the inn there, where they were welcomed and given hospitality. Then there came cantering up the lord to whom the village belonged and from whom the innkeeper held his property. He was a good old knight, who was also fully intending to go to the festival where the young knight was proposing to attend the tournament. The excellent old knight also rode to the inn, and I tell you now, honestly, that it was the same knight who had shone the lantern at the good castle for his wife, who had trouble with her teeth down in the garden until the handsome knight quietly made love to her as if he were her lover.

The two lords took some water and sat down cordially together at the table. Neither recognized the other. The old knight asked the young one: 'Dear sir, be so kind as to tell me where you are going. I would really like to know.'

The honourable, true young knight told him in all honesty: 'Sir, I am on my way to a tournament and adventure; that's what I have come for. I am riding to the festival in the town. There are lots of knights and fine fellows going there.'

'I'm glad that's where you're going,' said the old knight. 'I'd like to accompany you and share your luck.' That suited the young knight admirably and they promised each other companionship, accepting that the wrong done to the one would be accepted as done to both of them. The noble old knight paid for fodder, food and wine and the rest of what they had consumed as a confirmation of this. The young knight and the old man then departed in high spirits.

When they came to the town, the old knight asked the young one to join him in his lodging, to which he agreed, thus strengthening their friendship. The excellent young knight was a fine fellow and honourable, which made the upright, wealthy old man take to him. He supplied him with everything that he needed in the way of equipment and armour for the tournament and his amusement. The knight was provided with a good, handsome horse for the joust, which he mounted happily. The old knight rode in high spirits with him on to the meadow. Plenty of knights were already there. A clever knight lowered his lance at him, and he quickly knocked him down. The old knight was pleased that his companion had so swiftly laid one low with the first thrust. A short while afterwards he sent four others from their saddles.

107

The old knight hurried to hold the good young knight's bridle. They were both elated. What more shall I say? He rode up and down through the crowd, sending countless knights from their saddles. He succeeded so well with them all that in the end no one wanted to lower his lance to him. The magnificent knight continued as long as the festival lasted and didn't even get a hair injured. In addition he came out best in the tourney as well. That pleased many of the noble, splendid ladies. He brought them all happiness. He won public recognition over all the others. Great lords and beautiful ladies without number congratulated him and paid their respects at his lodging. There was plenty of entertainment with tripping and dancing. There was music with harps and violins and singing with great merriment performed for him.

When the festival was over, the young knight was sitting at table one night with his companion. They were drinking claret and were in good spirits. Plenty of tales were being told by the jolly landlady and her husband. The old knight also began to relate a few amusing things. The handsome young knight was also urged by the old knight to tell them something. He said: 'In all my life I never heard of an adventure to beat what happened to me on my way to this town. It happened that once I was out late in the fields, spending the night underneath a tree. The time hung heavy on my hands, so I left my servant with the horses and happened upon a good adventure. I came to a splendid castle, which was beautiful and well protected. Below it was an orchard, in which I heard a charming lady complaining with toothache. Her husband came and shone a light up at a little door in the castle to see if he could alleviate her pain. In fact, she hadn't any toothache at all. She was longing for her lover, with whom she had made a rendez-vous. But the lady fell to my lot. When I entered the garden and she noticed me, I went quietly up to her just as if I were the person she was expecting. She whispered: "Darling, is that you?" I quickly replied, "Yes." I immediately made love to her, after which she soon realized that I was not the proper person. Angrily, she said to me: "Who are you? How despicably you have deceived me! I thought you were my lover. He is a fine, splendid knight. I had been waiting a long time for him." She wouldn't believe that I was also of good birth, until I gave the charming lady sixty *gulden* in cash. She took a gold ring from her hand and gave it me in exchange. When I left in high spirits, her good husband was still making a light for his wife to see if she was getting any relief.'

Following this account the old knight got very upset. He said: 'Show us the ring to prove it.' The young knight showed him the ring without delay. He recognized it immediately as his wife's and concealed his sorrow at it.

In the morning as soon as it was day, the mayor of the town and the whole council came there, knowing that it was time for their departure. The honourable young knight and also his companion were congratulated by them. The town paid for their fodder, hay, food and wine as a reward for winning the prize. His companion, the elderly knight, also benefited from this. They then got ready and returned happily home.

When they got within sight of the old knight's castle, he said politely to his noble companion: 'Look, sir, that's my castle. Be my guest here tonight. I will give you a good rest. Please stay the night here.' The knight immediately agreed, and a servant was sent on in advance. His master told him: 'Tell my dear wife to get the house ready. I am coming and bringing a fine, noble knight with me. Tell her to put on her beautiful dress and receive him well, as he has won the crown of honour.'

The servant did exactly as his master told him. The lady also got everything ready and in good order that the servant had said. Since I am bound to tell the truth, the steadfast young knight became very dejected when he saw the castle properly. He said to his servant: 'I think that this is in fact the very castle at which I had my adventure a short time ago. That is the little door from which the lord showed a light to his lady. That is the orchard below, the high fence and the hedge, alongside which I walked for a long time before I left it. And now I've told him all about the adventure. Tell me what I ought to do! I'm afraid that our host will make things unpleasant for us.'

'If he is a decent fellow,' said the servant, 'he will neither harm nor disgrace us while we are in his house. If he desires to harm us when we leave, he will suffer for it from us.'

They had reached the drawbridge. The lady had heard them coming and went out to meet them. She welcomed the guest and also her husband extremely courteously. She took their guest by the hand and led him to a good and well-furnished room, where he was to get changed. There was hospitality in abundance. The lord and his lively wife showed their guest every honour. They had wine and food and every type of provision brought there.

When it grew late and time to go to bed, the handsome guest was made to promise his host and hostess not to leave early the next morning, as his host wanted to be up in good time and go hunting. He told him to wait for breakfast, since he would certainly get some good game for the kitchen. With this the guest was persuaded to stay the morning and get a good night's rest. Before dawn his host set off riding with his hunters into the forest. They soon caught a big huge stag and had excellent sport.

When it was light, the guest awoke from sleep, got up and said his prayers. This done, the lady came to look after him. She said: 'I hope you don't mind waiting until my husband gets back.' The honourable fine young knight replied: 'I'll do just what you say.'

The lady said, 'Well, let's amuse ourselves with a game of chess.' That

109

was soon done. They sat down together and played at the board. Now the lord had put the ring on his hand. The lady noticed this with a shock and began to cry. She said: 'For God's sake, dear sir, where did you get that ring from?'

He said: 'You know very well where I got it. You gave it me yourself for sixty *gulden* in cash.'

The lady replied: 'Dear good sir, has my husband seen it on you? Tell me!'

He answered her good-humouredly: 'Unfortunately he has seen it frequently. It happened quite innocently, because I knew neither of you.'

The lady said quickly: 'Oh, what a terrible thing! I shall die from it.'

In this state of trouble the hunter returned with a big stag. They opened the castle to them, and the lord also came riding in. The guest and the beautiful lady were very upset. They no longer dared to be together by themselves. Then the handsome host hurried to his noble guest. He said: 'Aren't you bored here in my house?' He had food and wine brought in, and the game was soon prepared. The cheerful knight sat at table and was joined by his host and charming wife. Both game and good fish were quickly brought to them. What more shall I tell? The guest was well looked after, and the goblets from which they drank the wine were kept filled.

When the cook came in and the tables were cleared, the lady sat there in great distress. As the guest now wanted to depart, she feared that her husband might cause her trouble. The guest could clearly see this, and it troubled him too. The noble and good host said to his wife: 'Now tell me honestly, do you not know our guest?'

She replied: 'Why do you ask me, dear sir? Honestly, I tell you, I do not know at this time where he comes from or who he is.'

The host retorted: 'How dare you say that you have no knowledge of him? Where are the sixty *gulden* that he gave you? Go and fetch them for me straight away!'

The lady was terrified at what he said and answered: 'I can't fetch what I am in no position to possess. In all my life I have never seen our guest apart from here. Honestly, he has never given me any money either.'

He said: 'Where is the ring that I married you with?'

He would not spare her on pain of death from producing the sixty *gulden*. Sadly, she brought them before the two men. The host placed them on the table and said to the two of them: 'In every game the thrower of the dice gets something. The person who provides the board gets something as well. The person who provides the light should also get the light.' He divided the *gulden* into three equal parts. Each pile was twenty *gulden* and no more. He gave one share to the guest and said: 'Now take your win from the dice you have thrown on the board.' The second share the host gave to his wife, saying: 'Look, wife, take the gold! That shall be your reward from the good game-board that you set for him and on which he had his amusement. The third pile remains for me for providing the light.'

When the division had taken place, the guest said politely: 'Take heart, dear sir! Let's have it now good and proper, and vent your anger on me! Your wife has lost your goodwill. I will not leave here until you have forgiven your wife for this misdemeanour and guilt. I beg this of you, dear sir, for the sake of the companionship that we two have enjoyed with each other.'

The host said: 'In God's name! You have admonished me very severely. I certainly dare not refuse you. He promised sincerely that he would never inflict any injury on his wife in the future. The guest brought about a restoration of friendship and reconciliation between them, which made the lady deeply happy. The guest promised his host that he would eternally be his companion with all his strength and in addition serve him and share his destiny.

The honourable and handsome guest departed in great amity. He rode back home, which made his friends happy. His fame spread far and wide and in a short time he won more honour and wealth, as is the case with many knights who know how to use their physical skills. He owed this to the honourable man who expressed friendship to him and first brought him out. He repaid him sincerely. With this the story ends.

5.   Three Wily Women

No one on earth is, I believe, more tricked and deceived with ruses and adroit talk than a man is by his wife. I will tell you a tale about this that has just come to my notice.

There were three pretty peasant women whom we all know: the first is called Mistress Jutta, the second Mistress Hildegard; the third – not to hold matters up – is Mistress Mechthild. They were getting ready to go to a beautiful town, where they were taking eggs to sell at the market. They quickly agreed to share equally the money that God gave them for selling the eggs. On this trip they sold the eggs for seven *haller*, which they divided up noisily, each getting two. Afterwards there arose a lot of trouble and dissension among the women about the odd *haller*. They quarrelled long and much about it. Each wanted to have it. Then Mistress Hildegard said to them: 'Listen to my plan. I have a good suggestion. I think it would be a good idea, which of us three can most trick and deceive her husband with a clever ruse, that she should without any further ado have the odd *haller*.' The suggestion attracted them all, and they promised to keep to it.

When Mistress Hildegard got home, she soon realised that her husband was back home from the fields and was sitting at the table over a big dish of porridge. She went into the room and wickedly began to see how she could deceive the good man. He was called Farmer Berthold. She was neither faithful nor true to him. She groaned terribly in front of him and couldn't get any respite from her pretended pain. She said: 'Oh, what a state I'm in, I think I'm going to die! Only you can do something to make it better, my dear husband. If you are kind to me now, I'll soon be fit and well again. But if you leave me in this plight, I shall die before your very eyes.'

Her husband said: 'My dear wife, whatever you want, it troubles me. How can I help you? Tell me. I love you so much that no pain is too hard for me to bear if it will help to put an end to your illness.'

Hildegard said to her husband: 'You have a bad tooth in the middle of your gullet that causes me this pain. It smells horribly from your mouth. That's what makes me ill and will make me die before my time. Honestly, I tell you, no other medicine will be as useful in preventing me from dying as if you had that tooth pulled out. It will give me a good many more days to live.'

The husband replied to his wife: 'That's an extraordinary tale. I've never had any toothache up to now. God gave me teeth that are strong and healthy.'

The wife immediately began to act worse than before. The husband was an utter fool and imagined she was about to pass away since she was behaving as if she were in great pain. He considered the matter deeply and came to the conclusion that he must have a stinking tooth; he would have sworn a hundred oaths on it. He was made a fool by his wife's trickery.

He had a servant who was bold and very fond of his wife. He used to drive away her pain. They both liked each other. He came from the fields as usual with his plough as they were in this state of misery. He came into the room, and his master urgently asked him: 'My dear servant, help your mistress so that she doesn't perish and die a swift death. Here in my mouth I have a bad tooth. Pull it out of my gullet to lessen my wife's pain.' The servant quickly got ready to do this for the wife. He bound the peasant securely on a table so that he couldn't move. The wife then handed the servant a big, clumsy pair of tongs. The peasant was terrified when he saw them, but he suffered this trouble gladly for his wife's sake. The servant did a good job with him. He seized him inside the left cheek and pulled out a strong, good tooth with the tongs so that blood spurted out of the simple man's mouth. He had never suffered greater pain in all his life. I tell you truly: his wife wasn't satisfied with this. She began to hatch out plans as to how she could trick her husband further. You'll probably like to hear this. She shouted out: 'Oh, the agony! I shall die. The pain is getting worse. Honestly, I tell you,' she said to the servant, 'that's not the right tooth that you have pulled out of his left cheek. Listen to me: the tooth that is causing my death is in his right cheek.' The servant took the tongs into his hand again, and the husband was forced to suffer greater pain. He had already been too much deceived. A good tooth was removed from his right cheek. He fainted and neither heard nor saw anything of this great distress. He had completely lost consciousness, which his wife noted and wanted to trick him one more time. She said to the servant: 'Go quickly and bring the priest to your master so that he can make confession of his sins, for death is creeping on him.'

The priest came straight away. The wife lamented about her trouble to the priest. She wept and cried without moderation like a person lamenting in all sincerity. The peasant made a complete confession. In his misery he had accepted that he was going to die. The priest gave him the benediction and departed. The wife sat in front of the good man and wept openly so that the peasant himself imagined that he was worse than he actually was. All of this she did to trick him further. She brought the candles and put them in his hand. She said, 'God has sent his messenger here. The soul is now departing from his lips. Lord God, come without delay and receive his soul and take it to the throne of God, where it shall be for eternity. God have mercy on you, dear husband.' When she had finished saying this, the wife deftly took a cloth and covered him with it. The peasant himself imagined that his soul had departed. The wife cried out: 'Oh, what agony! My dear husband is dead. Alas for my dear husband. I can never lament you enough, your love was so great that enfolded me in your heart. I must mourn eternally when I now think of you. Oh, my dear Berthold, you were always so dear to me! Now having lost you like this, I shall always be sorrowful.'

The news was publicized in the village that Mistress Hildegard had become a widow. She carefully saw to closing up the house both in front and behind and had her husband quietly put in a lidless coffin, over which she deftly spread a poor cloth through which the peasant could see what was going on. When she had finished this, the house-door was opened. Mistress Jutta and Mechthild and the other neighbours' wives came in. They lamented with this dejected woman that she had been bereft of her husband so suddenly in the prime of his life. Mistress Jutta and Mechthild realized just how this event had taken place, but dared not say anything about it. They went out with the others.

No one remained in the house apart from the woman and the servant, which suited them both. The woman sat by the coffin. She had a crazy idea. She bewailed her husband for a while then made a proposition to the servant. She said: 'You shall now console me in the future, and I will be obedient to you, live and die with you.' The servant immediately promised to give her his help. He seized her lovingly and laid her underneath him, bothering little about her husband. He laid himself between her legs and made love to her without the least anxiety. The peasant looked out of the coffin, as his face was uncovered. He saw for himself that they were lying on top of each other and playing the game of love. He said: 'Heinz, if I were alive, as I actually was this morning, I would be deeply upset by this disgraceful action. I would not leave it unavenged: I'd get my knife out to you. However, I shall have to put up with it as I can't hurt anybody any more, on my word, because of death's bitter blow, which has laid me low and torn my limbs apart.' There we must leave things. This was how Mistress Hildegard tricked her husband. I don't know whether she got the odd *haller* yet.

Now let me tell you how Mistress Jutta deceived and tricked her husband. He was called Farmer Konrad. When evening came, Farmer Konrad learnt that Farmer Berthold was dead, as did also Mistress Jutta. She sent for mead and plenty of wine and managed with fair skill, as she was well able, to fill her husband with wine and get him quite drunk so that he didn't know what he was doing. In this excessive drunkenness he fell fast asleep on the bench beside his merry wife. She rested no longer, but got hold of a good pair of scissors with which she sheared her husband and gave the monkey a tonsure like an unordained priest. After this she got him to bed. Mistress Jutta lay down beside him, and he slept soundly all night.

When day came and they began to ring the church bell, Mistress Hildegard had arranged for her husband to be taken to church. What more shall I tell you? Mistress Jutta gently touched her husband in bed and woke him up carefully. 'Get up quickly, Sir Heinrich,' she said to her husband (that was the priest's name – he had meanwhile set off). She woke her husband very cleverly and gently just as though he were the real priest. His head was heavy with drinking so that he paid no attention to what his wife said. She gave him a dig in the ribs. 'Get up, dear sir! Can't you hear the bell ringing. You're sleeping a long time today. Get up and receive the offering you'll get from Farmer Berthold, whose funeral is taking place in the church today.' Then Farmer Konrad said: 'What do you mean? What is deceiving you to want to make a priest of me now. You know very well that I can't read or write.'

Mistress Jutta answered her husband: 'Why are you talking like that, Sir Heinrich? Go to the corpse in the church at the holy altar and say a public mass for his soul. That is a much more useful thing for you to be doing than lying here, if you want me to tell you the truth.'

Farmer Konrad said: 'I don't know how to take what you're saying. You're having a fine time with your joke. You call me "Priest Heinrich", but I'm more like Farmer Konrad.'

Mistress Jutta replied: 'On my word of truth, I say: you are Priest Heinrich. Just touch your head and you'll realize that I'm speaking the truth.' At this he grasped the front of his head and found he had a broad tonsure such as a priest is supposed to have. He said: 'Now I see that I really am a priest. Yet I still think it can't in fact be so, because I am entirely uneducated. I can't read or write.' Mistress Jutta refused to stop: 'Go straight away to the church,' she said. 'God will not forsake you. As soon as you step before the altar, you will be able to read what is in the book.'

This Farmer Konrad believed. He hurried off quickly to the church, accompanied by Mistress Jutta. She stood him at the altar and put his surplice on. She said: 'Stand quietly here until the people come. It's still a bit early.' Farmer Konrad stood there like a priest at the altar (he was getting old with worry). When the people arrived, no one realized that it was actually Farmer Konrad standing in front of them dressed like a priest. Mistress Jutta had tricked him nicely, which should give her some satisfaction. There we must leave him for the present.

We must quickly go on to tell how Mistress Mechthild disgraced her husband. He was called Farmer Siegfried. When he went to sleep that night, Mistress Mechthild secretly stole all her husband's good clothes. When the night came to an end and day dawned, she woke him up and said: 'Don't sleep any more. We must go to church. The priest is going to read mass. Farmer Berthold has died. Get up fast, dear husband, let us make our offering there. You know what a good friend he was to us.' When Farmer Siegfried heard that, he got out of bed quickly. 'I can't find my clothes,' he said to his wife. 'On my word,' she replied, 'you've already got them on. Don't stand around any longer. We shall miss the service: the mass will soon be over. Go on quickly and stop talking.'

Farmer Siegfried said: 'I won't go to the church naked. I'd not be spared any mockery going to church. Stop your chatter and give me my clothes.'

His wife immediately answered him in an angry, ruthless way: 'You must be out of your mind; you can't see with your eyes open. Ask all those at church. They won't be able to tell you anything else than that they see you standing there in your clothes.'

Mistess Mechthild so persisted in swearing this was so that her husband didn't dare to gainsay her further. He was taken in by the ruse and would have sworn a hundred times that he was handsome and nicely dressed. That was the point his wicked wife had got him to. He then went with his wife completely naked to church. Farmer Konrad stood at the altar, Farmer Berthold lay there in the coffin, and Farmer Siegfried went up to the altar without any clothes. He wanted to place his offering there for his friend Farmer Berthold. He took hold of his testicles, thinking he had a pouch hanging there that he wanted to open. He looked for the two thongs there, but couldn't find them. He wanted to get his money-offering out. Mistress Mechthild had come up to him as he stood there confused. She was about to open the pouch. She took out a good knife and said: 'You are so stupid, you can't do anything like that. Let me see if I can open your pouch for you.' She then cut off his testicles. Farmer Siegfried suffered agony losing this good member and screamed so that it echoed through the church. He ran out making an enormous noise as if he had gone mad. He shouted with rage against his wife's crime. When Farmer Konrad heard it, he ran from the altar and shouted with a loud voice: 'My wife has also tricked me; the devil take her!' He also ran out of the church and found Farmer Siegfried in great torment outside. He was running up and down like a rabid dog, and he was wounded terribly. He bellowed and screamed like a cow. Farmer Konrad was furious with anger. The two of them ran together over the common to the wood, having gone wild. This was what Mistress Jutta and Mechthild had hatched up light-heartedly for an odd *haller*.

All the people, old and young, big and small, took note of what had happened. They did not, however realize what had happened to the two of them. They wanted to find out and ran out leaving no one in the church apart from Farmer Berthold in his coffin. He shouted: 'What am I doing here? I have been tricked by my faithless wife, but I don't know how. The devil enter her!' With these words he jumped up. He made a frightening appearance. He ran in front of the people and cried out in great anger: 'Where is cursed Mistress Hildegard? I won't delay her reward any longer. I will kill her with my own hands. No one shall stop me.' At this the people were terrified and started running in all directions. They were all scared of the dead man and fled from him every single one of them. Anyone who saw this happen would have gone grey through fear. Farmer Berthold decided, having seen Farmer Siegfried and Farmer Konrad run off in agony over the common, to go after them. He wanted to discover what had happened to them. He hurried after them in haste to get to the wood.

Now we'll let the idiots go to the wood, until they understand that they're all drunk and can't see with their eyes open. When they realize that they will return home and let the matter rest with regard to what they have suffered. Now I'd like to know which deceived and tricked her husband best. If anyone can tell me that, I'd regard him as wise. Whichever woman managed that, she would deserve the odd *haller*. I myself certainly don't know. That's the end of the story.

6. The False Messiah

In a town in Silesia there was a Jew who had the most beautiful daughter. At the back of the Jew's house there were two windows near together that faced each other. One of them belonged to a Christian's room, in which a student lived who was sorry for the daughter's pitiful situation. He got into conversation with her and eventually came to an agreement about the matter. At night he fixed a board across between the two windows and crawled along it over to her. What they then undertook you might as well preach to a fool about; an intelligent person will easily understand anyway. The fact that the daughter then became pregnant gave them both a great shock. The student said: 'Don't worry about it, I know how to deal with the matter. Just indicate to me which is your father's room, and I'll do it straight away.'

This the daughter did, and he went away. He got a joiner to make a pipe, and when it was ready the student climbed in to the daughter again at night, as he had done previously, first did his business, and before the time of the first sleep had finished, he bent down underneath a beam, from which he could reach the Jew's bed with his pipe. Through this pipe he then began to speak: 'Abraham, most dear father, and you, Sarah, his wife, listen to what I have to say! God tells you both that this very night your daughter has conceived the true Messiah. It is God's command that neither of you should enquire from where this noble birth comes. But, if you refuse to believe this, God will deprive you of honour and blessedness and damn all your people.' 'Now, in God's name, amen!' they both said. 'Praised be God who has given us so high a blessing.' The student said: 'Sleep and take your rest and care diligently for your daughter so that you may have success and gain benefit for yourselves and all the Jewish people, who have long been despised. Behold, this child will rule over all heathen and Christian multitudes. With this I commend you to the Lord.' Thereupon he very quietly turned away. They talked a long time about these things.

When they awoke in the morning, they came into their daughter's room and found her fast asleep, for the student had only just gone and had not let her get any sleep up to then. But he had told her, if she were showered with great honours, that she should accept it with a good heart, since he intended not to come to her any more until she gave birth to the child.

Now old father Abraham ordered the school-messenger to summon the four eldest Jews together. He quickly discussed the matter with them, as a result of which an order was circulated that the assembly of the synagogue should be summoned, both old and young. After this the eldest Jew put on his robes and stepped in front of the almamor and began with great reverence: 'Dear people, before I inform you of this new event, let us first sing a song of praise to God.' There then began, believe me, such a howling, in which the dogs also joined, with such terrible gesturings as if they were all possessed by devils. And when this furious, cruel screeching was finished and they were requested to be silent, the rabbi started again: 'Oh, chosen people of the Lord, that He now at last will grant our long cry and prayer and not abandon us, praised be eternally the seed of the first father Abraham, who is this time symbolized in our own Abraham today, who stands present here, in whom the Lord has put His mercy and revealed to him this very night that the Messiah has been made flesh in his only daughter, and that he will save us from the suffering of the revenge of the most evil Goyim and also from the scorn of all the heathen, and will lead us into the land that is often named in the scriptures, where we shall have our great feasting with the Leviathan with oats and geese. There we shall have revelling with gorging, carousing and running to the stream, there we shall drink milk mingled with honey, but it will be a little time yet. For this sing another song of praise to give God praise, honour and thanks.' Well, there struck up the greatest cry, and the voices were so varied with crying, shouting, howling and singing, that all the people began to press forward to ask what was the matter with them. They said: 'You will soon see what our great happiness signifies, unless Jews are not like other people.'

Now when the diabolical rejoicing had ended and everyone went home, the Jewish elders began again to consider zealously how the daughter should be looked after in the future so that the divine honour should in no way be tarnished. A plan was then devised to make her a new apartment, room and chamber, the ceiling of which was decorated with the finest blue studded with bright, pure, golden stars. The walls were painted green all over with trails of flowers everywhere; the seats were covered with cushions and green velvet; the floor spread with silken carpets all over; the bed and chairs were of cypress ornamented with gold fittings. Only when that was all finished was she publicly informed by four of the most learned wise men that all this dignity and beauty was done only for the sake of her virtue and especially for the mighty seed that God had implanted in her body. This immediately caused her to think fervently of her tender, fine student with the result that she sighed deeply in her heart and fell into a great faint to think of her pain in now having to do without him for nine long months. Now to continue with our story, she was well cared for with food and drink. If a princess had sat at table, she could hardly have been as well treated. And when she retired to bed, two servants preceded her with candles, and she had three maids and a manservant ready at all times to serve her. Yet her greatest trouble was that she never saw the student whose lesson she would much rather have listened to than had three more maids.

But we must leave the matter there. Letters were written to all Jewry to inform them of what was happening. Then from all Jewry she was brought the most splendid gifts, about which she thought all the time: 'Oh, if only the student could have the half of them and I could have a bit of his gorgeous body in my hand in exchange this very night, however virtuous they consider me to be,' for she thought about him all the time.

Then soon her confinement drew near with great pain, as with other women, but when they began to examine the child, it did not have one little member that is usually seen on boys. Whether a sow had bitten it off and torn it out root and all or however else it might have occurred, I do not know, but I must declare that there was never greater lamentation, howling and roaring in all Jewry. The father and mother of the girl hid themselves and neither ate nor drank for several days, so upset were they.

The student had been thinking seriously about how matters would go especially for the daughter, but also for the child. The Jews' singing had stopped. The student had previously discussed this with the senior members of the town council and said that he would marry the girl if there were no other way of keeping her safe. People had swiftly been sent to the town to prevent the girl from being strangled and to protect the child. The Jews were ordered, on pain of losing their lives and possessions, to hand over the two into the custody of the Christians, if they were agreeable to this. In this way the matter was kept quiet until the six weeks were up and the student publicly married her. Both child and mother were then baptized. All the student's troubles then ended, as they were given so great presents that they had more than enough. The Jews' disgrace was made public. They pulled the hair out of their beards and heads, they swore, cursed and continually attempted to get at father and mother. They would have liked to have torn them apart and got their teeth into them. What more shall I tell you? The Jews remained in disgrace, and no matter was more grievous to them. Well, should it not be made known? Each one of them ought to be tonsured. That is what Hans Folz, the barber says.

7. The Smith in the Baking-Trough

In Dettelbach there was once a smith, a foolish man, who had a beautiful wife whom the chaplain used to court. Now the smith was at home both night and day, which meant that the chaplain could not reach his goal. For this reason he made up a fantastic tale. On Sunday morning, when he had finished his sermon, he said: 'Dearly beloved, listen carefully! There is going to be a terrible flood at midnight tonight. Take refuge on the hill or however else you can escape.' The smith's house was down by the stream, so he quickly began to think up a plan and hung his baking-trough up under the roof with four strong ropes and got into it secretly so that as soon as the water came all he would need to do would be to cut the ropes and he would descend nicely in the trough and float on the water.

When it was night, the smith's wife thought that he had gone away and surreptitiously sent her maid for the chaplain, who crept equally surreptitiously into her room. Previously the smith's wife had also had an affair with their servant, who imagined that he was her only lover and now supposed that the smith had deserted the house. No sooner had the wife lain down than the servant came knocking at her bedroom door and woke her up with his pleas. She said: 'Go away from me, you silly fool: death will be about tonight.' He said: 'Just give me a kiss then before we die.' The bedroom had a little window, the priest got up and stuck out his backside at him. The servant kissed him on the anus, which stank horribly. The servant was incensed at this, realized it was the priest and thought up a trick.

He went to the fire and heated upon an iron rod, went with it to the window, opened it and said: 'Kiss me for the last time, turn to someone who does not hate you!' The priest pushed out his arse and farted at the servant, who then stuck the red-hot iron rod up his backside. The priest screamed: 'Water, water, oh water!' and his cry was heard by the good smith, who was lying happily in the baking-trough under the roof. He got up and loosened the ropes and descended as though the house were being struck by thunder. The priest jumped out naked, thinking he heard a clap of thunder. The smith lay underneath in the house with all his ribs broken. The smith was too stupid and was made a dupe. The priest was too clever for that and was repaid in the measure he had himself measured out and was not in a position to complain about it to anyone.

8. How Howleglass was Made Clerk of Büddenstedt

When Howleglass was parish clerk of the church, he had to help the priest to sing Mass. And once, as he stood before the altar with the priest, the priest let out such a great fart that all the church rang with it. Then Howleglass said, 'Sir Parson, what do you offer there? Frankincense for our Lord?'

Then the parson answered, 'Mind your own business! For I can shit in the middle of the church, if I want.'

Then Howleglass said, 'I bet you a barrel of beer that you will not shit in the middle of it.'

Then the priest said, 'I'll bet with you; do you think that I'm too scared to do it?'

Then the priest turned round and went and shat a great heap in the church, and said, 'Clerk, I've won the barrel of beer.'

Then Howleglass said, 'Oh no you haven't, for we will first measure whether it is exactly in the middle of the church or not.'

And then they measured it, and it was more than six feet from the middle. And then Howleglass won the barrel of beer. And so the priest's mistress was angry, and said, 'If you keep this uncouth yob much longer, you mark my words, in the end he'll make a fool of you.'

And then at the end of Lent, when Howleglass was parish clerk, at Easter they had to act out the resurrection of Our Lord; and because at that time the men were not learned, and could not read, the priest took his mistress and put her in the grave to be an angel. And seeing this, Howleglass took to him three of the most stupid people in the town; they played the three Marys, and the parson played Christ, with a banner in his hand. Then Howleglass said to the stupid people, 'When the angel asks you who you seek, you must say "The parson's mistress, with one eye".'

Then it happened that the time came when they had to act. And the angel asked them whom they sought, and then they spoke what Howleglass had shown and taught them before; and they answered, 'We seek the priest's mistress, with one eye.' And then the priest saw that he was mocked. And when the priest's mistress heard that, she rose out of the grave and would have hit Howleglass with her fist on the cheek, but she missed him and hit one of the stupid people who played one of the three Marys. And he hit her back, and then she took him by the ear, and, seeing that, his wife came running quickly to hit the priest's mistress, and the priest, seeing this, threw down his banner, and went to help his woman, so that they were all giving each other huge blows, and made a din in the church. And then Howleglass, seeing them set by the ears in the body of the church, went on his way out of the village and came there no more.

9. How that Howleglass would Fly from the Town House of Magdeburg

After that Howleglass came to Magdeburg, where he did so many marvellous things that his name was well known there. Then the mayor of the town asked that he should do something that had never been seen before. Then Howleglass said that he would go to the highest point of the Council House, and fly from it; and soon it was known through all the town that Howleglass would fly from the top of the Council House, so that all the town assembled there and gathered in the market place to see him. Upon the top of the house stood Howleglass with his hands flapping as if he would fly, and the people looked when he should have flown. Because of this he laughed, and said to the people, 'I thought there were no more fools but myself; but I see indeed that here's a whole town full. For even if the lot of you said that you would fly, I would not have believed you. And now you believe one because he says he will fly, which is impossible for I have no wings, and no man can fly without wings.'

And then he went on his way from the top of the Council House and left the folk standing there. And then the folk departed from there, some cursing him, and some laughing, saying, 'He is a clever fool, for he tells us the truth.'

10. How Howleglass Set his Hostess upon the Hot Ashes on her Bare Arse

As Howleglass was coming from Rome, he came to an inn where his host was not at home. And when he was within, he asked his hostess if she knew Howleglass. And the hostess said, 'No, but I hear it said that he is a false deceiver and trickster.'

Then Howleglass said, 'Why do you say so? You don't know him!'

Then the hostess said, 'That's true, but I have heard a lot said about his trickiness.'

Then Howleglass said, 'My good woman, he has never done you any harm; why do you slander him because of what other people say?'

The hostess said, 'I say nothing more about him than everyone does; for I have heard him spoken of by many of my guests who have lodged here.'

Then Howleglass kept quiet, and said no more until the morning; and then he scattered the hot ashes on the hearth. And then he woke the hostess up and set her on them on her bare arse. And so his hostess was well burned. Then he said to her, 'Now you can say bravely that you have seen the false deceiver and trickster Howleglass!'

Then the hostess cried for help and scowled at him. Then he went out of her doors and said to her, 'Shouldn't you correct and reprove slanderers and backbiters, who say things about men they never saw, or had never done harm to them? Yes, it is a charitable thing to do.' And then he took his horse and departed from there.

DUTCH TALES

1. The Resourcefulness of Women

You have heard many a time of women finding clever solutions to their problems, be it in Haarlem or in other towns. Listen now to what a certain maiden did.

She was a sensuous creature, but she was locked up in a house surrounded by high walls. Her father thought to himself that he would preserve her honour until some knight or young nobleman should come to seek her hand and bring him much honour. It was for this reason that he kept her secluded, so that she might not enjoy the company of anyone except for the chambermaids with whom she was wont to spend her time. Yet she fostered feelings of true love and friendship for a certain young man.

She resourcefully set out to inform him by what means they might meet one another in order to converse. She sent for a friar and bade him come to her. She said that she wished to give confession, 'For no one is without fault,' she said, 'neither man nor woman. Father, because I trust you utterly, in God's name give me advice, for I am troubled by a burden: a young man, who lives not far from here, has driven me to distraction; I could tell you his name. He has been here three times, loitering near these walls. I fear for what the neighbours will say. Father, I must implore you earnestly, tell him to desist and to spare me his love-longing before I complain to my family. It cannot fail to spawn rumours, so often does he show himself here.'

Good man that he was, the friar said that he would gladly speak to him and tell him to desist, and impress upon him that she was a woman of honour. The good friar went immediately to where he might find the young man with whom the woman had asked him to speak. The two of them stood off to one side and talked privately.

'You have wronged the maiden with whom you have tried to speak these past weeks,' said the friar. 'She wants nothing to do with you and asks that you desist.'

The young man swore by our Lord: 'I don't know what you're talking about.'

'I urge you, behave yourself from now on,' replied the friar curtly. Thus ended their conversation.

I shall tell you – understand me well – what the gentle maiden then did as she sat in her chamber. I shall tell you here and now. She put a purse of costly material on a belt and filled it with coins of gold. Neither her father nor her mother knew of this. She again sent for the friar and he came as called.

'Oh Father, I asked you to speak with this young man of whom I cannot seem to be rid. Did you not speak with him, dear Father?'

'I earnestly admonished him!' said the friar. 'He said he would never say another word about you.'

'Oh Father, this past week he came near these walls; this belt and purse he threw through my window – the one was wrapped in the other – and it is a source of embarrassment to me. At the same time he called out to me that it contained gold coins with which I might buy clothes, stockings and shoes. May the Lord be praised, I have no need of it, for I have a rich father who may buy me whatever it is his will that I should wear. Father, I ask of you now, take this trinket and return it to him and repeat to him exactly what I have said: that I do not desire his gifts and that he may wear them himself.'

The friar took the gifts from the maiden and, putting both purse and belt in his sleeve, went immediately to the place where he found the young man. He spoke with him privately, saying: 'Young man, you are wrong to tarnish the honour of this fine woman with your prowlings. In this you sin quite seriously.'

The young man responded in a haughty tone that he would certainly refute anyone at any time who should accuse him of having transgressed against her.

'Come what may,' said the friar, 'I do not believe you. See here the belt that you brought her and the silken purse filled with gold coins. She does not want to receive any gifts from you; take here your belt and your money, untouched, in the purse. She wants no gifts from you, neither great nor small.'

The young man realized that the maiden was after love. The friar gave him the purse and the gold on the silken belt then and there, and impressed upon him that the woman who had sent it wanted no part of his friendship and did not desire his gifts. The young man feigned the rejected lover and said: 'Father, I shall take care. You need not ever again suspect that I should address that woman at any time. I relinquish her utterly.'

Now, having completed his errand, the friar returned home. The lad was a handsome young man; he wore expensive clothes and behaved in a proper manner. The maiden – understand me well – who had thus enriched him, as I have said, thought of a quite ingenious plan. She summoned the friar by means of a messenger, and bade him for the sake of God to come to her. The friar sat reading but put down his book and went once again to the maiden. Having welcomed him, she said: 'Oh Father, how sorely troubled is my heart! Last night the young man of whom I have complained to you came entirely unbidden. He made bold to use something without my permission (I shall tell it you in confidence). In the place where my father's turfs are stored there has always stood a ladder. Last night he put it up against the ledge that borders on this window. Now I do not know what to do, I am sure this will be the death of me! Father, could you just one more time ask him to leave

128

me alone; I would offer you my friendship and such reward as will be to your benefit.'

'When I have finished reading my hours,' said the friar, 'I shall go and see to it that he leaves off his importunities.'

At that the friar departed and he spoke to the lad on the field where he was playing with his young fellows. What I tell you now is the truth. The friar signalled to him to come closer. As soon as he perceived this, the lad asked: 'Father, what is your wish?'

'It pleases me ill that you prosper,' replied the friar. 'You behave in a discourteous fashion! I have told you before and I will tell you again today, that you must never again desire to go where you were last night.'

'Where was that?' asked the youth. 'If it truly displeased you I would indeed be sorry.'

'Do you suppose that I do not know how you set out last night equipped with a ladder? The maiden told me herself. In her father's storehouse there is such a ladder; last night you put it up against the ledge outside her window. The wall there is water-logged and unsound, damaged as it is by heavy rains; you were fortunate indeed that the wall did not collapse or that she did not push you off.'

The youth solemnly declared that he would behave himself and that it would not happen again. At that the friar went home and never again did he speak to that youth. That evening the young man went and took up the ladder which he found standing there, just as the friar had told him according to the maiden's directions. Then he put up the ladder behind the house and climbed in through the window. The maiden saw that the young man had arrived and she welcomed him warmly as she helped him inside. At once they began to put mouth to mouth, but of that I will say no more. Yet Pieter van Iersele has said that the young man laid her upon a bed and taught her the ways of love, so that they remained good friends; and never again did they wish to see the friar who had performed this errand.

2. Concerning the Lad from Dordrecht, a Funny Jest

Hearken now, one and all, and listen to what transpired – as many know full well – not long ago within the gates of Dordrecht. Folks in that town began to take notice of a certain young man with long hair. He loved ostentation and sumptuous living. Each day before the first mass had been said he would be enjoying his wine in the tavern. He insisted that only the finest foods in the land be purchased and brought to him at the tavern. The lad was so generous that whoever wished to drink with him, whether he was of any importance or not, it was the lad and the lad alone who paid the bill.

The bailiff's servants, who had observed his behaviour for seven days, tried secretly to discover the occupation of this man who every day spent so much money. But they saw no indication that he practised any craft. So they brought the matter before the bailiff, that here was a man who lived so sumptuously, and yet there was no one, neither within the city nor without, who knew how he came by his money.

When the bailiff learned of this matter he wasted no time in looking for the lad. And he found him in the street. The bailiff clasped him by the hand and said: 'Young man, you must explain something to me. I see you drinking wine all day with the lads. You buy the rounds and pick up the tab for many a man in the tavern. Just how you can afford to drink and eat in this fashion is what I want to know from you.'

The lad replied: 'My dear sir, I shall tell you my occupation. But it must remain a secret. I bed other men's wives for money.'

The bailiff grabbed him by the hood and said: 'Is such a thing possible? I won't believe you unless I see some proof with my own eyes.'

'Follow me, sir bailiff, and you shall witness how my services are engaged,' said the lad.

'I've never heard of such a splendid occupation,' said the bailiff. 'Henceforth you'll have nothing to fear from me, so long as I see proof of it.'

So the lad took leave of the bailiff. Shortly thereafter the bailiff saw an old woman approaching. She headed for where the lad was standing, limping on both legs. She asked the lad if he would render her his services. They reached an agreement. After this the lad walked over to where the bailiff stood watching, and he said: 'Sir bailiff, I shall have earned 20 pounds before morning.'

'May you live and prosper! You're a good fellow for sure, for you earn your living by the sweat of your brow.'

It was three days later that the bailiff had a meal prepared for his family. At table he told them of the handsome young man and his occupation, and of how he had made the lad show him how he would earn 20 pounds in one night. They all replied: 'That's a good craft!'

When the meal was over, the bailiff's wife got up and immediately went to her room, where she found her chambermaid. She said: 'Have you heard about the lad in town? He'll satisfy one's needs for money. I must have him or I shall die. Search until you've found him. Promise him enough money that he'll come tonight and ply his craft on me.' The chambermaid ran out and scoured the town until she found the man. They were soon agreed that he should earn twenty pounds.

Now it was the bailiff's custom that he himself held watch together with his men. And so our craftsman went to bed, and he performed his craft so well that the fair lady praised him more than her husband. But as dawn approached, the lady was the first to speak, saying: 'Young man, get up! It's time for you to leave. You'll be paid tomorrow.'

'I'm afraid I don't work for credit,' said the lad. 'I must receive my money before I get up. I've never worked anywhere where my wages have not been slipped into my purse in the morning.'

The lady replied: 'But my husband – it's morning – he'll be here soon! We'll both be killed!'

As they thus lay there, the dawn's light shone ever more brightly. The bailiff wanted to go to sleep, so he took leave of his men, went into his room and removed his clothes, shoes, socks and all. Then he turned towards his bed, and the first thing he saw was the lad's beard. The bailiff grew very upset, at which the lad sat up and, like one knight to another, he exclaimed: 'Welcome, Sir Bailiff!'

The bailiff recognized him immediately and said, 'What are you doing here?'

'Practising my trade,' retorted the lad.

'Put your clothes on and go away,' said the bailiff. 'You have caused me more grief than any other man has ever done before.'

To which, full of self-assurance, the lad replied: 'Sir Bailiff, be so kind as to have my money fetched, for I have sweated hard enough for it. I should have been dressed and away from here long ago, if only I had received my wages.'

'Tell me, how much are you charging?' asked the bailiff.

'The price agreed upon before ever I came into this house and undertook this work was twenty pounds,' the lad replied.

Then the bailiff said: 'Please, I beg of you, do not bring shame upon me in these parts. I shall give you twenty pounds, but never before have I paid out money that caused me more pain. I shall never have need of your services again!'

The lad received his money. Once he had it in his possession, he thought he had done well for himself. What further transpired within those walls between the bailiff and his wife, of that I find no written record. Therefore I shall end the tale here. May God bless our souls. Amen.

131

3. Concerning the Unfortunate Lacarise, who Saw another Man Screw his Wife

I shall tell you an adventure in few words, just as I heard it, and you'll thank me for it. It was ten years ago or so that there lived a woman in Lokeren, on the Scheldt, who was called Machtelt. Her husband's name was Lacarise; he was soft-headed and simple.

Now this woman secretly loved a priest, whom one day she had called to her by means of a servant. She wished to talk to him, for she was burning with passion and consumed by love for him. She sent the servant out of the room. The priest sat down next to the woman, whose passion was promptly aroused. She looked at him and he at her, until they were aware of Lacarise returning from the neighbour's. They did not greet him, which annoyed him greatly, and moreover it was dinnertime. Lacarise was a foolish and repulsive man.

'Dame Machtelt,' he said, 'why are you sitting there? Hurry up and prepare my dinner! Why do you neglect me so?'

Then the woman replied in an angry tone: 'My dear Lacarise, what demon has brought you here? How ugly your cheeks are! You are pale and wan. It seems to me that the man who was carried off on a bier yesterday looked exactly like you. It's little wonder I'm frightened! My husband is dead, though he doesn't know it! Behold, Father, the condition of this poor devil. See how pale he looks!'

The priest said: 'By my faith, it would do no good to try to give him a drink. I shall be happy to bury him tomorrow morning.'

Lacarise spoke: 'This is a great marvel! I hear, and I see with my own eyes – and yet you make me out to be dead!'

Dame Machtelt spoke: 'Calm down. You're dead, I know this for certain.'

'Oh dearest lady, then you have no choice but to cover me with the shroud I am to wear when I depart this world. And see to it that people, poor and rich alike, attend my wake. Still, it's a shame that I am to be buried when there is so little wrong with me.'

Dame Machtelt spoke: 'That doesn't matter.' At that she reached for the cloth and began to cover him with it, and Lacarise stretched himself out on the floor under the burial shroud. Then both the woman and the priest laughed so hard that their heads hurt, because he lay there on the floor.

It was a clear, beautiful day, and the sun shone brightly upon the burial shroud at that moment, so that Lacarise could see through it. Dame Machtelt had lifted up her legs and in a flash the priest lay between them, pounding hard, and Machtelt laughed.

Lacarise spoke: 'By my faith, Father, you'd be better off in a brothel. Has the devil got into you? What are you doing on top of my wife? This is a crime and a sin. If I were alive now, as I was yesterday, you would pay for this debauchery.'

The priest answered the old fool immediately: 'Lacarise, you're not supposed to be able to see. Shut your eyes and lie as still as a millstone. That is what bodies do that lie in state. You're frightening us.' When the priest had addressed him thus, Lacarise said: 'I shall, Father.'

And so it was that the priest had his fill of pleasure while the poor wretch thought he was dead, and his wife was being screwed. He was a foolish and ignorant man. Now people have changed. Few folk so stupid are to be found today. Women are full of all manner of evil, though I do not speak now of courtly women, from whom one may expect only virtue, for good women deserve to be honoured; whoever says otherwise is a scoundrel. An evil woman must needs act according to her nature, though she be surrounded by a wall.

But I do not know how it fared with Lacarise, who remained lying there on the floor; whether he was released or not, I haven't heard. This then is the story of Lacarise. May God bring us to the eternal paradise. Amen.

4. Concerning the Priest whose Bacon was Stolen

Once a year, everywhere in the world where the Christian faith is embraced, there comes a time when people go eagerly to confess the sins they have committed and to accept such penance as their priest prescribes for them. It is for this reason that I extol this time of year, for people are mindful of their sins more than at any other time, as I shall illustrate for you based on what happened to a young lad who lived a riotous and lawless life. He thought little of his spiritual ruin, which was evident by his behaviour: he seldom went to church to hear God's word, and moreover he chose a fate far worse for the salvation of his soul.

It came to pass that this wicked young man became anxious, and he considered many of the things that he had done in order to support himself: he had spent all his own wealth, so he had stolen everything he could lay his hands on. He began to feel remorse for all this, and wished to make his confession and admit to the sins that weighed on his conscience.

So he went to where a priest sat alone, one who had heard the confession of many a man, both great and small. The lad sat down before the priest and

133

began to tell him how previously he had for so long lived the riotous life with his companions in undisciplined indulgence, that he had spent all his own goods and since then supported himself by such disreputable means that his soul was in grave danger.

The priest spoke: 'You must desist, or else I take you to be beyond salvation.'

The lad answered: 'Dear Father, now that I have come to you here, I'd like to speak to you of a certain matter that would be to our mutual advantage, and ask your advice. I know a place where there are two fat sides of bacon, one of which I should very much like to steal. Father, if you would help me conceal it, I will mend my ways afterwards.'

When the lad had spoken thus, the priest laughed and said: 'My friend, reconsider your words. Such talk amazes me.'

'Indeed, Father, though I would it were otherwise, I cannot do without it, and if you grant me absolution, I shall bring you half of it.'

Now you shall hear a novelty: I shall tell you how the lad's bribe helped him outsmart this priest. One of them was devious, and the other greedy. Where these two work closely together, men eat well. The priest thought to himself that half a side of bacon was always a good thing, no matter how the lad came by it (it is in the nature of some priests that they eagerly allow themselves to be bribed). Then he said: 'What is the meaning of this, that you propose such a thing? May I drown in evil waters before I did it for even twenty pounds.'

The lad answered him immediately: 'You'll change your tune. I have only to fetch the bacon from a rich man's house, and then half of it will be yours.'

The priest spoke: 'If that is the way it must be, then I advise you to proceed; but first you must promise me in the name of God above that you will forever keep this to yourself.'

'Father, you may be sure of it,' said the lad.

Then the priest laid his hand on the lad's head and absolved him of all sin. Without saying another word the lad took leave of the priest.

Now you shall hear further news. The priest himself had two fat sides of bacon of the choicest quality. The lad had noticed them earlier. He stole the best of the two that very night, from the very house where the priest had unsuspectingly allowed himself to be tricked into absolving him of that deed.

In the morning the lad returned with the bacon, laid it down at the gate, and called out. The priest was fast asleep, but as I understand it, his maid-servant got up and went to the gate, and she asked the lad what he wanted. He answered resolutely: 'My holy Father the Priest knows what I want, and no one else.'

134

'Well, he's fast asleep now, and I'm not allowed to admit any guests.'

'Go, and even if you have to wake him from his sleep, tell him that there's a lad here who's brought the goods that he purchased from him yesterday, and that he's to come down and claim his portion or I'll keep everything.' Thus spoke the lad from where he stood.

The maidservant hastened to where the priest lay in bed. Day was just dawning when she took the message to him. The lad knew what he was about when he ordered her to run so hard. The maidservant cried out: 'Father, a young man has come, and commanded me to give you this message. He has brought something of great value. Come and claim your portion. He says you will know what he means.'

'I do. He is my friend. Go quickly to him and tell him that what he requires of me, he should arrange with you. It's still a bit too early to my liking to be getting up just yet.'

The maidservant hurried zealously back to the lad standing at the gate, and told him what she had just heard: 'My master sends his thanks and bids you leave his portion of the goods with me. I am to receive it.'

The lad, who was eager to be away, was now very pleased, so he gave the maidservant the side of bacon, though the priest would be none the better off for it: he himself had fattened the pig that the lad had stolen. Hastening on his way the lad went straight home. He gave little thought to the priest's anger, for it seemed to him that the priest got what he deserved, and so he put his portion of the bacon in safekeeping.

Now you may hear new tidings of the priest who lost his bacon, yet thought that he stood to gain half another to be added to the two he already possessed. That was before the lad stole one side of bacon by means of a cunning trick, and carved off half of it, with which he paid the priest, and which, to his great satisfaction, the maidservant had collected from him when they took leave of one another. But the priest had not made the lad tell him where he had got the bacon. The priest would come to regret this sorely when he came out of his room and learned the truth.

But before that moment he was so pleased with himself that he cried out, 'Ho, ho, ho, ho! My, this is a fine side of fat bacon!' when he saw it lying there before him on the counter, so fat and choice. He gave little thought to how the lad had tricked him into stooping to such low moral depths.

Then he called for Molly to come to him without delay. 'Father,' she said when she stood before him, 'what is your pleasure?'

'Molly, what do you think, should we hang this bacon with the others?'

'Father, whatever you do with it seems right to me.'

I do believe the priest sang out in jubilation: 'This bacon is fatter than my own!' At that point he cast his eyes upwards for a moment, and then back again at the bacon that was supposedly better than the two hanging there.

135

He suddenly left off his singing, and said: 'This is scandalous! That thief has pulled a fast one on me!'

So it was that the priest's joy was short-lived. Consumed with rage, he wasted no time in chasing down the lad, and spoke to him thus: 'You there, thief! What have you done to me?'

'By my faith, Father, only what I promised.'

The priest nearly exploded when he heard the lad taunt him in this way. 'I'll have you hanged by the neck!' was the priest's angry reply.

The lad answered him sensibly: 'Father, if you consider the matter well, you will realize that you stand to gain little by bringing a charge against me. I told you yesterday that I knew where I might steal two sides of bacon, but I wanted you to conceal the goods, and you gave me absolution then and there.'

Then the priest thought to himself: 'It's true, I have got what I deserved.'

Thus the lad got off scot-free, but the priest returned home, angry and ashamed, for he stood in fear of a scandal should word of the incident get about. This caused the priest to keep silent about it, though he did so against his will, for he could not recover the bacon that had belonged to him before.

I wish that everyone who is moved to sin for a bribe, wherever they be, would always be made a fool of in this way; many a man might guard himself better against sin. This is the sincere wish – and I know this for certain – of Willem van Hildegaersberch, who wrote this story, and no one else.

5. Concerning a Monk

Constant vigilance against sin is to be praised by everyone, for fear compels one to avoid many a shameful deed, and the pain, anger, and other harmful things that accompany them. When ladies and maidens at various times have secret dealings now with this man, now with that one, and lay their trust in any and every man, it brings them neither honour nor wisdom, for secret meetings lead many a man to sin in such a way that he brings dishonour upon himself. And because opportunity makes the thief, one should avoid the kind of privacy that leads to sin and vice. Nature is weak when resistance is necessary. If one goes secretly where opportunity presents itself, then the Will takes over, and Reason is silent, wherever people meet in private. I would not particularly trust my confessor to meet privately with beautiful women, for the Devil is a cunning one.

There once was a holy man, a Dominican, who fell into sin. He had for a number of years been a mendicant friar. It was his custom to fast and pray, and to deliver stirring sermons, so that the people listened to him so often and with such pleasure that they took his message to heart and voluntarily shared their goods with him out of love and Christian charity. He had so thoroughly foresaken worldly things that his life seemed holy indeed. He used to comfort the people who repented their sins, in order that they might henceforth with a burning passion render service to God. Those who are feared by no one may perform many miracles.

A fair maiden of good family visited this friar frequently because she wished to learn how she might win her place in heaven. Not for a fortune of gold would she continue in her sinful ways. Thus with great zeal she used often to go to the friar when she considered herself guilty of some sin. She would confess with ardour, and the friar would grant her absolution. So often did she find her way to the friar, that opportunity made the thief. The friar blessed her with his own personal trinity, and so well did she learn the Pater Noster and the Creed during her lessons that the loose folds of her gown began to fill out at her waist, compelled by the wooden stylus with which one marks those hours that are written according to Nature's laws.

Such games are pleasurable as long as they remain a secret, but after throwing snake eyes several times in a row, one is bound to get lucky. The friar learned that the maiden was pregnant. People got wind of it and began to gossip about it. He stood in dread of a scandal, and of losing his good name. So he sought desperately for some way to conceal his guilt, for he expected that if the congregation learned the truth it would either cost him his life, or he would suffer some unendurable torment.

This friar of whom I speak worried constantly about his predicament, and he took frequent secret, solitary walks. Doubt gave him many painful thoughts, despair he could hardly stave off. As he walked thus consumed with worry, the Devil befriended the friar and spoke with him, taking on the guise of a master who could read his thoughts, so that before long the friar asked the Devil in disguise for a solution to his problem. Now the Devil was out for revenge, though the friar did not know this. The cause of his wish for revenge lay in the past. It was the friar's custom to speak to the people in his sermons of the Devil's ugly, frightful countenance, so that many of them immediately repented of their sins. So when the Devil perceived that the friar was in such dire straits, he came to him and spoke to him thus:

'I am a man who has the power to conjure the Devil. I shall cause the people to believe that you do not possess the necessary tool – whether large or small – by which either maiden or lady could come to shame. You will be entirely cleared of suspicion concerning such an act.'

'Help me prove my innocence without delay!' said the friar in reply. 'It shall be done,' said the master. So without any discomfort or pain he removed the friar's poperin pear, so that only smooth skin remained between his legs. When the friar groped down there, he found neither this nor that, but only a little hole through which he might purge himself.

The Devil said: 'Now put those evil folk publically to shame, and reprimand the liars who spread such rumours.'

'This is a fine arrangement, for after my innocence is established, I will more readily be able to procure women's favours', said the friar.

'Certainly!' was the Devil's immediate reply. 'As soon as your innocence has been shown, you shall be restored to your previous state.'

The friar said: 'I wouldn't want it any other way.'

The Devil's counsel was very much to his liking. Then he set about reading and studying until he had written a sermon that met his needs, and, as was his wont, he went to the pulpit one holy day, when a great crowd had gathered. The part of the Gospel proper for that holy day, he read first. Then he preached to the congregation concerning malicious backbiters; and he also spoke out against liars who had slandered many a man, and of how he himself had been slandered and his honour sullied by rumours concerning the maiden. All this he offered for their moral instruction, and then he brought his sermon to a close in proper fashion.

'This is my situation, and I must persevere', said the friar from the pulpit. 'I must now do what simply must be done. Though it pains me to reveal it, you may now see with your own eyes that I am smoother between the legs than a woman, and that it is because of malicious backbiters that I suffer this indignity.' At that he opened wide his garment at the front.

The Devil awaited his opportunity. As soon as the friar revealed himself to the congregation, he restored the friar's Father Confessor to its original place, harder and more rigid than it had ever been before. The people saw it standing there, erect, before the friar felt or even suspected that his plumbing had been restored. Then the Devil laughed heartily, because he had brought ruin upon him, and helped to renew his suffering. The people began to curse and spit on the friar, treating him with great scorn. All of this was brought about by the Devil, from start to finish! Such desserts, such profits does the Evil One give his followers, especially hypocrites. And it is with great glee that he causes them to do such foolish deeds, as he did with the friar. He was treated with mercilessness by the people, who repeatedly called and clamoured for him to be put to death.

The friar expected that he would die a humiliating death, or else endure unbearable torture, but how his suffering came to an end, I am not able to tell you here. Either he was spirited away in secret, or he was slain. But it should be a lesson to one and all to avoid such a fate, and to consider beforehand what will come of it if one drinks one's draughts in secret just as the maiden did, who so often sought out the friar for secret meetings that Nature compelled them to come to intimate terms.

A woman's favours, her fair countenance, will often cause a man to forget the dangers involved, and in reckless company one often plays a foolish game. Nature is strong, the wit is fleeting, in those of more feeble self-discipline, and even wise men may succumb to it. For if a man finds a maiden who is quick to loosen her belt, and she is short-heeled, it takes but a short prayer to get her on her back; for women are most loath to stumble forwards. This is because their hearts are weak. If they hurt their noses or mouths, their hearts do not remain unscathed; if they hurt either knees or elbows, it does nothing to improve their spirits. And because they are so apprehensive, they would much rather fall over backwards, though they suffer a little for it, than that they should risk their lives or endanger their spiritual health; for women are always eager for fulfilment.

6. Concerning Three Companions Who Stole a Side of Bacon

You good people, listen to me: you have never heard such a jest as I shall tell you now. There once were three companions who for fully twenty years had plied the trades of robber, thief and murderer. Upon a day they took from one man – believe me – no less than a hundred gold coins. One of them said that he no longer wished to earn his living in that way. He would cease and desist, for those who continued in their business were in the habit of dying in their boots, or else they knelt down before the hangman, for you often see them swinging from the gallows. Therefore he decided to work for a living.

He soon took leave of the other two and found work with a farmer. The former thief was adept at ploughing the land, sowing grain, threshing, winnowing, cutting and mowing. So well did he perform his duties that at the end of a year the farmer gave him his daughter for a wife, and all his goods upon his death.

One day this man was missing one of his sheep, so he went out in search of it till he found it. Then he saw approaching the estate none other than his two companions, dressed in rags and begging for their bread. The man went to his wife and said: 'Two poor wretches are coming this way, dearest, whom you will sit down to table. See them there approaching in their rags?' Thereupon the man went out of the door and locked himself in the barn.

It wasn't long before the two entered at the doorway. Just how they behaved – what they did, said, or asked – I cannot recall, but before long they knew that their former companion was master of the house. They sat down in front of the hearth. One of them looked up and saw a side of bacon hanging from the ceiling. He began to rub his chin, and said: 'Friend, by St Bavo, I'll have it off before morning comes!' The wife, who had heard this, thought he wanted to have his beard shaved. 'Indeed,' she said in all earnest, 'it is so black and rough, I'll give you tuppence for it now.'

When the meal was done, the two of them left. It was a great plot they forged, that during the night they would steal the bacon, no matter how closely it was guarded. The husband asked his wife what she thought of the two companions. She said: 'One of them looked at the ceiling and was continually rubbing his beard and saying: "It has to come off." I gave the fellow tuppence to that end.'

'Oh, dearest, they're after our bacon. They'll come for it tonight. Quickly now, let's get it down and hide it deep in the straw at the foot of our bed. We'll tell no one about it.'

The two thieves agreed that they would break into the house that night. One of them came for the bacon, but when he couldn't find it, he was angry. The other, who remained below, said: 'Say, do you have it?'

His fellow replied: 'The bacon's gone.'

'No,' said the other, 'is it true?'

The first thief ran boldly to where the wife lay sleeping with the good man, her husband. The thief roused the wife out of her slumber and said to her: 'Tell me, dearest love, did you bring the bacon in here? Where have you put it?'

The wife answered the thief at once, mumbling drowsily: 'You brought it in here last night and put it in the straw at our feet.' The thief said: 'So I did.' The wife was soon fast asleep. The thief threw the bacon over his neck and carrying it thus he made off with it. The husband did not sleep much longer: he started awake. His wife said the following to him: 'This night I had to remind you where you had put the bacon. Your memory's not worth an egg!'

The husband said: 'My bacon is gone! The two scoundrels who ate here yesterday have made off with it; but they'll suffer in hell for it, and I'll steal it back!' The husband got dressed and set out after them. He soon caught up with the one who was carrying his bacon; he toiled under the weight of the burden, while the other thief kept the dogs quiet. The husband spoke to the thief in a muted voice, as if he were his companion: 'That bacon is too heavy for you. Give it to me, dear friend; I'll carry it for a while.'

'Here, take it,' said the thief, 'it's breaking all my limbs.' The husband's spirits improved immediately, and he set off for home carrying the bacon. The thief who had just unloaded the bacon ran ahead. He soon ran into the other thief. The latter thief said: 'May God cause you grief! What have you done with the bacon?'

'What? Didn't I just give you the bacon?' replied his fellow.

'You've done something that will grieve both you and the good St John! I know full well that the good man has plainly stolen his bacon from your very neck.'

'I believe it,' said the other, 'for he's stolen many a load before. But wait here for me. I'll get it back.'

Hastily the thief dropped his trousers, and wound them on his head in the same way as wives are accustomed to wearing their headdresses. He ran back to the husband's house, over dry land and wet, until he stood at the entrance to the farmyard. The husband approached with the bacon and thought it was his wife whom he saw there. He said: 'Help me, dearest.' The thief whispered in reply: 'Give me the bacon, sweet love. Those two thieves should be broken on the wheel!' The husband unloaded the bacon from his own back to the thief's. He thought it was his wife.

The thief made off with it, and the husband entered his house and called out in a loud voice: 'Now at least I've got my bacon back!' His wife, who lay in the bed in the loft, yelled down to him: 'Dearest, is the bacon ours again?' The husband spoke: 'Are you up there? I've never been so miserable! I thought I had given you the bacon, but they've stolen it from my neck, those two wretches! But I won't let them keep it.' The husband ran out after them. He soon found them in a desolate and isolated barn.

Now listen to what the husband did! Just below the roof he stuck his naked arse – no pants at all! – through a hole in the wall. One of the thieves saw it. He said: 'Look, friend! Just before my mother died her face was horribly swollen. Her cheeks were as big as balls, her hair hung down over her eyes, and her nose hung down over her mouth. Look, friend, there she is! Let's get out of here while we can!' The two thieves took to their heels.

The husband grabbed his bacon and carried it home. The two thieves returned, shaken, to the barn. But when they couldn't find the bacon, they realized that the husband had tricked them out of it. They were determined to steal it back, though they should hang for it. They returned to their former companion's house under cover of darkness, and they made a big hole in the back door, under the threshold. But the husband, who by rights was intent upon keeping his bacon, saw them. There he saw one of the thieves stick his arm through the hole. The husband drew his sword and struck off the thief's arm, but the thief didn't utter a sound. Instead he said: 'Friend, come here; the bacon is too heavy for me. I can't budge it, though I have got hold of it. Put your hand in through the hole as well, and the bacon will surely be ours.' The second thief did as his companion asked; the husband struck off a thief's arm for the second time, and that thief cried out:

'Woe is me! I've lost my arm!' The other one said: 'I lost mine here just a minute ago too. It's pennies, ha' pennies, and coppers we'll have to go begging for throughout the land. And if our work here becomes known, we'll swing on the gallows. It would be best to keep silent about it. Let's be gone.'

By this examplum it may be seen that if a man earns his living by evil deeds, he should desist in time, before great harm or sorrow surely befall him because of it. He who does not, will suffer for it. May God protect us from all evil. Amen.

MEDIEVAL LATIN TALES

1. Ruodlieb and Rufus

[The knight Ruodlieb is accompanied on his travels by a malicious and lascivious red-headed man. When night approaches, they ask a shepherd where they might seek lodging in the nearby village. The shepherd recommends the house of a very hospitable and virtuous couple: an elderly lady with a much younger husband. The red-head, however, asks the shepherd if there isn't instead a lodging owned by an old man with a beautiful young wife. The shepherd tells the red-head of an older man whose wife had died and who had recently been re-married to a young foolish wife who despised him and deceived him by having many lovers. The knight Ruodlieb decides to seek lodging with the first virtuous pair.]

Meanwhile, let us not pass over what the red-head was doing. As the knight entered the house where he found such bounty, the red-head asked him why he wished to go to where the old she-ape was. The knight said, 'If you wish to come with me, you'll be glad you did later. I've found what I wanted; what you want you'll get'. The many people who were standing around advised the red-head not to desert his travelling-companion, since he would nowhere be so well looked after. But the red-head, with great disdain, left him quickly. He speeds to the 'cousin' – where he'll ultimately get nothing but his own death. When he arrives, he finds the door of the old man's place closed with an iron grate. The old man is standing in the courtyard with his two sons in front of him. Then the red-head pounds on the gate, shaking it violently, and says, 'Open up as quickly as you can, and don't leave me out here!' When the old man said, 'Look through the iron grate and see who it is,' the boy ran back and said, 'A man is hammering and breaking down the door'. The red-head says, 'Open up! You're making inquiries as if you didn't know me.' At this point the young men were exceedingly angry and irritated. The old man, fearing the violence of the malicious fellow, ordered the door to be opened for him. The red-head, charging very boldly and arrogantly into the courtyard, did not take off his cap and, leaping from his horse and slinging the reins around a post, he drew his sword in an insane manner and took his stand before them like a heathen. At length he says to the old man, smiling, 'If you recognize me, I'm surprised you don't say something.' 'I don't know who you are,' he replied. 'You behave stupidly. I don't know who you are nor what you want from us now.' 'Your wife is a very close cousin of mine; allow me to meet her alone, by myself.' The old man said, 'Do so,' and ordered her to come to him. She came. When the red-head saw her, he burned inwardly to possess her. He smiled with delight at her; she too smiled joyfully at him. 'Your father and mother send you all their best wishes. I'll tell you something else alone, somewhere else.' Then they stand by the gate and lean on the grate. The red-head says: 'First of all, note carefully what I say. Our conversation shouldn't be too long. Don't cry, don't laugh, behave seriously so that the old dog doesn't sniff out our plot. If you follow my plan, you'll soon be free of him. You have here a young man full of all kinds of goodness; not short, not tall but of medium height, with flaxen hair and ruby cheeks: there's no one more beautiful in the world than him. When this young man learned how beautiful you were and what hardships you suffered daily, his heart ached, and sighing he said to me, "If ever you were faithful to me, dear friend, go, and say to that martyred woman that, if she wishes, I will free her and take her from her prison. When tomorrow she hears the slender horn calling, speaking to no one – not even to a trusted girlfriend – she must leave the courtyard and stand in the open street inconspicuously until I come running to her with several companions to carry her off. After that she shall be lady (of the manor) and shall do whatever she pleases." Now ask of this young man what you will, my dear sweet cousin.' As she listened to all this, standing calmly but rejoicing inwardly, she nonetheless said to him, putting on a sad face (for the benefit of her husband), 'I will do all these things willingly, be sure of it, and I give you my word.' Taking her right hand the red-head hesitated no further: 'I want your promise to submit to me three times as a reward.' 'If you can do it ten times, do so,' she said, 'or as many times as you like.' 'I'll make as if to go: you forbid it.'

He returned to the old man and said, 'Allow me to take my leave.' The old man would gladly have done so, if he'd had any authority over his wife. She asks insistently that he not let the red-head go. 'If he wishes, let him stay here: let what is ours be his as well.' She had very quickly led the red-head's horse to the stable; neither she nor the red-head thought further about it – it could eat whatever it could find there in the way of hay. As the red-head enters the house his 'cousin' receives him well. They sit down together and engage in playful conversation; they entwine their fingers and kiss each other. The old man comes in – who was more serious than anybody: a face so hairy that no one could see what expression it wore through its shagginess, only that his nose was hooked and full of thick veins. His two eyes were gloomy like caverns, and a forest of tangled hair overshadowed them; nor could anyone see where the aperture of his mouth was, so greatly did his long and dense beard spread over his face. In any case he ordered his servants to prepare enough to eat. Since the antics of his wife and the red-head displeased him exceedingly, he sat down between them and separated them with his buttocks. For a while they were silent, and were unhappy that someone was sitting between them. They exchanged a good many jokes by leaning around him. When he became disgusted with it, he ordered the table to be covered and said to his wife: 'That's enough. Now stop, for the sake of decency. A woman ought not to be so flirtatious, nor a man either. And with her husband present it's not proper for her to flirt with another man.' Saying this he got up, as if to go to the privy, but he peeked back at the scene through a hole in the wall. Alas, the red-head jumped into the old man's chair itself: one hand fondled her breasts, the other her thighs – which she concealed by spreading a fur over them. All this the old man watched like a thief. When he goes back in, the red-head doesn't withdraw, for she won't allow it. And then, sitting very indignantly in the guest's seat, he repeatedly urges his wife to have the dinner brought. She, making derisive gestures at him, jokingly delays the dinner. He asks the servants whether dinner is ready. They say: 'You can eat as soon as you wish.' 'Now, madam,' he says, 'let us eat and go to bed. It's time too for your dear friend to rest. You've tired him enough; now let him rest.'

[This fragment of the *Ruodlieb* breaks off here. The subsequent fragment (VIII) pictures a priest giving the last rites to the dying old man; following this the wife and the red-head are arraigned before the village judge. Apparently, then, the red-head and the wife had been discovered during the clandestine meeting (had the neglected horse awakened the old man by its neighing?), with the result that the old man was mortally wounded by the red-head. Eventually the red-head is hanged and the woman reprieved on the condition that she undergo perpetual penance.]

2. Cambridge Songs

(a) The Snow-Child (§ 14)

Pay attention, everyone, to an amusing story, and hear how a woman deceived a Swabian, and he her. A Swabian from the town of Konstanz, transporting his merchandise in ships across the seas, left his exceedingly lascivious wife at home.

Scarcely have his oars touched the gloomy water when suddenly a storm blows up: the sea rages, the winds battle, the waves rise high; after a long time the south wind deposited the wandering exile on a faraway shore. In the meantime, his wife is not idle at home: mime-players arrived, and other young men followed, whom the wife – forgetful of her distant husband – joyfully received. Becoming pregnant on a subsequent night, she produced an illegitimate son on the proper day.

After two years had passed, the aforementioned 'exile' returns. His faithless wife runs to meet him, dragging the little boy with her. After they exchange kisses the husband says to her, 'Where might you have gotten this child? Tell me, or I'll kill you.' But she, fearing her husband, covers everything with a lie: 'My . . .', at length she says, 'my husband, once upon a time in the Alps I was very thirsty and quenched my thirst with snow. Because of that I became pregnant and, alas, I produced this boy with painful labour.'

After this five years or more passed, and the wandering merchant took to his oars again; he rebuilt his shattered ship, bound up the sails, and took the snow-child with him. They crossed the sea. He produced the boy, and for a small consideration sold him to a merchant and received a hundred pounds, and having sold the boy he returned home rich.

Entering his house he said to his wife: 'Console yourself, my wife, console yourself, my dear one; I have lost your son whom even you yourself didn't love more than I. A storm arose, and furious winds drove us aground, exhausted, on sandy shallows. The sun scorched us all fiercely and he, born of the snow, melted.'

Thus the Swabian deceived his faithless wife; thus deception overcame deception. For the sun rightly melted him whom the snow had engendered.

(b)   Alfrad and her Ass (§ 20)[1]

There's a place called Homburg in which Alfrad pastured her strong and faithful ass. When it wanted to go into a large field, the ass saw a greedy wolf running towards it; it hid its head and displayed its tail. The wolf ran up and bit its tail. The ass kicked up its two hind legs and fought a long war with the wolf. When it felt its strength failing it let out a mighty howl, and calling its mistress, died. Hearing the great lamentation of her ass Alfrad ran out: 'Sisters,' she said, 'come quickly, help me! I sent my beloved ass out to pasture. I hear its mighty wail. I think that it's fighting with a savage wolf!' The shouting of the sisters reached as far as the cloister; crowds of men and women gathered in order to catch the blood-thirsty wolf. And Adela, Alfrad's sister, looking for Rikila, found Agatha: they went to lay low the mighty enemy. But the wolf, having broken the ribs of the ass, gulped down

---

1   This curious little story would seem to be a mock-serious account of a girl's loss of her virginity (represented by the ass), with the wolf being her obdurate lover and so on. Her girlfriends console her with the prospect of more enjoyable encounters to come (see discussion by Peter Dronke in *Romanische Forschungen* 85 (1973), 285–7). The ambiguity of the story can partly be sustained in English by translating *asina* as 'ass' rather than as 'donkey', the customary translation.

148

the river of blood and all the flesh, and went into the woods. Seeing this, all the sisters tore out their hair and beat their breasts, lamenting the innocent death of the ass. It turned out that it was carrying a small foal: Alfrad wept for the foal most of all; she'd hoped that the offspring would have grown to maturity. Gentle Adela and sweet Fritherun had both come in order to fortify Alfrad's spirit and to cure her of her misery: 'Dear sister, abandon your sad complaints. The wolf doesn't care for your weeping. The Lord will give you another ass.'

(c) The Parson and the Wolf (§ 35)

Let those who have the inclination for a joke and funny song listen to this amusing story; it's true, not fictitious.

There was a country parson of declining years who loved his flocks of sheep – it's common behaviour among rustics. Everything was as he liked it, if it hadn't been for the nearby forest, a breeding ground of wolves. The wolves diminish the number of sheep one by one, turning odd numbers into even, and even into odd. The parson, lamenting this loss of revenue, sought revenge through craftiness, since he mistrusted his strength. He dug a rather large pit, and put a lamb in it; and so the pit wouldn't be discovered by the enemy, he covered it over with branches. There is nothing granted to human kind more useful than its wit! A wolf, while prowling around at night, seduced by the hope of booty, fell into the pit.

In the morning the priest ran to the pit and rejoiced to have overcome the enemy in this manner. He poked his staff into the pit and threatened the wolf's eye. 'Now,' he said, 'you foul beast, I'll pay you back what I owe you. Either this staff will break, or your eye will burst.' Having said this, he jabbed at the wolf. But the deed failed to match the word: for the wolf, his eye intact, held the stick in his jaws. But while the wretched old man was regaining his balance, the edge of the pit gave way, he tumbled down, and ended up in the wolf's company. Here stands the wolf, here the priest: both afraid, but to a different degree, for – if I may hazard a guess – the wolf's position was more secure.

The parson mutters prayers to himself, and regurgitates seven psalms, and frequently returns to 'Lord, have mercy upon me!' 'For this piece of bad luck,' he said, 'comes about through my people's wishes, whose souls I have neglected, whose tithes I have consumed.' For the benefit of the deceased he chanted 'Placebo Domini', and for the prayers of the living he chanted the entire psalter. After the completion of the psalter, the timidity of the priest and the sagacity of the wolf together provided a common benefit. For when the parson, bent over in prayer, would have finished the 'Pater Noster' and would have shouted to the Lord 'deliver us from evil', the wolf jumped onto his back and with a bound leapt free of the pit – and so used as a ladder him by whose art he had been captured.

But the parson, exceedingly happy, chants 'Laudate Dominum' and promises that he will henceforth pray for his people. His neighbours look for him and when they find him he is taken out of the pit. But he never afterwards prayed more devoutly nor with greater faith.

(d) Little Abbot John (§ 42)

In the lives of the ancient Church Fathers I read a certain amusing story, very appropriate as an example, which I reproduce here for you in rhythmic verse.

Abbot John, small in stature but not in virtue, said to his elder who was with him in the wilderness: 'I wish to live serenely like an angel, and not to use clothing or food which has been produced by manual labour.' The elder said, 'I warn you, brother, not to be too hasty to begin something which it might be better afterwards not to have begun.' But the younger said: 'Who doesn't strive doesn't fall, but neither does he conquer.' And, naked, he went into the heart of the wilderness. He endured scarcely seven days on a grassy diet, and on the eighth day hunger compelled him to return to his companion. It was late, and with the door locked the elder was sitting securely in his little cell when the younger with a feeble voice called, 'Brother, open up! John, in need of help, sits outside these familiar doors. Let not your clemency reject him whom necessity has driven back.' The elder replied from within: 'John was made an angel; he's contemplating the turning of the heavens; he's no longer concerned with men.'

John sleeps outside and spends a miserable night, and does this extra penance unintentionally. Next morning he is received and is blistered with a tirade; but, intent upon a small crust of bread, he endures it all patiently. Warmed again to life he gives thanks to the Lord and to his friend; next he attempts to wield a hoe with his tired arms. Chastized by hardship for his high-flown ideas, since he could not be an angel, he has learned to be a good man.

3. Pamphilus

Characters: *Pamphilus, Galatea, An Old Woman*

[Pamphilus enters complaining of a deep and painful wound: he is in love. His only hope is Venus, whom he invokes. Venus appears and Pamphilus explains his plight: he is in love with a young lady, Galatea, who is his next-door neighbour. Unfortunately, Galatea is of more noble birth and of a richer family than Pamphilus. Pamphilus has kept his love hidden even from Galatea, but he is in doubt and despair. Venus replies in a sententious (and Ovidian) speech, telling Pamphilus to be resolute: diligent effort will overcome anything; don't be afraid to tell the lady of your love; if you don't succeed at first, try and try again; conceal your poverty at any cost; frequent the lady's company; if the occasion presents itself, take her by force – she'd rather lose her virginity that way than by saying 'Take me if you wish.' Venus concludes by urging Pamphilus to get at it: if he applies himself eagerly, he will succeed.]

Pamphilus: Someone in good health easily offers consolation to someone who is ill, but the sick person doesn't feel any less the presence of his illness. My anguish is not alleviated by the counsel of Venus; love still reigns in my sad heart. Previously all hope of assistance was placed in Venus: my hope is gone but the anguish remains. Poor wretch! – I won't get out of it: the ship's pilot abandons me on the high seas. I seek the port, but I can't find it. But what shall I do now? My spirit now looks to the young lady herself: it's only fitting that at last I go to speak to her.

(*Galatea appears*) My God, how beautiful she is! She comes with her hair uncovered! What an opportunity it would be to speak to her now! But suddenly great anxieties come upon me; I'm no longer in possession of my wits, nor can I speak; I'm powerless; my hands and feet tremble. It's no proper appearance for one so thunderstruck! In my mind I've prepared several things to say to her, but my fear has driven out what I wanted to say. I'm not the man I was. I can scarcely recognize myself. My voice doesn't come forth properly . . . Nonetheless I'll speak.

(*To Galatea*) My cousin in the other town has asked me to send you a thousand greetings and to discharge her business. She knows you only by name and by what people say, but if there's a chance, she wishes to meet you. My parents wanted to keep me there: the whole town's full of their choices; they promised me a girl in marriage with a great dowry – but I don't care to speak further about that right now. I disregarded all these plans: you alone pleased me. For you I'd reject everything else in the world.

Galatea: We converse by bantering. That's often the way the young speak. A few words in jest won't start any wars!

Pamphilus: But now let us tell the secrets of our hearts in turn. But let no one else beside us know what we say! Let's give our word on it, and then I'll tell you. I started it first, therefore I'll speak first. We ought now to agree to tell the truth.
No woman in the world is more pleasing to me than you. For three years I've loved you, but I never dared to tell you of my wishes. But wisdom doesn't spend a long time speaking to the deaf, and it's not fitting that I speak too long to you in vain. I love you constantly. But I don't now want to say anything more to you until you tell me what pleases you.

Galatea: In this way many young men tempt many young ladies with many temptations, and clever love deceives many young ladies. You have taken measures to infatuate me with your speech and subtlety, but it's not seemly for me to be deceived by your wit. Look for some other young ladies who are suitable to your licentious manners, ladies whom your false faith and deceit will infatuate.

Pamphilus: How often the sins of evil men confound the just! Someone else's sin – not my own – is at fault here. But yet let your grace hear me kindly, and let me say a few words to you my lady. Accordingly, I swear by the God of Heaven and also by the divinities of the earth: I do not say these things to you in deceit or cunning. In this world there is no other woman so pleasing to me as you; my heart and soul look on no other so lovingly. But I speak in vain; your youthful soul and age don't yet know what is harmful from what is beneficial, even though youth is sharper than old age. For although the aged see a good deal, youth sees much more. But even though you're young, see if you can recognize what I am, what is my station and what the nature of my love. Prudence learns through the experience of many things; experience and theory teach what every man knows. I pray you, grant me leave to come and go, to talk with you and be together. We can't learn our innermost feelings except through conversation. You yourself can now say what pleases you.

Galatea: I shall not forbid you nor anyone else to come and go and to speak with me: each way-farer has all roads open to him. It's fitting, and etiquette requires, that response be given to one who seeks it, and that every young lady acknowledge whomever she sees. It's enough that I grant to you – or to anyone else – that you come to see me: thus is my honour safe. A young lady should listen and reply, yet it's fitting that she do this moderately. If you've spoken to me in jesting words, I'll reply in jest; but I won't allow it if perhaps these words are harmful to me. You ask that we get together: I won't allow us to be together alone. It's not decent for us to be together in isolation. For isolated places are harmful: gossip is born that way. I'll speak more confidently to you if other people are watching us.

Pamphilus: You've bestowed on me not small but mighty bounties! For mere permission to speak with you is enough for me. For these benefits I can't thank you enough: this bounty cannot be matched by mere words. But perhaps some time and occasion will arise when your friend might be able to show you what sort of lover he is. Don't be displeased – I don't dare say it – yet I would ask of you a few small favours: that we be able to exchange embraces, kisses, caresses, if the opportunity arose.

Galatea: Although embraces nourish illicit love, and kisses undo their mistress, I'll only allow this if you do nothing further. For I wouldn't grant such favours to anyone else but you.

But both my parents are now coming back from the temple; I ought to be back home so I don't get scolded. Plenty of times will come when we two may speak together. Meanwhile, let each of us think of the other. (*Galatea departs.*)

Pamphilus: There isn't and never was anyone in the world happier than me! My anchor is fixed in her shore! Suddenly God and Fortuna have blessed me, for I who was formerly a pauper return home rich. It was superfluous of her to ask that I think of her – even pain wouldn't drive her from my heart! She doesn't quite yet feel at one with me – she doesn't know how much I desire her. I'm as before; but let her think of me by all means.

I've accomplished a good deal, but further concerns urge me on, about which I myself don't know what to do. If I pursue her diligently, and meet her frequently, talking and joking, garrulous gossip will put obstacles in our course. If no deeper involvement confirms our affair, perhaps our love – not yet really stable – will pass. All love grows through frequent association and decreases without it; all unfed love grows thin and withers. The fire always grows so long as the wood is added; take the wood from the hearth and straightway the fire is out. Bothered by such cares and dangers I'm distracted in I don't know how many ways! I see no prosperity for myself in this affair. My mind hasn't worked out a safe plan. Fortune frequently opposes the deeds of men and allows no opportunity for the success of their undertakings. Thus fortune harms many, yet again she blesses many others: under such terms man lives in this world. God and our own hard work provide and grant all things to us; no work in the world progresses without God's help. Let God therefore be custodian and guide of my work; let Him govern all my affairs and undertakings.

My go-between won't be my brother nor my cousin, for one doesn't thereby easily find a guarantee of trust. A cousin doesn't know how to keep faith and loyalty with his cousin, nor brother with brother, if once the fury of love comes upon them. A trifle can cause great injury; the wise man avoids injury; therefore it's proper for me to choose another route. Near here lives a crafty and ingenious old lady – she's a suitable enough minister for the arts of Venus. I'll leave my troubles and direct my steps to her, and shall explain to her my situation. *(Pamphilus goes to the Old Woman)*

Pamphilus: The excellence of your reputation and the renown of your integrity have brought me to you for the purpose of seeking advice. May your mercy and grace hear what I say, and may no one else know of it without my assent. I love my neighbour, Galatea, whom you know. She says that she loves me, if I'm not mistaken. I'm not speaking as I would, for I'm avoiding a thousand dangers; I anxiously fear everything in the world. Rumour grows from the merest trifle, but does not quickly fall silent; even though it tells lies it nonetheless increases in its progress. Trifles injure those who are miserable; a thousand misfortunes attend the miserable; the outcome of their situation and of all their efforts remains in doubt. You see my troubles: let your counsel deal with them one at a time. I ask that you conceal our secret affair by being a go-between.

The Old Woman: Another man loves her whom you love, and what you seek this other man seeks as well. Nonetheless he hasn't my assent. He is exceedingly upright and worthy of an honourable wife, but he displeased me by the gift he offered me. He promised me some old clothes together with an overcoat! But his vile gift deprived him of my assistance. If it's given at the appropriate time, a gift bestows and confers benefits; it bypasses the law with its power. Without my help, I do believe, no one shall have the young lady you seek, for she is thoroughly subject to my authority. What is more, I'm her guide and confidante in this affair, and she does everything in accordance with my advice. I shall not myself speak any longer with you; I've another pressing concern. Let each of us make his own way and look after himself.

Pamphilus: For me this business is all-important; no other concern is pressing for me. If you could give me Galatea, you'd have excelled everything. Often it's worthwhile to pay for outside help so that the help thus hired may obtain the goal. In no way shall your efforts be in vain, believe me, if you provide me with those things I now lack, I ask only this: name your price, and I'll give you whatever you ask.

The Old Woman: Those who are needy want and seek many things; I'm ashamed to say how many things I need. When I was in the flower of youth I had much wealth, but the abundance decreased, and now I'm in need of many things. My age and my weakened condition have thoroughly despoiled me; my wit and my efforts confer no benefits on me. If you feel that my assistance can be to your avail, I ask that your house henceforth be at my disposal.

Pamphilus: From now on my house and all my estate shall be at your disposal. Let all my wealth be at your command! I am delighted that an agreement now binds us, and the pledge of faith shall exist between us. Therefore I pray that your wits and your efforts be awake and attentive to the business as they will. Let your discretion look at once to the beginning and outcome of the affair: the outcome brings with it either disgrace or honour. Look too to the beginning and also to the end of your discourse so that you may better be able to deliver words which you have thought out beforehand. (*Pamphilus departs*)

The Old Woman (speaking so that Galatea can overhear her): In this town there is an extremely attractive young man; he grows excellent in all his behaviour. There was none kinder nor sweeter in my time; he has taken my poverty upon himself. Pamphilus excels all his contemporaries in every form of goodness and surpasses all his companions in integrity. He behaves fool-ishly with the fools, and is as gentle as a lamb with someone gentle. As a wise man he properly resists foolishness. Nor is there in this town another youth of such probity. No gluttony devours the riches he acquires. He is exceedingly upright, because he's of a good family: sweet apples fall from a sweet apple-tree. Nature frequently distinguishes its offspring by charac-teristic marks; the son is usually like the father.
But what's this I see? – Galatea standing at the door! Perhaps she will have heard what I said. I thought there was no one here, Galatea, but nonetheless the things I said were quite true. Pamphilus certainly excels all others in this town. He disposes of his affairs in an excellent manner. His renown and praise and esteem are always growing, and no one – rightly – envies him. He's exceedingly rich but yet not proud of the fact: his wealth carries no disgrace with it. I wish, Galatea, that he were your husband! You'd wish so too, if only you knew the situation well. I've revealed my wish, but Pamphilus hasn't asked me to do so. My better judgment decrees that you two should be together. The kin, the excellence and the beauty of you both persuade me that you are two of a kind. But now we're passing leisure time with empty words. A small concern nevertheless provokes a larger; from the smallest spark a great fire is born; a small beginning generates great offspring. I was mentally aware of the beginning of this discussion, and I began to speak after my own inclination. But if your heart and soul are inclined to these things, if it pleases or rather displeases you to speak at this point, speak, I pray you. What you shall say, I shall myself keep quiet about, if you wish me to

conceal it; or if you wish me to pass it on, I shall. Tell me. Don't hesitate. Put aside your silly shame: shame like this comes from boorishness alone.

Galatea: Not my boorishness nor any foolish shame stands in my way. But I wonder from whence this talk of yours comes. I wonder now whether it was chance or Pamphilus which brought you to it, and whether your discourse is seeking a reward?

The Old Woman: The crimes committed by evil men always confound the deeds of good men; often a man pays a penalty which he doesn't deserve. Although I'm very poor, I'm not seeking any payment in this way, for my poverty is sufficient for me. As I said in the first place, this business is the product of my mind. No one else knows of it, there's no accomplice. It can be enough if you two wish to be together; both of you can permit this without shame. He is noble indeed, and you are no less noble yourself; both of your families are well enough known to me. He is more attractive than his companions; you are more beautiful than your friends. Beauty agrees pleasantly with beauty. The equal wealth and youth of each of you approves of it, and even if gossip knew of it, it would likewise approve. When you are equals, you can duly be united. There's nothing lacking between you, except perhaps love.

Galatea: What you say to me now ought to be said to the close relatives by whose assent I hope to obtain a husband. Speak to them first – either you or this Pamphilus. The affair will be more satisfying if it meets with their approval.

The Old Woman: It's only right that your marriage take place with the consent of your parents; but in the meantime let the fire of your love fight on its behalf. Subtle Venus superintends the hearts of the young. Whoever applies himself to this end gains her support. She arouses enthusiasm, gives to those who are generous, disparages those who are greedy, puts sadness to flight and brings on happiness. No one could say how much the skill of Venus can avail; unless you obey her, you'll always be a boor.

Galatea: In following the discipline of Venus a young lady quickly loses her reputation: that fiery fury knows no moderation. The violent arrows of Cupid do not make light wounds, and a girl can unfortunately be seduced by them. Often gossip accuses undeserving girls; greedy envy doesn't stop gnawing at all things. I would agree to what you ask, if I didn't fear words of gossip which in such an affair most quickly take the limelight.

The Old Woman: In matters like this infamy is far and away greater than truth; but truth comes to the fore, and rumour itself falls away. I shall remove the murmurs, rumours and cares that you fear, and cover up you and your frolicking by my craftiness. For I know the behaviour of Venus and her arts; the affair shall be safe in my management.

Galatea: Tell me what to say when I see him. If you tell me beforehand I'll speak more securely. I hesitate to confess my wishes and my secrets to you, for deceit sets its traps everywhere. But yet I shall find out the quality of your speech and loyalty, and where your finesse is leading me. Pamphilus recently sought my love himself; a true friendship joined us together. But keep this thoroughly hidden: reveal it, please, to him alone. Yet don't begin speaking to him in this vein: tempt him first with great temptation. Perhaps he himself will say to you what I have said. Now leave; and, I pray, do all this cautiously, and tell me tomorrow everything he says. (*Galatea departs*)

The Old Woman (to Pamphilus): Many times the hopes and undertakings of men are frustrated. Our affair isn't coming along as we wish, Pamphilus. I've been called to your assistance much too late; my craft and effort can't be of any use to you. As report has it, preparations are underway for Galatea's wedding. I'm astonished at the decorations with which she's preparing her house. There are a hundred reasons why I suspect this is so, but yet both parents have concealed it all thoroughly. Please accept what I say to you with equanimity. Dismiss what cannot be; seek what can be.

Pamphilus: Alas! My strength and life are fled! Neither my wits nor my tongue are any use to me. Poor me! There's no force in my limbs and they refuse to do what they're supposed to. My hope has killed me. Through hope Venus clung to my bones. My hope departs, but the fire's still there. My ship's sails see no port anywhere, nor can my anchor feel the harbour floor. My cares don't know where to seek a remedy: Galatea alone has the power to cure me – she's the cause of my death and the cause of my salvation! If I can't have her, then it's better to die!

The Old Woman: Fool! Why are you raving? Why does empty anguish propel you? Your moaning won't get you anything. Therefore let moderation and prudence temper your weeping. Wipe away your tears. Look to what you can do. A mighty need takes hold of great souls and very often this need makes a man clever. The eager intelligence of a man overcomes great risks, and perhaps effort, intelligence and attention will be helpful here.

Pamphilus: Alas, what effort could overcome this disaster? All my hope perishes; the hour of the wedding approaches. As long as her husband's alive she won't marry me: it's a sin to violate a legitimate marriage. All my efforts are straightway reduced to nil. My desire has lost its store of ingenuity. No day and no night will give me any peace and quiet: an unfulfilled love will always gnaw at me.

157

The Old Woman: Very often a mighty grief falls away in the hour of need; a mighty wind dies down bringing small rain showers. Serene weather is more pleasant after long rainstorms, and health itself is more pleasant after a depressing illness. You may now breathe again – away with your grief, weeping and anger. Great joys follow right behind your sadness. Your Galatea will do what we wish: she will give herself utterly to our commands.

Pamphilus: As the loving care of mothers tempts crying children with vain promises so that they'll be quiet, so perhaps you are feeding me with false consolation so that my grief will leave my heart?

The Old Woman: The bird just freed from the talons of the ferocious falcon is hesitant and thinks it still sees the falcon everywhere. There's no reason for me to lie to you now; rather you will find all the things I have said to be true.

Pamphilus: If you're telling me the truth, and if she told the truth, then all anguish leaves my heart! But the end does not always follow on from the beginning; chance often impedes an operation that is underway.

The Old Woman: No man's mind knows the course of the Fates; it is the province of God alone to know the future. Yet it's harmful to despair; persistent effort fulfils one's prayers. Determination and concentration often accomplish great deeds. All hope and effort are subject to an ambiguous outcome, yet hope itself grows from a good beginning.

Pamphilus: Can't you tell if she loves me or not? Love can scarcely conceal the innermost recesses of the heart.

The Old Woman: When I'm speaking her whole heart and soul hang on what I say; she listens joyously to every word. She puts her arms around my neck and asks me to tell her what you have said. And when the course of the conversation turns on your name, she becomes enraptured at the mere mention of your name. As she savours all my words she grows pale or blushes frequently, and if I become weary and fall silent she entreats me to keep talking. By these and other means we recognize her love: nor does she deny to me that she is in love with you.

Pamphilus: Now my hope feels that success is near as a result of your efforts, and my exultation grows through your assistance. Persistent labour sometimes brings doubtful projects to completion, whereas inert laziness puts great benefits out of reach. Work to advance what you've begun as much as you can; let no slack delay put off your work.

The Old Woman: Your wishes are being fulfilled, I think, by me; but what you promised me remains in doubt. Often one's intention is contrary to one's speech, nor do we always follow up all we say by deeds. Ineffectual promises deceive labours that have been purchased. When you're happy, perhaps you'll give me nothing?

Pamphilus: It's a mighty crime if the rich deceive the needy, and if I deceive you, there's no honour in it for me. My intentions have deceived neither you nor anyone else at any time. My reputation, if you ask, is without blemish. And my loyalty is consistently faithful to my word: it will make safe for you everything you now doubt.

The Old Woman: The humble people fear that they will be overwhelmed by the ingenuity of the powerful. Laws give way where a poor man is involved, and everywhere loyalty is despoiled of its pristine radiance, for it is covered up by the innumerable arts of sin. No private fortune can resist the Fates. The sea often gives rise to fears even though it isn't dangerous. What bounties you have promised me I consign to fortune; but what gifts I've promised you, you'll get.

It's convenient for me to go now to ask the young lady if she agrees to come here to speak with you alone. If my clever management gets you both together, if there's a chance, I pray you, be a man. The heart and soul of a lover is always capricious. Perhaps a small while longer will get you what you want. *(Pamphilus departs)*

A great fire can't conceal its light, nor can Venus conceal her wishes. The whole range of your feelings is laid open to me. When I mull them over in my mind, I can scarcely contain my tears. For I recognize now that you're both loving without discretion: the business itself announces its foolishness. A pallid face makes clear a secret love: without any intention on your part your skin has become languid.

(To Galatea): That poor Pamphilus! He's miserable around the clock! What obstinacy he's discovered in you! He toils quite foolishly by day and night, but the hard field returns no crop. Who – except someone mentally deficient – would plant his seeds in the sand? Labour is usually more pleasant when it offers some reward. It's firstly your beauty and secondly your words that have undone him. Bitter love wounds him with those two weapons. You have not been to him the medicine you promised to be, and his grief was more profound than he would have hoped. Now his wound lacks a remedy; his grief is continual and excessive. And you, although you're silent, are consumed by the same fire. A wound that is not revealed often results in a foul death; a love that is kept hidden usually oppresses us. Therefore, pay attention to your wishes with an alert mind, and let your words explain to me your heart's desire.

Galatea: Impudent Venus frequently overwhelms me with her fiery weapons, for she does me violence in always urging me to love. On the other hand shame and fear urge me to be modest. Driven by these opposite impulses, I don't know what to do!

The Old Woman: Keep away from this sort of fear! There's no cause for this fear – in this affair there'll be no traitor. That Pamphilus might be yours is the only thing he desires; all his care and trouble strive to this end. He has told me in a thousand ways of his wretched state of mind, the fire of his love, and weeping he said to me the following grave words: 'Galatea is my sorrow and the medicine for my sorrow. She alone can give me my wound and also its cure!' Compassion drove me to weep at his tears, and yet I was silently rejoicing in my heart. I saw that all things were going as I myself wished, and I felt that you two were burning with an equal flame. But flame can also cause injury: I pray you, spare yourselves, and let love join you two together through my management.

Galatea: I desire what you request, but this would be dearer to me still if both my parents would consent to it. It's not seemly for it to take place through our boldness alone. And even if we wished it devoutly there'd be no opportunity for it. For my mother who is my custodian is always with me: I'm kept at home all day and all night.

The Old Woman: Ingenious love opens locked doors; ingenious love overcomes whatever is in its way. Put away your empty fears, amend your childish worries: sweet love asks that you come with me!

Galatea: You are now made confidante to the secrets of my heart, and you are the better part of my counsel. I ask that you give me beneficial advice, and that you not be ashamed for having advised me. It's a shame and outrage to seduce young girls by deceit: this advice could bring either honour or great infamy.

The Old Woman: I'm not ashamed, and I won't cover my head in the face of chattering gossip; nor shall my behaviour disguise the fact that I've been your adviser. For whosoever would now wish to disagree with me, let him advance whatever arguments could support his opposition. Let him come with all his might to do battle with me; let him either be silent if he's beaten, or depart quickly with his victory. How quickly would reason – supporting me – restrain him! With reason on my side he could say nothing to me! Pamphilus is good, handsome, his family distinguished, his wealth great. Sweet love shall be my contribution to the advice! Let chattering gossip be silent, let iniquitous murmur be silent. This affair has its own way, and that way is without shame.

Galatea: O God! How greatly the soul of a lover is perturbed, whom fear and earnest love drive now here, now there! These two discords torment him day and night: love says yes, fear says no. The lover doesn't know what to do; he wanders always along the by-roads and feeds the wound of his love by his wanderings. Love conquers me, even though up till now I've fought with him: the more I struggle, the more forcibly love compels me! So long afflicted, and exhausted with vain labour, it's sad to say, but I'd rather die than live like this.

The Old Woman: As great fires surge up under their own impulse, and as battle and fury increase through continuous struggle, so Venus herself rises against those who struggle against her, and keeps conflict alive by means of her strife. For that reason you can't extinguish your flames by your continuing struggle, but if you make peace the flame will be more gentle. Do what Venus commands, so long as you're a soldier in her army, in order that your struggle and effort won't be to your loss. By beginning rashly you unfortunately lose the joys of life, and a harmful delusion will have you in its spell for the rest of your days. You see with your mind's eye only the face of your absent lover; no less does he himself see only your face day and night; each of you has only the other's face in his eyes. If you delay, this affair will lead to death for you both. But I suspect you care to dismiss what you love lightly? A cruel death will be the outcome of such a rupture!

Spare your youth. Embrace the joys of life. It's proper for joyous hearts to feed on joyous delights. And now come along by yourself to my house for a little while: there'll be nuts and apples for you at my place. My little garden would scarcely ever be without fruit of some sort; you can enjoy whatever of it you like. (*They go to the Old Woman's house*)

But now someone is violently hammering on the door. It was a man . . .? Or else the wind. But I think it was a man. It *is* a man! He's looking at us through that crack! It's Pamphilus! I recognize his face! He cleverly draws back the bolt bit by bit . . . He comes in to us . . . Why do I stop talking? Why did you furiously hammer on my door, Pamphilus? You've destroyed the lock which I bought from my landlady. What do you want? Have you come to us as someone's messenger? If you've anything to say, say it quickly and then go!

Pamphilus: O Galatea, above all things the cause of my salvation! Kiss me a thousand times after such long delays! Not even after such kisses will my thirsting ardour be quenched, but it grows more bitter with these pleasant delights. Now I enclose all my joys within my arms! Now I embrace my sweet and beloved burden! A happy fate has directed my footsteps here, for in this very place is that which I love most!

The Old Woman: My neighbour's calling me. I'll go and speak with her and then I'll be back: I'm extremely worried that she may come here just now. (*To the neighbour:*) Why are you shouting? I'm coming right away. I'm locking my door behind me as I come, because there's no one here except the house itself. I'm extremely busy. Tell me quickly what you want: I haven't got all day to spend with you.

Pamphilus: Now delicious love and flowering youth, and the right situation, all urge us, Galatea, to feed our hearts with pleasure. Now lascivious Venus compels us to her joys and urges us now to indulge in her practices. Why do I delay? Whose divine guidance do I need? I pray that you allow me to do as I wish!

Galatea: Pamphilus! Take away your hands! You're trying in vain! . . . This effort's for nothing . . . What you wish can't be. Pamphilus, hands off! Now you're seriously offending your lover! The old woman'll soon be back! Hands off, Pamphilus! Alas, what little strength women have! How easily you overcome both my hands, Pamphilus! You're hurting my breasts with your chest! Why do you handle me like this? It's a sin and an outrage! Stop! I'll call out! What are you doing? It's nasty to undress me like this! Woe is me, when will that deceitful woman come back? Get up! Please!! The neighbour'll hear our struggles! The old woman did a foul deed in entrusting me to you! I'll never be caught here again with her, and she'll never again deceive me as she did now! You'll be the victor in this fight – although I struggled! – but all love between us is now broken off!

Pamphilus: Now it's time for both of us to relax a little while; having finished the course, our race-horse takes a breather. Why do you avert your glance from your beloved? And why are you weeping, covering your face with tears? I'm entirely guilty: now mete out some punishment; and let your punishment be greater than my rewards. Here I am ready to endure whatever blows you wish to administer. Nevertheless it wasn't my fault that I sinned in this way. If you wish, let's now come to an equitable judgment: either I'm innocent, or else guilty by demonstration. Your burning eyes, radiant skin, noble face, your sweet chatter, your embraces, the delightful kisses, the playfulness – these were the source of my crime, these gave it its start. Love was the instigator of this affair. Through these things my madness swelled up, the insanity of sexual desire burned and urged me on to my nefarious deed. This foul error subverted my senses, as a result of which my better sentiments were deaf to your entreaties. Because of these things I stand accused; you would more justly be guilty. You were the fountainhead and the material cause of the wrongdoing!
It's not proper for there to be such a serious anger between lovers. If it comes by chance, at least let it be brief. A lover must always tolerate what pleases her lover. Bear patiently the burden of our common guilt. When the old woman comes back, put away your sad expression so that she won't think – because of your tears – that we've sinned.

The Old Woman: That woman kept me in front of my door with empty chatter. She could beat Cicero with her eloquence! Why, Galatea, is your face disfigured with weeping? What are you trying to tell me? Where does this complexion come from? What did Pamphilus do with you while I was away? I beg you, Galatea, tell me everything in its proper order.

Galatea: Is it decent for you to ask what befell me as if you didn't know, although the deed was done through your connivance? The tree is recognized by its fruit: you yourself are recognizable by your deeds. It wasn't nice to arrange to give me apples and nuts while your Pamphilus himself was right outside the doors! So there'd be an opportunity for it, your neighbour called you, in order that I'd be deprived of my virginity! O, what important business was it that made you dawdle outside? How well your cleverness covers up your tricks! Craft and deception have run their course: see how the fleeing hare has fallen into the trap!

The Old Woman: I'm unjustly accused! Far be it from me to commit such a crime! I'll account for myself satisfactorily in whatever way you wish. The accusation of this crime squares poorly with my old age, nor is my cunning desirous of such an evil deed. If in some way an argument arose between you from your pleasantries, how can I – who was absent – be at fault? Let be whatever may be: your argument, which your foolish love produced, has nothing to do with me! Nevertheless, Pamphilus, tell me one by one the things that happened without my knowledge, so that the origin of the wrongdoing won't be hidden from me.

Pamphilus: I am the accused for the smallest of offences, if you would know things from the start, and the anger against me is more severe than I deserve. But lovers ought always to conceal their secrets. For it would be a disgrace to have spoken of it, when there's no disgrace involved. It's convenient for you to mitigate our quarrels; for the rest it's better kept between us two.

Galatea: Pamphilus, tell her what happened to us – as if she didn't know nor realized how it came about. She, who advised you throughout, asks *you* as if she were unaware – so that it will appear that she didn't do anything to harm me! *(To the Old Woman:)* You led me down many garden paths with your innumerable tricks, but nevertheless your trickery is revealed through the evidence. Thus the fish already caught recognizes the curved hook; thus the captured bird sees the fowler's trap.
But what will I do now? Shall I flee a captive through the world? Both my parents will rightly close the doors of their house to me. I'll travel here and there through the whole world, with my eyes wide open – yet no joyful hope comes to miserable me!

163

The Old Woman: It's not right for a wise person to grieve seriously, since sorrow brings its master no reward. Retain in moderation what can't be restored by craft, what an immoderate love unfortunately drove you to. Moderation and prudence are fitting in our circumstances, and it's only decent that we seek what counsel is to be followed. Discord gnaws horribly the hearts of lovers, and nourishes the lovers' blind wounds in its wars. Grant each other a suitable peace which will foster your love: let her be your wife, let him be your husband! Each of you is now in possession of what he hoped for through my assistance; both are happy because of me: now don't forget me!

4. Medieval Latin Anecdotes

(a) The Quarrelsome Woman

I heard about a certain quarrelsome woman, who frequently disparaged her husband, and, among other abuse, she called him 'lousy' in front of everyone. When the husband frequently asked her to stop her abuse, and she no less frequently accused him of being a wretch and a louse, at length he forbade her to say such things under the threat of serious penalty. But she, contemptuous of his threat, did not stop reviling her husband more bitterly and frequently than before. Finally he pushed her into the water. When she had almost drowned, and couldn't open her mouth without it filling with water, she stretched her hands above the water and began by gestures to indicate – with the two nails of her thumbs as if she were killing a louse – in a gesture what she could not with a word.

(b) The Deceit and Cunning of Old Women

I heard tell of a certain old woman, who could not persuade a certain lady to give in to the advances of a young man. At this point the old woman said to the young man: 'Pretend you're sick, and indicate to the lady that your love for her is the cause of your illness.' Meanwhile the old woman made her little dog starve for three days, and after that gave him bread mixed with mustard to eat. She took the dog with her to the lady's house; the dog began to weep because of the bitterness of the mustard. When the lady asked why the dog was weeping, the old woman said with a sigh, 'This little dog was once a lady who allowed a young man to die for love of her. When the young man was mortally ill, he thought about how he might be able to avenge himself on the lady and, by means of certain sorcery, he transformed her into this puppy dog. God condoned this because of her sin, inasmuch as she'd allowed a young man to die whom she could have saved from death. And you can see that she's now weeping in penitence because she wouldn't consent to the young man's wishes.' Then the lady, fearing that the same thing might happen to her, said, 'Woe is me! A certain young man is now mortally ill because I wouldn't give in to his wishes!' And thus the old woman induced the lady to give in to the young man.

(c) The Peasant and the Sheep

A certain peasant took a sheep to market. Six crafty peddlers noticed him entering the village. One of them said to the others: 'We could well get this sheep from the peasant if we wished.' When they asked how, he said, 'Let's station ourselves in six separate streets, so that none of us is with another, and each one of us ask the peasant if he wants to sell his dog.' This was done; they went up to him one after the other. When the peasant swore that it was a sheep, they said it was a dog. At length, impelled by his shame, that so many times so many people had said it was a dog, he said to the sixth, 'I don't want to sell it, but take it for nothing, and for God's sake don't make fun of me any more.'

(d) The English Nobleman and his Three Sons

A certain English nobleman who owned land in England and Wales had three sons. When he saw himself approaching death, he called his three sons and said to them: 'If you had to become birds, what sort of bird would you like to be?' The eldest replied, 'I would be a hawk, since it's a noble bird and lives off prey.' The middle son replied, 'I would be a starling, since it's a sociable bird and flies in a flock.' The third and youngest son said, 'I'd be a swan, since a swan has a long neck, and if any word were produced in my heart, I could think about it before it came to my mouth.' Hearing all this the father said to the first, 'You my son, I perceive, wish to live off prey: to you I give my lands in England, since it's a land of peace and justice, and you won't be able to prey off England with impunity. You, my son, since you love society, shall have my lands in Wales, which is a country of discord and war, since through your courtliness you will moderate the wickedness of the

165

inhabitants. To you, my younger son, I assign no land, since you will be wise and through your wisdom will acquire whatever you need.' When the father died, therefore, the lands were divided as the father had advised. The younger brother, progressing in wisdom, was made the Chief Justice of England.

(e) The Woman who Greased the Judge's Palm

I heard about a certain venal judge, that when a very poor little woman had not been able to obtain justice from him, someone said to the woman: 'The judge is such that, unless his palm is greased, you won't get a just settlement from him.' The woman, understanding these words simply and literally, arriving at the judge's court with some pork fat, began to grease his palm while everyone was watching. The judge said: 'What are you doing, woman?' She replied, 'I was told, Milord, that unless I greased your palm I couldn't obtain justice from you.' The judge, confused, altered his decision in her favour.

(f) The Fable of the Fox and the Wolf

By chance, a fox fell into a well in one of its buckets. A wolf came along and wanted to know what the fox was doing there. 'My good fellow,' said the fox, 'I've got many fish down here, and big ones too, and wish you could share them with me.' Ysengrimus said, 'How can I get down there?' The fox said, 'There's a bucket up there; get in it, and you'll come down.' There were two buckets: when one went down, the other went up. The wolf got into the bucket which was up and descended; the fox ascended in the other. When they passed each other the wolf said, 'Where are you going, my good fellow?' And the fox said, 'I've eaten enough and I'm going up; you'll find wonderful things down there.' The unfortunate wolf descended, and found nothing there but water. The next day the peasants came along, hauled out the wolf, and thrashed him to death.

(g) The Two Companions

Two companions were forced to cross a desert. Said the one: 'I'll bet you that I gain more by means of falsehood than you gain through truth.' The other replied, 'I'll accept your bet.' The wager agreed, the liar fell into an assembly of apes, and the apes said, 'How do we appear to you?' The liar said, 'You are the most beautiful of all animals on earth, and men resemble you: never have I seen so beautiful an assembly'. And he flattered them greatly. The other truthful man arrived, and the apes asked how their assembly appeared to him. He replied, saying, 'Never have I seen so ugly and so foul an assembly'. And the irate apes clobbered him thoroughly, so that he scarcely escaped from their hands.

(h) Reynard and Tibert

A fox, or Reynard, met Tibert – that is, a cat – and Reynard said, 'How many tricks of the trade do you know?' The cat replied, 'When dogs chase me I know how to climb trees and so escape.' And the cat asked, 'And you, how many do you know?' Reynard replied, 'I know seventeen, and I have them here in this full sack: come with me and I'll teach you my tricks so that the dogs won't catch you.' The cat consented; they set off together. Hunters and dogs chased them. The cat said: 'I hear dogs. I'm afraid!' And Reynard replied 'Don't be afraid: I'll instruct you well in how you may escape.' The dogs and hunters drew near. 'For sure,' said the cat, 'I'll go with you no further: I want to use my own trick.' And he bounded up a tree. The dogs abandoned him and chased Reynard, and finally caught him, some by the legs, some by the stomach, some by the back, some by the head. And the cat, sitting aloft, shouted down, 'Reynard, Reynard! Open your sack! – All your tricks now aren't worth an egg!'

(i) The Demon and the Robber

It happened that a demon and a robber ran into each other and the demon said to the robber, who had asked where he was going, 'I'm going to strangle that hermit who has committed a sin and has gone to sleep without confessing it.' And the robber, on being asked in turn where he was going, replied, 'I'm going to steal the hermit's cow.' 'Let's go together,' they said, 'and let's be companions and friends, and let's help each other.' Standing at the door of the hermit's house, they argued about which of them should first commit his crime. When the demon said that he would begin, the robber disagreed, lest perhaps while the hermit was being strangled he made a noise, and the people aroused by it would keep the robber from his booty. When the robber said that he would go first, the demon disagreed, lest perhaps the cow awakened the hermit with mooing or noise, and thus kept the demon from his booty. While they were arguing the demon shouted out, wishing to be avenged, saying, 'Get up, my lord hermit, and catch the thief who's come to steal your cow: I'll help you catch him.' When it was done, the demon said to the hermit, 'You ought to love me well, since I'm your faithful friend who thus diligently guards your house.'

(j)   The Man who Pretended to be Dead

When a certain man turned over in bed, not being able to sleep, and was asked by his wife the cause of such great worry, he said that he had calculated how with his income he would get through that year, and that he had enough for the whole year except one day, 'And therefore,' he said, 'I'm worried how I'll get through that day.' Although his wife comforted him he was not quiet but said, 'I've found a good method, which is as follows: I'll pretend that I'm dead for one day, and you'll put me in the hall and cover me, and thus on that day I won't eat anything, nor will you nor the family because of your grief and concern; and by economising in that way we'll avoid that day, and we'll have enough for the remainder.' When this had been done, the wife placed herself at the door, and when the household was returning from the fields she lamented, saying that the cause of her weeping was the death of her husband. When they had said 'Pater Noster' over the corpse one of them said, 'Even though he's dead we have to eat.' 'You shall not eat today,' said the wife, 'because of grief and the bother of arranging what's necessary for the funeral.' But the opinion of the family prevailed. While they were eating, the unfortunate man, hearing that his precaution had been of no avail, raised his head from the cover. One of the servants saw this and, thinking that the devil had harassed the corpse, picked up an axe or staff and knocked his brains out. When the wife screamed that he'd killed her husband he said, 'No – I drove the devil from your husband's corpse.'

(k) The Lawyer and a Devil

A certain man, who was the lawyer of various villages, was merciless, greedy
and made heavy demands of those in his power. On a certain day, when he
was going to a village for the purpose of collecting a debt, a devil in the
disguise of a man accompanied him on his way. The lawyer, as much from
his horror as from their conversation, recognized him to be a devil. He was
quite afraid to go with him, but in no way – neither by praying nor by
making the sign of the cross – could he separate himself from the devil. As
they went along a certain poor man ran up to them leading a pig on a noose.
And when the pig would go this way and that, the angry man shouted,
'Devil take you!' Having heard these words, the lawyer, hoping by such an
occasion to be freed from the devil, said to him, 'Hear that, my friend? That
pig is given to you; go ahead, take him.' The devil replied, 'In no way did he
give it to me with all his heart, and therefore I can't take it.' Then, as they
were passing through another village, when a child was crying, the mother,
standing at the door of her house, shouted in a disturbed voice, 'Devil take
you! Why do you irritate me with your crying?' Then the lawyer said, 'See
that! You've gained another soul! Take the child, he's yours.' The devil
replied as before, 'She didn't give him to me with all her heart; but such is
the way men speak when they are angry.' As they began to approach the
village of their destination, men from the village, seeing them from afar, and
not being unaware of the lawyer's mission, shouted together in one voice,
'Devil take you! You even come with the devil!' Hearing this, the devil
cocked his head and, laughing, said to the lawyer, 'See: these men have
given you to me from the depths of their hearts, and therefore you're mine.'
And the devil carried him off at that very moment, and what he did with
him is unknown. The words of their conversation and what happened are
related through the words of the lawyer's servant, who was with them on the
journey.

(l) The Jew's Daughter

There was a certain young student who slept with the daughter of a Jew, who
became pregnant by the student. And the student took a reed and went by
night to the Jew's house and spoke through the reed through the window of
the room where the Jew was sleeping with his wife, saying, 'Rejoice and
glorify God, since the Lord has visited His people and since your daughter is
pregnant, she will give birth to the true Messiah who is promised in the Law
and Scriptures.' The student did this three times. And when the parents

knew that their daughter was pregnant, they believed the words of the insinuator, and told this to the other Jews who all rejoiced, and glorified God, and held the girl in great honour. And when the time of birth came, all the Jews assembled to see such a great spectacle. At length the girl gave birth with great pain not to a boy but to a girl. When the Jews saw this, they were all confused, and saw that they had been deceived.

(m) The Bailiff and his Wife

A bailiff arranged for the marriage of his son. A certain man, who had important business dealings with him, gave him a handsome ox, asking that he take his side. Hearing of this, one of the man's enemies sent to the bailiff's wife a beautiful cow, asking that the wife represent him. She was in such standing with the bailiff that he promised to do whatever she wished. When judgment was given, and the bailiff would not stand for the man who had given him the ox, the man said, 'Why not?'[1] And the bailiff then replied, 'The ox cannot speak, since the cow won't permit it.'

(n) Aristotle

Aristotle instructed Alexander to restrain himself from frequent intercourse with his wife, who was extremely beautiful, so that he would not prevent his soul from fulfilling its common destiny; and Alexander consented. The queen was sad when she learned this, and began to seduce Aristotle to her, inasmuch as she very often went out alone with bare feet and hair hanging loose in order to attract him. At length he was attracted by her and began to seek an opportunity to make love to her; she said, 'I won't do this at all unless I see a sign of your love, so that you don't trick me. Therefore come to my bedroom crawling on your hands and feet and carrying me like a horse; then I'll know that you're not deceiving me.' When he agreed to this condition, she advised Alexander of it. Alexander waited and caught him carrying her. When Alexander wished to kill him, Aristotle excused himself by saying, 'If it so happens that a wise old man be deceived by a woman, you can see that I've taught you well concerning what could happen to a young man like you.' Hearing this Alexander spared him, and made great progress in his learning.

---

[1] These words, or something similar, have been omitted from the text.

(o) The Blind Man and his Wife

There was a certain blind man who had a very attractive wife, and who watched over his wife's chastity with great anxiety: he was fanatically jealous in this respect. It happened one day that, when they were sitting pleasantly in their garden next to a pear tree, the blind man agreed to the wishes of his wife that she climb the tree to pick some pears, and in order that no other man would get to her, he embraced the trunk of the tree with his arms. It was a broadly branching tree in which, before the wife climbed it, a certain young man had hidden himself, awaiting the wife's coming. They meet joyously, embrace each other, kiss each other, and the plough of Venus digs deep into the shaggy field and shady grove. When the youth was engaged in his work as strenuously as could be, and the woman was providing opportunities for him to indulge his energies, the blind man heard their panting and, saddened, shouted out, 'You foul woman! Although I'm blind my hearing and my perception are all the stronger: I sense that you're with an adulterer. Therefore I lament this most disgusting outrage to Jove the highest god, who can bring joy to the hearts of those who are sad, and can restore sight to the blind.' With these words the blind man's vision was suddenly restored and, looking up in the tree, he saw the adulterer. He suddenly shouted out, 'O falsest of women, why do you torment me with this deceit, when I believed you to be virtuous and chaste? Woe is me! For I'll never have another happy day in your company.' But the woman, hearing her husband abusing her, although a bit terrified at first, yet with a happy face quickly thought up a lie and replied to her husband with an exclamation, 'I give thanks to all the gods and goddesses who have heard my prayers and have restored sight to my beloved husband! For, sweet husband, know that you can see because of my effort and prayers. Although until now I had spent a good deal on physicians in vain, I urged the gods that they would make you healthy and would restore your sight. Finally the god Mercury at the command of mighty Jove appeared to me in a dream saying, "If you climb a pear tree and consummate the game of love with a young man, your husband's former eyesight will be restored." I did this in order to heal you. Therefore you owe me a great reward for such a deed, since I have restored your sight.' The blind man gave in to the lies and deceit of his wife, and forgave the whole sinful affair, and reconciled her with gifts, as if she had been shamefully corrupted against her will.

(p) The Fasting Abbot

I heard about a certain abbot who was accustomed, before his promotion, to frequent fasting on bread and water. When, however, he was made an abbot, he began to eat huge meals. When he was asked about this extremely sudden change, he replied, 'I fasted for a long time as the vigil to this feast; for that reason I ate small little fish so that some day I'd be able to eat big ones.'

(q) The Old Woman who Made a Pact with the Devil

There was a certain man of a noble and aristocratic family who, when his father died, by reason of his patrimony joined himself in marriage to the exceedingly chaste and beautiful daughter of a famous man. While they were joined in this way by God's law, for no short time they embraced each other in holy love, and were as pleasing to God as to men. Through their holy works they aspired deeply to the glory of the heavenly realms. The enemy of mankind, in no way able to tolerate their holy relationship, attempted to devise a corporeal rift between them, or at least a spiritual blemish on their souls, by sending several of his followers. But through the help of the Saviour's grace, the more energetically he encouraged them to sin, the more firmly these servants of God were rooted in a good resolution. Therefore the crafty Serpent, seeing – although only after some time – that by no application of his wits was he able to make headway by this method against this holy couple, turned his attention to something astonishing and unthought of: just as if a fighter, stripped of his own arms and impotent in himself, miraculously armed another combatant for the battle.

For, having taken on the appearance of a human being, he became a young man and appeared to a certain hag who had come from the city in which the holy couple lived, saying, 'Where have you come from?' She replied, 'I come from the city to which you seem to be going.' And he: 'I have a certain secret to reveal to you, if I knew that you wouldn't repeat it.' And she: 'Go on. I'll keep quiet.' He said to her: 'Do you know of a man and his wife who, as report has it, because of their manners and virtue, are praised not only by their fellow citizens but even by people in faraway places who have heard stories about them?' She said, 'Of course I know them.' And he: 'Would you know anyone in the world so wise and clever who could sow hatred between them and separate their unanimity a little? For, having heard of their marvellous mutual devotion, I made a bet with one of my friends that I could perhaps create some dissension between them.' The old

172

woman replied, 'He would have to be a man of astonishing genius. But if perhaps I were to show some affection, I think I could do what you say.' And the demon said: 'And I shall pay you well if you will try to do this for me.' Accordingly this miserable and unhappy woman is paid to the tune of five pieces of silver for committing so foul a deed. When this was settled, they parted from each other, giving assurances that they would meet again the following day to discuss the outcome of the business.

Thus the crafty old woman, first approaching the wife when her husband was away, said to her, 'My lady, I suffer exceedingly at seeing your naiveté, in so far as you have been deceived by your husband for such a long time without your knowing about it. You evidently assume that he has the same constancy of affection towards you which you have towards him, he who – in my estimation – you ought surely to know is attached to a certain pretty young lady with all the fondness of his heart.' The wife said to the old lady: 'Are these things that you say true?' 'I'm speaking the truth,' she said, 'and unless he mends his ways quickly, I fear that you yourself will find out abruptly – perhaps through some dreadful deed.' The wife said, 'Alas, what shall I do? I thought that I'd got through all my troubles quicker than that. But what course remains for me? I ask you now, if you know any, that you won't refuse to give me useful advice about this.' And she: 'I advise you, when your husband's asleep at night, that you don't forget to shave off four hairs from his beard for me, and with them you may be assured that I'll prepare such a medicine that he'll change his mind about that love affair and return to you forever, more ardently than usual.' The wife said to her: 'It seems that this can be provided easily enough. I'll do what you suggest.'

After she had done this the old woman spoke to the husband separately as she had previously with the wife, as follows: 'Surely you're not unaware, my lord, that your wife, whom you think chaste and modest, being loved for a long while by another man, and deeply in love with another besides you, is now plotting your death? Whence, unless you act wisely, you'll die tonight. For daily anticipation of the crime did not deter her from her intention, but rather she required a deliberately plotted murder. And if you suspect that I'm telling lies, pretend that you're asleep even if you have to lie awake all night, and the things I've said will be clear to you from this test.' Having been forewarned by hearing this about his wife, he thanked the old woman and parted from her. When night came the wife of loving and simple conscience, not forgetting the old woman's warning, called to her husband coming in from the street with a happy face. Now with food, now with drink she plied him, trying to get him drunk so that she could more freely fulfil her intention. The husband, warned by that mother of error, accepted gracefully whatever his wife gracefully brought him, pretending to show a cheerful face although in his heart he was anything but glad, so that with such dissimulation he could plainly see the outcome of the business.

Therefore, when it came time for bed, the husband lay down on the bed and straightway closed his eyes; with his body motionless as if he were half dead, he pretended to be asleep. Seeing this, and having prepared her instruments, the wife went up to the husband. And when she touched her husband's moistened beard with the razor, he grabbed her hand with the razor in it, and suddenly getting up, he spoke as follows, 'For a long time, you foulest of wives, you've concealed this poisonous plot under a cloud. Although you've tried – through God's help – you've failed in your present purpose. You shall die by the very judgment you passed on me.' Without any hesitation, as if he couldn't contain his rage, he snatched up a knife and cut the throat of his chaste wife with his own hand, even though she didn't deserve to die.

The next day when daylight came – not as a good labourer worthy of his hire, but as a most foul operator who deserved eternal punishment as her pay – the old woman proceeded along the same path towards her employer, seeking her payment. While she was looking about her across a huge wide river, she recognized the demon her master standing on the other side, holding up the silver pieces in his hand, which he urged her, with nods, to catch when he threw them. When she entreated him to come closer, he replied that he wouldn't dare, fearing that she might perhaps kill him, just as she had killed the good wife, and added that, not even if he had ten years and a legion of accomplices could he have accomplished what she had brought to completion in the space of only one night.

(r) The Woman who met a Priest

There is the example, so the story goes, of the woman who made the sign of the cross in the morning when she met a priest, and replied that she did it so that no misfortune would befall her that day. He said to her, 'Do you think that something bad will happen to you because you've met me?' She said, 'I fear so.' He said, 'Indeed it shall happen just as you thought, for you'll have one misfortune through meeting me.' And he grabbed her by the shoulders and threw her into a muddy ditch, saying, 'It's fitting that it turned out just as you thought.'

(s) The Peasant and the Ape

A certain man entered the hall of a particular nobleman, and saw an ape dressed in the style of the nobleman's sons. Since the ape had its back to him, he thought it was his master's son, to whom he spoke with the deference that the situation demanded. He found out that it was an ape laughing at him. He said to it, 'Damn you! I thought you were Jenkin, my master's son.'

NOTES ON TEXTS AND TRANSLATIONS

The following notes have been compiled by the translators. To them have been added references, where available, to the Folktale Type of which the tales are literary versions, derived from A. Aarne and S. Thompson, *The Types of the Folktale* (Helsinki: Academia Scientiarum Fennica, 1973).

French Tales

These ten examples of the medieval French *fabliau* all date from the thirteenth century, the period when this genre flourished in Northern France, particularly in the Picard area. The translations are based on the versions edited from the original manuscripts by R.C. Johnston and D.D.R. Owen as Nos I, II, V, VI, VIII, X, XIII, XIV, and XV of their *Fabliaux*, published by Blackwell, Oxford 1957. The great majority of *fabliaux* are anonymous. Of the present selection, three are attributed to named authors. 'The Three Hunchbacks' is attributed to one Durand, of whom nothing else is known. The attribution of 'The Knight who Won Back his Estranged Lady' to 'Pierre d'Anfol' (Petrus Alphonsi) is certainly spurious. Rutebeuf, the named author of 'The Donkey's Last Will and Testament', was a major poet of Champenois origin who flourished in Paris from c.1250 to c.1280.

Eight major studies may be usefully consulted:
1. J. Bedier, *Les Fabliaux* (5th edition, Paris, 1925).
2. P. Nykrog, *Les Fabliaux* (Copenhagen: Munksgaard, 1957).
3. J. Rychner, *Contribution à l'étude des fabliaux*, 2 vols (Geneva: Droz, 1960).
4. O. Jodogne & J.C. Payen, *Le Fabliau, Le Lai narratif* (Turnhout, 1975).
5. P. Ménard, *Les Fabliaux: contes à rire du moyen âge* (Paris: P.U.F., 1983).
6. C. Muscatine, *The Old French Fabliaux* (New Haven and London: Yale University Press, 1986).
7. R.H. Bloch, *The Scandal of the Fabliaux* (Chicago and London: The University of Chicago Press, 1986).
8. A. Lecoy de la Marche, *Le rive du prédicateur*, ed. J. Berloiz (Brepols, 1992).

Folktale types:
3. 'The Three Hunchbacks'. Type 1536B.
5. 'Brownie, the Priest's cow'. Type 1735.
6. 'The Donkey's Last Will and Testament'. Type 1842.
7. 'The Peasant Doctor'. Type 1641B.
10. 'The Covetous Man and his envious Companion'. Type 1331. This widely known medieval story has been noted in 1995 in the former Yugoslavia currently told to illustrate the behaviour of Croats and Serbs to each other. (Elizabeth Payne, letter, *The Daily Mail*, 26 July 1995, p. 43.)

Spanish Tales

General background:

A.D. Deyermond, A *Literary History of Spain: The Middle Ages* (London: Ernest Benn; New York: Barnes and Noble, 1971). The bibliographical references given below for individual tales include the best edition(s) of the original, translations, and useful studies in English. Much of the best scholarship on medieval Spanish tales is of course in Spanish, but I have assumed that those who wish to read the tales in translation will not, in general, have a good reading knowledge of Spanish, and I have therefore not listed books and articles in that language (or in any languages other than English). I have made an exception for two major general studies in Spanish and one in French, listed in the next paragraph. Bibliographical references to studies in Spanish and in other languages will be found in the more recent studies listed here.

On medieval Spanish tales in general, see John Esten Keller, *Motif-Index of Mediaeval Spanish Exempla* (Knoxville: Univ. of Tennessee Press, 1949). Rameline E. Marsan, *Itinéraire espagnol du conte médiéval: VIIIe–XVesiècles*, Témoins de l'Espagne, Série Historique, 4 (Paris: Klincksieck, 1974). Martin Favata, 'Static Society in Medieval Spanish Exempla', in *Oelschläger Festschrift* (Chapel Hill: Hispanófila, 1976), pp. 185–89. María Jesús Lacarra, *Cuentística medieval en España: los orígenes*, Publicaciones del Departamento de Literatura Española, 1 (Zaragoza: Univ., 1979). Harriet Goldberg, 'Sexual Humor in Misogynist Medieval Exempla', in *Women in Hispanic Literature: Icons and Fallen Idols*, ed. Beth Miller (Berkeley: Univ. of California Press, 1983), pp. 67–83. *Cuentos de la Edad Media*, ed. María Jesús Lacarra, Odres Nuevos (Madrid: Castalia, 1986).

1. 'The Well' is taken from the Hispano-Latin *Disciplina clericalis*, by Pedro Alfonso (born c.1062), a Jew who was converted to Christianity in 1106 and spent some time in England. A version of this tale also appears in the *Libro de los exenplos por a.b.c.*, and, though its authenticity is disputed, in the *Arcipreste de Talavera* (see below). Folktale Type 1377.

Editions: Alfons Hilka & Werner Söderhjelm (*editio maior*), Acta Societatis Scientiarum Fennicae, 28.4 (Helsingfors, 1911); (*editio minor*), Sammlung mittelateinischer Texte, 1 (Heidelberg: Winter, 1911). Ed. María Jesús Lacarra, Spanish transl. Esperanza Ducay, Nueva Biblioteca de Autores Aragoneses, 3 (Zaragoza: Guara, 1980).
Translations: Joseph R. Jones & John E. Keller, *The Scholar's Guide* (Toronto: Pontifical Institute of Mediaeval Studies, 1969). Eberhard Hermes & P.R. Quarrie, *The 'Disciplina clericalis' of Pedro Alfonso* (London: Routledge and Kegan Paul, 1977).
Study: Haim Schwarzbaum, 'International Folklore Motifs in Petrus Alfonsi's *Disciplina clericalis*', *Sefarad*, 21 (1961), 267–99; 22 (1962), 17–59 & 321–44; 23 (1963), 54–73. Barry Taylor, 'Wisdom Forms in the *Disciplina clericalis* of Petrus Alfonsi', *La Corónica*, 22.1 (Fall 1993), 24–40.

2–4. 'The Parrot', 'The Bathkeeper', and 'Book-Learning and Experience' are from the work generally known as the *Libro de los engaños* or *Sendebar*, but whose title was probably intended to be *Libro de los assayamientos de las mugeres*. It was translated from Arabic in the mid-thirteenth century under the auspices of Prince Fadrique of Castile, and is a version of *The Book of Sindibad*, which is of either Indian or Persian origin (one scholar has argued for a Hebrew origin). The *Libro de los engaños* represents the Eastern branch of the prolific Seven Sages tradition (the Western branch, *The Seven Sages of Rome*, gives rise to other medieval Spanish texts).

Editions: Ángel González Palencia, *Versiones castellanas del 'Sendebar'* (Madrid: Consejo Superior de Investigaciones Científicas, 1946); includes other Spanish Seven Sages texts, but for the *Libro de los engaños* use: María Jesús Lacarra, *Sendebar*, Letras Hispánicas, 304 (Madrid: Cátedra, 1989). A new edition is being prepared by Richard P. Kinkade.

Translations: Comparetti 1882 (below). John Esten Keller, *The Book of the Wiles of Women*, Univ. of North Carolina Studies in Romance Languages and Literatures, 27 (Chapel Hill: Univ. of North Carolina Press, 1956).

Studies: Domenico Comparetti, *Researches Respecting the 'Book of Sindibâd'*, tr. Henry Charles Coote, Publications of the Folk-Lore Society, 9.1 (London: Elliot Stock for the Folk-Lore Society, 1882); includes transl. of the text. George T. Artola, '*Sindibad* in Medieval Spanish', *Modern Language Notes*, 71 (1956), 36–42. B.E. Perry, 'The Origin of the *Book of Sindbad*', *Fabula*, 3 (1959), 1–94. John Esten Keller, 'Some Stylistic and Conceptual Differences in Texts A and B of *El libro de los engaños*', in *Studia hispanica in honorem R. Lapesa*, III (Madrid: Cátedra-Seminario Menéndez Pidal & Gredos, 1975), pp. 275–82. George T. Artola, 'The Nature of the *Book of Sindbad*', in *Studies on the Seven Sages of Rome and Other Essays in Medieval Literature Dedicated to the Memory of Jean Misrahi* (Honolulu: Educational Research Associates, 1978), pp. 7–31. Norman Roth, 'The "Wiles of Women" Motif in the Medieval Hebrew Literature of Spain', *Hebrew Annual Review*, 2 (1978), 145–65. Hans R. Runte, J. Keith Wikeley, & Anthony J. Farrell, *The Seven Sages of Rome and the Book of Sindibad: An Analytical Bibliography* (New York: Garland, 1984). Alan Deyermond, 'The *Libro de los engaños*: Its Social and Literary Context', in *The Spirit of the Court: Selected Proceedings of the Fourth Congress of the International Courtly Literature Society (Toronto 1983)*, ed. Glyn S. Burgess & Robert A. Taylor (Cambridge: D.S. Brewer, 1985), pp. 158–67. S. Belcher, 'The Diffusion of the *Book of Sindbad*', *Fabula*, 28 (1987), 34–58. John Esten Keller, 'The Literature of Recreation: *El libro de los engaños*', in *Hispanic Medieval Studies in Honor of Samuel G. Armistead* (Madison: Hispanic Seminary of Medieval Studies, 1992), pp. 193–200. Robert Irwin, 'Oceans of Stories', chap. 3 of his *The Arabian Nights: A Companion* (London: Allen Lane, The Penguin Press, 1994). Current bibliographical information is given in *Society of the Seven Sages Newsletter*, which may be obtained from Professor Hans R. Runte, Dept of French, Dalhousie University.

5–7. 'The Debate of Greeks and Romans', 'Pitas Payas, the Breton Painter', and 'The Youth and the Millstone' are from the *Libro de Buen Amor*, by Juan Ruiz, Archpriest of Hita. It was probably composed in 1330 (see, however, Kelly 1984, below), and – despite cogently-argued views to the contrary – it still seems likely that the poet expanded his work in 1343. These are the only Spanish verse tales translated in the present volume.

Editions: G.B. Gybbon-Monypenny, Clásicos Castalia, 161 (Madrid: Castalia, 1988). Jacques Joset, Clásicos Taurus, 1 (Madrid: Taurus, 1990). Alberto Blecua, Letras Hispánicas, 70 (Madrid: Cátedra, 1992).

Translations: There are six English translations, the first, in a Cambridge PhD thesis by John W. Barker (1923), being unpublished. Elisha Kent Kane, *The Book of Good Love* (Kane, PA: the translator, 1933); this hilarious and often inaccurate verse translation, with Kane's bawdy woodcuts, is a collector's item; the 2nd ed. (Chapel Hill: Univ. of North Carolina Press, 1968) is tamer. Rigo Mignani & Mario A. DiCesare, *The Book of Good Love* (prose, with verse transls of the lyrics) (Albany: State Univ. of New York Press, 1970). Raymond S. Willis, *Libro de Buen Amor* (ed. with prose transl.) (Princeton: UP, 1972). Mack Singleton, *The Book of the Archpriest of Hita* (verse transl.) (Madison: Hispanic Seminary of Medieval Studies, 1975). Saralyn R. Daly, *The Book of True Love* (verse transl., with ed. by Anthony R. Zahareas) (University Park: Pennsylvania State UP, 1978). The Mignani-DiCesare and Willis translations are the most reliable, though both suffer from the disadvantage of prose translating verse.

Studies: María Rosa Lida de Malkiel, *Two Spanish Masterpieces: The 'Book of Good Love' and the 'Celestina'*, Illinois Studies in Language and Literature, 49 (Urbana: Univ. of Illinois Press, 1961). Otis H. Green, 'Medieval Laughter: The *Book of Good Love*', chap. 2 of his *Spain and the Western Tradition: The Castilian Mind in Literature from El Cid to Calderón*, I (Madison: Univ. of Wisconsin Press, 1963). Anthony N. Zahareas, *The Art of Juan Ruiz, Archpriest of Hita* (Madrid: Estudios de Literatura Española, 1965). *'Libro de buen amor' Studies*, ed. G.B. Gybbon-Monypenny (London: Tamesis, 1970); see especially Ian Michael, 'The Function of the Popular Tale in the *Libro de buen amor*', pp. 177–218. John K. Walsh, 'Juan Ruiz and the *Mester de clerezía*: Lost Context and Lost Parody in the *Libro de Buen Amor*', *Romance Philology*, 33 (1979–80), 62–86. Dayle Seidenspinner-Núñez, *The Allegory of Good Love: Parodic Perspectivism in the 'Libro de Buen Amor'*, Univ. of California Publications in Modern Philology, 112 (Berkeley: Univ. of California Press, 1981). Gail Phillips, *The Imagery of the 'Libro de Buen Amor'*, Spanish Studies, 9 (Madison: Hispanic Seminary of Medieval Studies, 1983). Colin Smith, 'Juan Ruiz: *The Book of Good Love*', in *Medieval Literature: The European Inheritance*, The New Pelican Guide to English Literature, ed. Boris Ford, 1.2 (Harmondsworth: Penguin, 1983), pp. 275–86. Henry Ansgar Kelly, *Canon Law and the Archpriest of Hita*, Medieval & Renaissance Texts & Studies, 27 (Binghamton, NY: Center for Medieval and Early Renaissance Studies, 1984). Jeremy N.H. Lawrance, 'The Audience of the *Libro de Buen Amor*', *Comparative Literature*, 36 (1984), 220–37. Marina Scordilis Brownlee, *The Status of the Reading Subject in the 'Libro de Buen Amor'*, North Carolina Studies in Romance Languages and Literatures, 204 (Chapel Hill: Dept of Romance Languages, Univ. of North Carolina, 1985). John Dagenais, *The Ethics of Reading in Manuscript Culture: Glossing the 'Libro de buen amor'* (Princeton: UP, 1974).

Studies on individual tales: **5.** A.D. Deyermond, 'The Greeks, the Romans, the Astrologers and the Meaning of the *Libro de Buen Amor*', *Romance Notes*, 5.1 (Autumn 1963), 88–91. Sara Sturm, 'The Greeks and the Romans: The Archpriest's Warning to his Reader', *Romance Notes*, 10 (1968–69), 404–12. A.A. Parker, 'The Parable of the Greeks and Romans in the *Libro de Buen Amor*', in *Medieval Hispanic Studies Presented to Rita Hamilton* (London: Tamesis, 1976), pp. 139–47. **6.** Lucius Gaston Moffatt, 'Pitas Payas', in *South Atlantic Studies for Sturgis E. Leavitt* (Washington: Scarecrow Press, 1953), pp. 29–38. Donald McGrady, 'The Story of the Painter and his Little Lamb', *Thesaurus*, 33 (1978 [1980]), 357–406.

8. 'The Drunken Mouse' is from the *Libro de los gatos*, an anonymous version (probably late fourteenth century) of the thirteenth-century Anglo-Latin *Narrationes*, or *Fabulae*, of Odo of Cheriton. The moralizations attached to Odo's tales are significantly emended by the Spanish author, especially in the first half of the book. 'Gatos' here does not, despite the story translated, mean 'cats'; the most likely meaning is 'liars, hypocrites'.

Editions: John Esten Keller (Madrid: Consejo Superior de Investigaciones Científicas, 1958). Bernard Darbord, Annexes de *Cahiers de Linguistique Hispanique Médiévale*, 3 (Paris: Séminaire d'Études Médiévales Hispaniques, Univ. de Paris XIII).

Translation: Charles L. Nelson, *Book of the Cats*, introd. John Esten Keller ([Tokyo: Isamu Yamiguchi], 1984).

Studies: George T. Artola, '*El libro de los gatos*: An Orientalist's View of its Title', *Romance Philology*, 9 (1955–56), 17–19. James F. Burke, 'More on the Title *El libro de los gatos*', *Romance Notes*, 9 (1967–68), 148–51. Alan Deyermond, 'The Moralizations of the *Libro de los gatos*' (forthcoming).

9. 'The Reluctant Monk' is from the *Libro de los exenplos por a.b.c.*, a collection of *exempla* alphabetically arranged by theme for ease of reference (cf. the Middle English *Alphabet of Tales*). It was written in 1436–38 by Clemente Sánchez (sometimes called Sánchez de Vercial; died 1438), Archdeacon of Valderas, and, with 550 tales, is the longest medieval Spanish *exemplum* collection (there is an even longer one in the sixteenth century).

Edition: John Esten Keller (Madrid: Consejo Superior de Investigaciones Científicas, 1961).

Translation: There is no published transl., but Keller is preparing one.

Studies: Alexander Haggerty Krappe, 'Shepherd and King in *El libro de exemplos*', *Hispanic Review*, 14 (1946), 59–64. Harlan Sturm, 'A Note on the Sources of the *Libro de los ejemplos por a.b.c.*', *Kentucky Romance Quarterly*, 17 (1970), 87–91. Harriet Goldberg, 'Deception as a Narrative Function in the *Libro de los exenplos por a.b.c.*', *Bulletin of Hispanic Studies*, 62 (1985), 31–38.

10. 'The Timid Lover's Expedition' is from the *Arcipreste de Talavera* (often mistakenly called the *Corbacho*, or sometimes *Reprobación del amor mundano*), written in 1438 by Alfonso Martínez de Toledo (1397/98–1468), Archpriest of Talavera. Martínez de Toledo was also a historian, and was for a time in charge of the Corpus Christi plays in Toledo. Despite the title of Simpson's translation (below), the *Arcipreste de Talavera* is not a series of sermons, but a treatise whose structure owes much to that of the sermon; it includes *exempla* drawn from a variety of sources including the author's experience and observation. The tale translated here comes from the section describing the effects of sexual love on each of the four humours (see J.B. Bamborough, *The Little World of Man* (London: Longmans, Green, 1952)), and the timid lover depicted represents those whose dominant humour is phlegm.

Editions: E. Michael Gerli, Letras Hispánicas, 92 (Madrid: Cátedra, 1979). Marcella Ciceri, Colección Austral, A95 (Madrid: Espasa-Calpe, 1990).

Translation: Lesley B. Simpson, *Little Sermons on Sin* (Berkeley: Univ. of California Press, 1959).

Studies: D.P. Rotunda, 'The *Corvacho* Version of the Husband-locked-out Story', *Romanic Review*, 26 (1935), 121–27 ('The Well', the story discussed here, is included in some early editions but not in the only medieval manuscript, and its authenticity is disputed). Christine J. Whitbourn, *The 'Arcipreste de Talavera' and the Literature of Love*, Occasional Papers in Modern Languages, 7 (Hull: Univ., 1970). E. Michael Gerli, *Alfonso Martínez de Toledo*, Twayne's World Authors Series, 398 (Boston: Twayne, 1976). Colbert Nepaulsingh, 'Talavera's Imagery and the Structure of the *Corbacho*', *Revista Canadiense de Estudios Hispánicos*, 4 (1979–80), 329–49; revised in his *Towards a History of Literary Composition in Medieval Spain*, Univ. of Toronto Romance Series, 54 (Toronto: UP, 1986), pp. 143–60. Marina Scordilis Brownlee, 'Hermeneutics of Reading in the *Corbacho*', in *Medieval Texts and Contemporary Readers*, ed. Laurie A. Finke & Martin B. Schichtman (Ithaca: Cornell UP, 1987), pp. 216–33. Roberto G. González-Casanovas, 'Rhetorical Strategies in the *Corbacho*, Part III: From Scholastic Logic to Homiletic Example', *La Corónica*, 20.1 (Fall 1991), 40–59.

English Tales

1. 'Dame Sirith' is preserved in a single text of 450 lines in Bodleian MS Digby 86 of the late thirteenth century, containing a miscellaneous selection of poems. It is written in a mixture of tail-rhyme and roughly octosyllabic couplets and tells the story, widely known in Europe, called 'The Weeping Bitch' (Folktale Type 1515). For an earlier Latin version see above, pp. 164–5. It was told as late in English as William Baldwin's *A marvellous hystory intituled beware the cat*, 1570, 1584, though the bitch is changed to a cat. In the present translation the passage put into verse marks where the author parodies the *clichés* of contemporary love poetry (as Chaucer does in 'The Miller's Tale'). For editions see *Middle English Humorous Tales in Verse*, ed. G.H. McKnight (Boston and London, D.C. Heath, 1913) and *Early Middle English Verse and Prose*, ed. J.A.W. Bennett and G.V. Smithers (Oxford, Clarendon Press, 1966).

2–5. These tales are all to be found admirably edited by Melissa M. Furrow, *Ten Fifteenth-Century Comic Poems* (New York and London, Garland, 1985), to which the reader is referred for further information. They have been translated as literally as possible with the editor's permission. The redundant slack oral style and many paratactic sentences have not been smoothed out.

2. 'The Lady Prioress' is found in only one miscellaneous manuscript, British Library Harley 78, where it was probably bound in the sixteenth century. The booklet constituted by the poem was probably written in the late fifteenth century somewhere in the Midlands. The poem is composed of nine-line stanzas of mixed alliteration and rhyme, four long lines and five short, comprising 243 lines. The form was perhaps a little too ambitious for the poet. The story is well known.

3. 'The Tale of the Pot'. This tale is more usually, and in Furrow, entitled 'The Tale of the Basin' but in modern English 'basin' is unknown as a word for what is clearly a chamber-pot, i.e. kept under the bed for night use. The general theme of an object which people become unwillingly attached to is a popular folktale motif and found e.g. in the story of 'The Golden Goose'. (Cf. Tale Type 571A) The poem is found only in University of Cambridge MS Ff.5.48, a substantial miscellany of pious and secular items. The poem is written in the same stanza form as that of 'The Lady Prioress', comprises 223 lines, and derives from the same general area, written in the late fifteenth century. Priests were conventionally entitled 'Sir', better rendered in modern English as 'Parson'.

4. 'The Friar and the Boy'. This well-known tale is edited by Furrow under its alternative title, 'Jack and his Stepdame', which is more significant of the main point of the story, the revenge of a boy on his (by tradition) unkind stepmother. The title 'The Friar and the Boy' is more widely attested, and the versions under that name have further though variable extensions by up to some 140 lines. The longer version ends with a ludicrous trial scene before 'the official', omitted from the present translation, which finishes at line 426. There are four manuscripts of the fifteenth century, of the usual miscellaneous kind, and the seventeenth-century Percy Folio, and five early printed texts, the earliest by Wynkyn de Worde, 1510–19. The poem continued to be reprinted in England widely well into the eighteenth century, and was popular in Europe generally. Cf. Robert Darnton's interesting essay 'Peasants Tell Tales' in his *The Great Cat Massacre* (Harmondsworth, Penguin Books, 1985: originally Basic Books Inc. 1984). Darnton prints German and French versions of the same tale, attributing the differences to oral tradition. He does not refer to the English versions. Furrow takes the text in Bodley MS Rawlinson c.86, of the usual miscellaneous kind, for copy text. The poem is written in rough 6-line stanzas with lines of three or four stresses and three end-rhymes. The place of origin of this version is roughly North Midland. The story is Tale Type 592.

5. 'Dom Hugh Leicester'. This is a version of a widespread folktale summed up in the title 'The Corpse Killed Five Times', Tale Type 1537, with versions known in three thirteenth century French *fabliaux* and in a late fifteenth-century Italian *novella*. Its only surviving text in English is a printed chapbook dated between 1560 and 1584, Bodleian S. Seld. d.45(6), *Short Title Catalogue of Early Printed Books* 13257. It is written in 326 very rough rhyming couplets, perhaps modernized from a fifteenth-century version written somewhere in the Midlands.

6–13. These tales are taken from the anonymous work *A Hundred Mery Talys*, 1526, of which only one perfect copy is known, in the library of Göttingen University. Traditionally known as a 'jest book', it is a collection of short tales and *exempla*, some of considerable antiquity, others apparently original. The probable author is John Rastell, brother-in-law of Sir Thomas More. See Introduction. First edited as

Shakespeare's Jest Book, A Hundred Mery Talys by H. Oesterley, with Introduction and Notes (London, John Russel Smith, 1866). A slightly modernized edition is found in *A Hundred Merry Tales and other English Jestbooks of the Fifteenth and Sixteenth Centuries*, ed. P.M. Zall (Lincoln: University of Nebraska Press, 1963).

6. Oesterley IV. No analogues. Interesting reference to acting (and believing in) devils.

7. Oesterley XVIII. For the long history of the telling of this tale from medieval Europe to twentieth-century southern U.S.A. see Introduction pp. xxx–xxxi. Folktale Type 1791.

8. Oesterley XXI. There are many medieval and modern tales (they are still being invented) using the notion of St Peter at the gate of heaven (cf. 12 below). Folktale Types 714A–K are jokes concerning St Peter, cf. types 785, 791. Types 1516 and 1516A–C are specifically jokes about marriage and 1516C tells of a man ejected from heaven for the folly of marrying twice, which is the nearest analogue to the present story; but these latter examples have small and late diffusion.

9. Oesterley XXII. Gotham is pronounced 'Gottam'. This story, well-known in England, is Folktale Type 1327, but of very narrow recorded distribution (Serbo-Croatian and Greek). Cf. S.J. Kahrl, 'The Medieval Origins of the Sixteenth-Century Jest-books', *Studies in the Renaissance*, XIII (1966) 166–83.

10. Oesterley XLII. Jokes about fools and cuckolds are common. There is no analogue noted of the present story, but it was repeated and caught the eye of Robert Burton who refers to it in *The Anatomy of Melancholy*, 1651 (Partition 3, Section 3, Member 4, Subsection 1), though he misunderstands, or disregards, the joke, and praises the Yeoman for his restraint.

11. Oesterley LXVI. One later sixteenth-century analogue noted.

12. Oesterley LXXVIII. An early ethnic joke, one of eight about the Welsh in *The Hundred Mery Talys*. The Welsh taste for toasted cheese became proverbial. No precise analogues noted. No title in original.

13. Oesterley XCV. One later remote Latin analogue noted.

For discussion and further references, besides the editor's, see F.P. Wilson, 'The English Jestbooks of the Sixteenth and early Seventeenth Centuries', *The Huntington Library Quarterly*, II (1938–39), 121–58, reprinted with revisions in F.P. Wilson, *Shakespearian and Other Studies*, ed. H. Gardner (Clarendon Press: Oxford, 1969), 285–324; S.J. Kahrl, 'The Medieval Origins of the Sixteenth-century English Jest-books', *Studies in the Renaissance*, XIII (1966) 166–83.

Italian Tales

The basis of this brief selection from the *Trecentonovelle* of Franco Sacchetti (born between 1330 and 1335, died between 1399 and 1401), is the selected *Cento Novelle*, a cura di R. Fornaciari, nuove presentazione di E. Li Gotti, Biblioteca Carducciana XVIII, G.C. Sansoni, Firenze, 1957, referred to as Fornaciari-Gotti. An English version, *Stories from Sacchetti*, translated by F. Steegman, was published in 1907, referred to as Steegman. Present titles are editorial.

1. *Novella* IV, ed. Fornaciari-Gotti 3, transl. Steegman 3. Bernabò Visconti shared the lordship of Milan first with his brothers, then a nephew, from 1354 until the nephew imprisoned him in May 1385. He died suddenly, still in prison, December 1385. Chaucer probably knew him, describes him as 'God of delit and scourge of Lumbardye', and devotes a stanza to him and his fall in the series of 'tragedies' of great men related in 'The Monk's Tale', *The Canterbury Tales*, *Works*, *Riverside Chaucer* 1987, VII, 2399–2406. Abbeys might be held as benefices in Italy at this period by those not in orders, who entrusted the spiritual affairs of the monastery to a deputy, who was a monk. Sacchetti adds another brief version of this same anecdote as applied to a pope, omitted by Fornaciari-Gotti and this translation. The anecdote is of course a folk-tale, not historical. Folktale Type 922.

2. *Novella* XLVIII, ed. Fornaciari-Gotti 19; transl. Steegman 8. It was believed that by touching another person one could pass on bad luck, such as that caused by association with death. Fornaciari-Gotti gives 1349 as the date of Lapaccio's journey.

3. *Novella* LXIV; ed. Fornaciari-Gotti 25; transl. Steegman 12. In the story Benghi appears to be a nickname, while *ser* (here translated Mr) was the appropriate designation for a notary, a kind of solicitor. However, a notary of Agnolo's name appears in Florentine records of 1299.

4. *Novella* LXXVI; ed. Fornaciari-Gotti 30; transl. Steegman 16. The subject of this anecdote appears in Florentine records between 1278 and 1313.

5. *Novella* CCXXV; ed. Fornaciari-Gotti 98; transl. Steegman 82. Agnolo Moronti appears as a court-jester in Novella CXLII. The name Golfo puns with *gufo*, 'owl', and 'fool'. The same plot appears in other popular Italian tales.

6. *Novella* CCLIV; ed. Fornaciari-Gotti, 100. Not in Steegman. The war between Catalans and Genoese took place in 1331.

German Tales

1. 'The Judge and the Devil' by the Stricker, translated from *Der Stricker. Verserzählungen*, II edited by Hanns Fischer (Tübingen: Niemeyer, 1967), pp. 31–42. Date of composition: probably second quarter of the thirteenth century. Folktale type 1186.

2. 'The Three Monks of Colmar' by Niemand, translated from *Neues Gesamtabenteuer*, I, edited by Heinrich Niewohner, 2nd edition by Werner Simon with variants by Max Boeters and Kurt Schacks (Dublin/Zurich: Weidmann, 1967), pp. 202–7. Niemand appears to be the pseudonym of an Alsation poet of the mid or late fourteenth century; nothing certain is known about him. Folktale Type 1536B.

3. 'The Lover in the Tree', translated from *Die deutsche Märendichtung des 15. Jahrhunderts*, edited by Hanns Fischer (Munich: Beck, 1966), pp. 485–92 (= 'Die Buhlschaft auf dem Baume A). Date of the only manuscript: *c*.1460–80. Folktale Type 1423.

4. 'The Returned Payment for Love' by Heinrich Kaufringer, translated from *Heinrich Kaufringer. Werkke*, I, edited by Paul Sappler (Tübingen: Niemeyer, 1972), pp. 53–72. Heinrich Kaufringer is the name of both a father and a son, documented in Landsberg from 1369 to 1404. Which was the poet we do not know, but the poems were composed probably during the last decade of the fourteenth century and the first decade or so of the fifteenth. Folktale Type 1420D.

5. 'Three Wily Women' by Heinrich Kaufringer, translated from *Heinrich Kaufringer. Werke*, I (see the previous item), pp. 116–30 (= 'Drei listige Frauen B'). Folktale Type 1406.

6. 'The False Messiah' by Hans Folz, translated from *Hans Folz. Die Reimpaarspruche*, edited by Hanns Fischer (Munich: Beck, 1961), pp. 92–8. Date of composition: *c*.1485/6. Folktale Type 1855A.

7. 'The Smith in the Baking-Trough' by Hans Sachs, translated from *Sources and Analogues of Chaucer's Canterbury Tales*, edited by W.F. Bryan and Germaine Dempster (New York: Humanities Press, 1941/1958), pp. 121–2 (= '*Sämtliche Fabeln und Schwänke von Hans Sachs*, III, edited by Edmund Goetze and Carl Dreschler (Halle: Niemeyer, 1900), pp. 163–5). Date of composition: 20 January 1537. Folktale Type 1361.

8–10. These are a very small selection from the 94 tales told of the jester Till Eulenspiegel, by an anonymous author about 1500, written in Late Middle High German prose, probably in the Brunswick area. Till Eulenspiegel, in English 'Howleglass', became extraordinarily popular in Europe.

The set of tales is an early example of the jest-book biography, in which a series of jests, often traditional, are attributed to one person, whose birth begins, and death ends, the sequence. The first, or possibly second, edition exists in only a fragment, published in Strassburg in 1510–11. Full editions of 1515 and 1519, with woodcut illustrations, are the basis of current scholarly work on the original. The first English translation was printed in Antwerp *c*.1510 surviving as a fragment. In 1528 the English printer W. Copland issued a book entitled *Here beginneth a merye jest of a man that was called Howleglas, and of many marveylous thinges and jestes that he dyd in his lyfe, in Eastlande and in many other places.* The tales given here are modernised from this edition by Caroline Palmer. The name 'Howleglass' has been much debated. It means 'owl-mirror' and is obviously meant to be satirical. Owls normally symbolised wisdom. Mirrors were thought of as means of perception. In some tales Howleglass leaves his sign scrawled in chalk or coal of an owl and a mirror and the Latin words *Hic fuit* – 'Howleglass was here' (cf. Tale 40, Oppenheimer). A full translation of the German version of 1515 with Introduction and Critical Appendix by Paul Oppenheimer was published as *A Pleasant Vintage of Till Eulenspiegel* (Middletown, Conn.: Wesleyan University Press, 1972) and as *Till Eulenspiegel His Adventures*, translated by Paul Oppenheimer, with Introduction, Bibliography, and notes, in paperback in The World's Classics (Oxford and New York Oxford University Press, 1995). References to 'Oppenheimer' are to this latest edition.

8. Cf. Oppenheimer 12. Büddenstedt is in Brunswick.

9. Cf. Oppenheimer 14. This traditional jest was also attributed to 'The Parson of Kalenborowe' in a thirteenth century German poem. It is recorded by Poggio and was printed in English at Antwerp in 1520, of which a fragment survives.

10. Cf. Oppenheimer 83. This may be a curious and ironic variant of Folktale Type 753 comprising numerous motifs. Christ visits a smith, 'takes off a horse's foot in order to shoe it and rejuvenates an old woman by putting her in the fire. The smith tries disastrously to do the same.'

Dutch Tales

1. 'Wisen Raet van Vrouwen' ('The Resourcefulness of Women'). From the Hulthem manuscript. The translation is based on the edition by Frank Brandsma and Orlanda S.H. Lie in *Klein Kapitaal uit het Handschrift Van Hulthem*, pp. 32–41. Previously edited by C. Kruyskamp, *De Middelnederlandse Boerden* ('s-Gravenhage: Martinus Nijhof, 1957), pp. 25–31. This *boerde*, or fabliau, deals with the well-documented theme of the 'Innocent confessor duped into being go-between for adulteress and lover' (Stith Thompson, *Motif-index of folk-literature*. Revised and enlarged edition (Bloomington, In.: Indiana University Press, 1989): K 1584). It resembles closely Boccaccio's version in *Decamerone* III, 3, though it does not appear to have any parallel among the French fabliaux. The style in the original has some puns.

2. 'Vanden Cnape van Dordrecht' ('Concerning the Lad from Dordrecht, a Funny Jest'). From the Hulthem manuscript. Translation based on the edition by Bart Besamusca and Erwin Mantingh in *Klein Kapitaal uit het Handschrift Van Hulthem*, pp. 104–112. Previously edited by Eelco Verwijs, *Dit Sijn X Goede Boerden*, pp. 4–10; and C. Kruyskamp, *De Middelnederlandse Boerden*, pp. 46–50. This fabliau has two medieval analogues, the Old French *Le Foteor* (Willem Noomen, ed. *Nouveau Recueil Complet des Fabliaux* (Assen, 1991), vol. 6, pp. 51–75) and the 'Schwankmäre' by Heinrich Kaufringer, *Bürgermeister und Künigssohn* (Heinrich Kaufringer, *Werke*, ed. Paul Sappler (Tübingen, 1972–1974), vol. 1, pp. 41–52). Fred Lodder discusses this *boerde* in relation to its intended audience in 'Corrupte Baljuws en

Overspelige Echtgenotes: Over het beoogde publiek van drie boerden', in H. Pleij et al, *Op belofte van profijt. Stadsliteratuur en burgermoraal in de Nederlandse letterkunde van de middeleeuwen* (Amsterdam, 1991), pp. 217–227.

3. 'Van Lacarise den Katijf die een Ander sach Bruden Sijn Wijf ('Concerning the Unfortunate Lacarise, Who Saw Another Man Screw His Wife'). From the Hulthem manuscript. The translation is based on Kruyskamp's edition, pp. 58–61. Previously edited by Verwijs, pp. 19–22. The motif is ubiquitous: 'Wife makes her husband believe that he is dead' (Thompson J 2311.0.1). It has close parallels in Old French fabliaux, especially 'Le Vilain de Bailluel' (*Nouveau Recueil Complet des Fabliaux*, vol. 5, pp. 225–249), as well as very close affinities with the poem *Von den dreyen frawen*, ed. by A.V. Keller in *Erzählungen aus altdeutschen Handschriften* (1855), pp. 213–16.

4. 'Vanden Paep Die Sijn Baeck Ghestolen Wert' ('Concerning the Priest Whose Bacon Was Stolen'). Translation based on the edition by W. Bisschop and E. Verwijs, *Gedichten van Willem van Hildegaersberch* 's-Gravenhage: Martinus Nijhof, 1870), pp. 59–61. Also edited by Kruyskamp pp. 64–71. Willem van Hildegaersberch was a professional poet who lived and composed in the second half of the fourteenth century. Willem was a *sprookspreker*, an itinerant writer and performer of metrical tales, usually of a moral and didactic nature. This *boerde*, and the next, demonstrate that he knew how to wield humour to good effect in his social and religious criticism. No parallels to this fabliau have been identified. A recent study of the entire oeuvre of Willem van Hildegaersberch is that by Theo Meder, *Sprookspreker in Holland: Leven en Werk van Willem van Hildegaersberch (circa 1400)* Amsterdam: Prometheus, 1991). Fred Lodder considers the moral in this and· other Middle Dutch *boerden* in 'De moraal van de boerden' *De Nieuwe Taalgids* 75 (1982), pp. 39–49. For a discussion of Willem's activities as a court speaker, see Frits van Oostrom, *Court and culture: Dutch literature, 1350–1450* (Berkeley: University of California Press, 1992), chapter 2.

5. 'Vanden Monick' ('Concerning a Monk'). Translation based on the edition by W. Bisschop and E. Verwijs, *Gedichten van Willem van Hildegaersberch*, pp. 179–181. Previously edited by Verwijs in *Dit Sijn X Goede Boerden*, pp. 25–32; and Kruyskamp, pp. 72–79.

6. 'Van .iij. ghesellen die den bake stalen.' (Concerning Three Companions Who Stole a Side of Bacon).This boerde was first published by J.F. Willems in *Belgisch Museum*, Gent, 1837–1846, and was also edited by C. Kruyskamp, *De Middelnederlandse Boerden* ('s-Gravenhage: Martinus Nijhoff, 1957), pp. 51–57. It has numerous parallels, among which Jean Bodel's *Barat et Haimet* (Willem Noomen, ed. *Nouveau Recueil Complet des Fabliaux* (Assen, 1991), vol. 2, pp. 28–75). A discussion of the Middle Dutch boerde and its parallels in a broad range of languages, including one in Old Norse/ Icelandic by the Icelandic Bishop Jón Halldórsson, is to be found in J. de Vries, 'De Boerde van .III. Ghesellen, die den Bake Stalen.' *Tijdschrift voor Nederlandsche Taal-en Letterkunde* (1926): 212–62.

I should like to acknowledge the generous assistance of Dr Geert H.M. Claassens of the Universität Bonn, who read and commented on all of these translations.

Thanks also to Dr Theo Meder of the P.J. Meertens Institute in Amsterdam, who did the same. I must also thank Dr Eugene Crook of Florida State University for bringing *The Country Wife* to my attention.

Medieval Latin Tales

1. *Ruodlieb* VII 26–126 (title of extract editorial). There are three useful editions of the *Ruodlieb* in English: G.B. Ford, *The Ruodlieb: Linguistic Introduction, Latin Text and Glossary* (Leiden, 1966); E.H. Zeydel, *The Ruodlieb* (New York, 1969); and C.W. Grocock, *The Ruodlieb* (Warminster and Chicago, 1985).

2. *Carmina Cantabrigiensia*, ed. K. Strecker (Berlin, 1926); also ed. J.M. Ziolkowski, *The Cambridge Songs (Carmina Cantabrigiensia)* (New York and London, 1994).

3. *Pamphilus*, ed. E. Evesque, in *La comédie latine en France au XIIe siècle*, ed. G. Cohen (Paris, 1931), vol. II, pp. 169–223; also ed. S. Pittaluga, in *Commedie latine del XII e XIII secolo*, ed. F. Bertini (Genoa, 1980), vol. III, pp. 1–137.

4. The texts of these Medieval Latin anecdotes are found in T. Wright, *A Selection of Latin Stories*, Percy Society Publications 9 (1842). For the text of each anecdote both the number in Wright's collection and also the manuscript sources cited by Wright are given, in so far as Wright's text is somewhat difficult of access.
(a) 'The Quarrelsome Woman': Wright no. VIII, p. 12 [MS BL Harley 463, f. 18r].
(b) 'Concerning the Deceit and Cunning of Old Women': Wright no. XIII, p. 16 [MS BL Harley 463, f. 20v].
(c) 'The Peasant and the Sheep': Wright no. XXVIII, p. 29–30 [MSS BL Arundel 52, f. 113v; Arundel 506, f. 46v; Royal 7 E. iv, f. 550v].
(d) 'The English Nobleman and his Three Sons': Wright no. XXXIV, p. 36 [no MS source given by Wright].
(e) 'The Woman who Greased the Judge's Palm': Wright no. XLIII, p. 43 [MSS BL Arundel 506, f. 47v; BL Addit. 11579, f. 89r. BL Royal 7 E. iv, f. 258v].
(f) 'The Fable of the Fox and the Wolf': Wright no. LVII, p. 54 [MSS BL Addit. 11579, f. 101r; BL Harley 219, f. 5r].
(g) 'The Two Companions': Wright no. LX, p. 56 [MSS BL Addit. 11579, f. 105v; BL Harley 219, f. 7r].
(h) 'Reynard and Tibert': Wright no. LXII, p. 57 [MSS BL Addit. 11579, f. 110r; BL Harley 219, f. 23r; BL Arundel 292, f. 16v].
(i) 'The Demon and the Robber': Wright no. LXXV, p. 68 [MS BL, Royal 7 E. iv, f. 46v].
(j) 'The Man who Pretended to be Dead': Wright no. LXXVI, p. 69 [MS BL, Royal 7 E. iv, f. 63v].
(k) 'The Lawyer and a Devil': Wright no. LXXVII, p. 70 [printed by Wright from the 15th-century *Promptuarium Exemplorum*, which exists in printed versions only].
(l) 'The Jew's Daughter': Wright no. LXXX, p. 72 [from the *Promptuarium exemplorum*].

(m) 'The Bailiff and his Wife': Wright no. LXXXI, p. 73 [from the *Promptuarium Exemplorum*].

(n) 'Aristotle': Wright no. LXXXIII, p. 74 [from the *Promptuarium Exemplorum*].

(o) 'The Blind Man and his Wife': Wright no. XCI, p. 78 [no MS source given by Wright].

(p) 'The Fasting Abbot': Wright no. XCVIII, p. 84 [MS BL Arundel 506, f. 41v].

(q) 'The Old Woman who Made a Pact with the Devil': Wright no. C, pp. 85–9 [MS BL Harley 2851 (not foliated)].

(r) 'The Adulterous Wife': Wright no. CI, pp. 89–91 [MS BL Harley 2851].

(s) 'The Woman who Met a Priest': Wright no. CXVIII, p. 110 [MS BL, Royal 7 E. iv, f. 560v].

(t) 'The Peasant and the Ape': Wright no. CXXIX, p. 122 [MS BL, Royal 7 E. iv, f. 252v].

Secondary source:

Dronke, Peter, 'The Rise of Medieval Fabliaux: The Latin Evidence', *Romanische Forschungen* 85 (1973), 275–97.

The following are the Folktale Types of the Latin tales where they have been traced:

2. (a) 'The Snow-Child'. Type 1362.
   (c) 'The Parson and the Wolf'. Type 31, where the parson's part is played by the fox.

4. (a) 'The Quarrelsome Woman'. Type 1365B.
   (b) 'The Deceit and Cunning of Old Women'. Type 1515.
   (c) 'The Peasant and the Sheep'. Type 1551.
   (f) 'The Fable of the Fox and the Wolf'. Type 32.
   (h) 'Reynard and Tibert'. Type 105.
   (k) 'The Lawyer and a Devil'. Type 1186.
   (l) 'The Jew's Daughter'. Type 1855A.
   (n) 'Aristotle'. Type 1501.
   (o) 'The Blind Man and his Wife'. Type 1423.
   (q) 'The Old Woman who Made a Pact with the Devil'. Type 1353.